KU-334-321

CAMBRIDGE LATIN AMERICAN STUDIES

GENERAL EDITOR
SIMON COLLIER

ADVISORY COMMITTEE
MARVIN BERNSTEIN, MALCOLM DEAS
CLARKE W. REYNOLDS, ARTURO VALENZUELA

67

THE DEMOGRAPHY OF
INEQUALITY IN BRAZIL

*For a list of other books in the
Cambridge Latin American Studies series,
please see page 302*

THE DEMOGRAPHY OF INEQUALITY IN BRAZIL

CHARLES H. WOOD

*Department of Sociology and Center for
Latin American Studies, University of Florida*

and

JOSÉ ALBERTO MAGNO DE CARVALHO

*Centro de Desenvolvimento e Planejamento Regional
Federal University of Minas Gerais, Brazil*

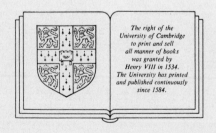

The right of the
University of Cambridge
to print and sell
all manner of books
was granted by
Henry VIII in 1534.
The University has printed
and published continuously
since 1584.

CAMBRIDGE UNIVERSITY PRESS

Cambridge

New York   New Rochelle   Melbourne   Sydney

Published by the Press Syndicate of the University of Cambridge
The Pitt Building, Trumpington Street, Cambridge CB2 1RP
32 East 57th Street, New York, NY 10022, USA
10 Stamford Road, Oakleigh, Melbourne 3166, Australia

© Cambridge University Press 1988

First published 1988

Printed in Great Britain by
Redwood Burn Limited, Trowbridge, Wiltshire

British Library cataloguing in publication data
Wood, Charles H.
The demography of inequality in Brazil. –
(Cambridge Latin American Studies; 67).
1. Equality – Brazil   2. Social classes –
Brazil   3. Brazil – Population
1. Title   II. Carvalho, José Alberto
Magno de
305′.0981   HN290.Z9.S6

Library of Congress cataloguing in publication data
Wood, Charles H. 1945–
The demography of inequality in Brazil/Charles H. Wood and José
Alberto Magno de Carvalho.
p.   cm. – (Cambridge Latin American studies: 67)
Bibliography.
Includes index.
ISBN 0 521 35174 X
1. Brazil – Population.   2. Income distribution – Brazil.
3. Brazil – Economic conditions – 1945–   1. Carvalho, José Alberto
Magno de.   II. Title.   III. Series.
HB3563.W66 1988
304.6′0981 – dc 19   87-32991 CIP

ISBN 0 521 35174 X

RB

Contents

v

Illustrations

Tables

Preface

The ideas we present here began to take shape long before we realized we were writing this book. In 1974, after I finished a PhD in Sociology at the University of Texas at Austin, I had the good fortune to find employment at the Centro de Desenvolvimento e Planejamento Regional (CEDEPLAR), a research and graduate training center at the Federal University of Minas Gerais in Belo Horizonte, Brazil. My arrival at CEDEPLAR coincided with José Alberto's return from England, where he had completed a PhD at the London School of Economics, under the direction of William Brass. José Alberto's knowledge of Brazil's economic and political history and his expertise in demographic methods nicely complemented my background in sociology and my interest in development studies. In the process of working together on several projects, our respective interests consistently gravitated to that grey area where population and development research overlap. Over the years, it became increasingly evident to us that the field of demography could benefit from a greater sensitivity to the macrostructural issues that concerned students of development and social change, just as the field of development studies could benefit from a solid dose of demography. But precisely how we were going to build a better bridge between the two posed a major problem. Unhappy with the tendency to resort to *ad hoc* solutions tailored to the particular topic at hand, we searched instead for some way to situate population variables within a larger model of socioeconomic and political organization. The task was made easier when we discovered that systematic attention to the idea of inequality was an effective way to construct a framework to conceptualize the relationships between structural change and demographic behavior. The result of our efforts is the model we use in this study of Brazil. We have no doubt that both the framework as well as the empirical analyses presented in this volume can be improved upon. Our hope is that we will have contributed something to the effort to understand the relationships between population and development in Latin America.

We have benefitted from the opinions of many people during the years that it took us to write this book. We owe our thanks to more colleagues and friends than we can name here. We are grateful to the students and faculty at CEDEPLAR and at the University of Florida, who probably contributed more to this effort than they realize. We gained much from the criticisms and suggestions generously offered by Harley Browning, Marianne Schmink and by the comments of the unnamed reviewer for Cambridge University Press. Special thanks are also due to Pamela Richards, whose sharp eye for awkward sentences and ambiguous ideas greatly improved the clarity of the text. We appreciate the help these people offered, and relieve them of any responsibility for the final product.

CHARLES H. WOOD
Gainesville, Florida

1

Introduction

Brazil is the largest and most populous country in Latin America. In 1980, the census bureau counted nearly 120 million people, a figure more than twice that of second-ranked Mexico. Brazil's 8.5 million square kilometers of national territory stretch from the Atlantic Ocean in the east to the foothills of the Andes in the west; from the Guiana plateau in the north to the Plate River basin in the south. The country's continental proportions dominate the geopolitical map of the southern hemisphere, making it the fifth largest country in the world, surpassed in area only by the Soviet Union, the United States, China and Canada.

In the nineteenth century, the change from colony to independent empire (1822), from monarchy to republic (1889–91) and from slaveholding society to a free one (1888) occurred essentially without violence. Brazil's early history thus imparted to the country a legacy of political stability and national unity rare in the New World (Burns 1970). Unlike many of its neighbors in the continent, direct military control of the state has been the exception in Brazil. From the late 1800s through the first three decades of the twentieth century, Brazil's presidents were duly elected. The democratic tradition was interrupted in the period 1930–4 and again in 1937–45 when Getúlio Vargas, a civilian backed by the military, ruled by decree. After World War II, Brazil experienced a succession of democratic regimes until 1964, when the military forcibly took power and initiated a period of authoritarian rule that was to last twenty-one years. Brazil's return to democracy in 1985 represents the most significant political event in recent decades.

Brazil was predominantly an agrarian society for most of its history. From the colonial period onward, the country's export-oriented economy relied heavily on a series of commodities such as hardwoods, sugar, rubber, cotton and coffee (discussed in chapter 3). Since the end of World War II, the economy, especially the industrial sector, grew in size and complexity. Two growth cycles were of particular importance

1

in the postwar period: the "inward-looking" import substitution industrialization (ISI) from the early 1950s through the mid-1960s; and
the "outward-looking" post-ISI export promotion cycle from the
1960s to the present. The first period emphasized the domestic production of previously imported finished goods. The second period saw the
diversification of industrial growth and a closer integration into the
world economy. Brazil continues to export traditional commodities,
yet, as a consequence of recent industrial and trade policy, the country
now produces a growing number of manufactured goods that successfully compete in international markets with products from the United
States, Western Europe and Japan.

A long-run perspective shows that Brazil's economy, although subjected to cyclical downturns, experienced an annual rate of growth that
averages out to around 7 per cent a year between 1956 and 1984 (chapter
3). Industrial sector growth in the postwar period nearly always surpassed the overall rate by 2 or 3 percentage points. With a Gross
National Product (GNP) of around $250 billion in 1980, the Brazilian
economy is approximately equal to Canada's and ranks as the tenth largest in the world. Per capita income reached $1,800 in 1981, placing
Brazil closer (in aggregate terms) to the advanced industrial nations
than to most countries in Asia and Africa. With the largest and the most
complex economy in Latin America, and with an abundance of natural
and human resources to draw from, Brazil is a country that vies for position in the small but growing class of world powers.

Social and demographic changes are closely tied to the structure of
Brazilian development. The industrialization of south-central Brazil
has lured migrants from rural areas to the country's more dynamic
urban metropolises, especially Rio de Janeiro, São Paulo and Belo
Horizonte. By 1980, the proportion of the population residing in urban
places for the first time surpassed the number of people living in the
countryside. The spatial redistribution of the population has been accompanied by substantial gains in educational attainment and greater
access to public services. Between 1970 and 1980 the mean number of
years of school attended rose, as did the proportion of households with
piped water and sewage facilities.

Changes in the structure of economic production, as well as the
increase in educational attainment and in provision of health-related
services have profoundly altered reproductive behavior in Brazil (chapter 7). There has been a sharp rise in the proportion of women using
contraception, and the fertility rate has fallen nearly 30 per cent, from
an average of 5.8 children per woman in 1970 to 4.2 in 1980. The decade

of the 1970s also saw a decline in death rates, causing the average number of years of life expected at birth to increase over six years during the period, reaching 59.6 years by the time of the last census. Today, the average Brazilian enjoys a higher standard of living, a smaller family size and a longer length of life than ever before.

Paralleling this promising picture lies another less positive side of Brazil. It is one of sharp socioeconomic inequalities, of entrenched and widespread poverty and malnutrition, and of an economy heavily burdened by a huge and growing external debt. Although average real income rose by nearly 50 per cent between 1970 and 1980, the structure of Brazil's recent development has done little to attenuate the high concentration of income in the hands of an affluent elite (chapter 3). The top decile of the income-earning population in 1980 appropriated nearly half (47.9 per cent) of all income earned, while the share of income accruing to lowest decile barely exceeded 1 per cent of the total. After rising in the 1960s, the degree of income inequality remained about the same in the 1970s despite increases in Gross National Product.

If the recent pattern of economic growth did not significantly reduce income inequality, the same can be said for the pronounced spatial differentiation that has long characterized Brazil. Ever since the decline in sugar prices in the eighteenth century, which left the once wealthy northeastern plantation economy in ruins, development has favored central and southern Brazil. Today the northeastern states of Ceará, Rio Grande do Norte, Paraíba, Pernambuco, Alagoas, Sergipe and Bahia lag far behind the rest of the country in terms of income level, educational achievement and other indicators of living standards.

The ability to capture regional differences is central to the study of population and development in Brazil. The five macroregion breakdown suggested by the Council of Statistics (NORTH, NORTHEAST, SOUTH, SOUTHEAST and CENTRAL WEST) offers a broad view of the most salient features of Brazil's spatial diversity. This study uses these divisions, which appear in upper case letters in the text, whenever further disaggregation is unwarranted or precluded by the absence of data. More detailed inter-regional comparisons subdivide the five macroregions into ten smaller and more homogeneous units (lower case letters). The states and territories included in the five- and the ten-region classifications are given in Table 1.1. Map 1.1 shows their spatial locations.

Table 1.1. *States and territories in each region and macroregion*

Macroregion	Region	State or territory
NORTH	Amazônia	Acre, Amazonas, Pará, Roraima, Rondônia, Amapá
NORTHEAST	Northern Northeast	Maranhão, Piauí
	Central Northeast	Ceará, Rio Grande do Norte, Paraíba, Pernambuco, Alagoas, Fernando Noronha
	Southern Northeast	Bahia, Sergipe
SOUTHEAST	Minas	Minas Gerais, Espírito Santo
	Rio	Rio de Janeiro
	São Paulo	São Paulo
SOUTH	Paraná	Paraná
	South	Rio Grande do Sul, Santa Catarina
CENTRAL WEST	Central West	Goiás, Mato Grosso, Mato Grosso do Sul, Brasília

In all regions of the country, land ownership in the rural area is highly concentrated in a small property-holding class, leaving the vast majority of rural families without land, or with plots too small to support themselves. In 1975, well over half of all agricultural establishments were less than ten hectares in size, yet occupied only 2.7 per cent of all land. At the other end of the distribution, landholdings in excess of 1,000 hectares comprised 0.8 per cent of all farms, yet appropriated 42.9 per cent of all land (chapter 3). Analyses of land tenure in Brazil indicate that the degree of land concentration, which is among the highest in Latin America, may have become even more skewed in recent years.

In the densely populated drought-prone rural NORTHEAST, subsistence farmers rely on centuries-old agricultural methods. Meanwhile, in central and southern Brazil, agriculture has become highly industrialized as farmers increasingly depend on machinery, fertilizers and other manufactured goods. The modernization of agricultural production has been accompanied by a shift away from labor-intensive crops, such as coffee, to machine-harvested soybeans sold mainly to buyers abroad. Developments such as these mean an increase in productivity and a contribution to foreign exchange earnings. Yet the benefits of changes in the structure of agricultural production also entail social costs which are disproportionately borne by those population groups

Map 1.1 Brazil: states, territories and regions

that can least afford them (chapters 9 and 10). Recent trends imply a slower increase in the production of domestically consumed food crops, a decline in labor absorption in rural labor markets and the substitution of permanent employees, sharecroppers and tenant farmers by low-paid wage workers hired only at harvest time.

The difficult conditions people face in the countryside enhance the lure of employment opportunities thought to exist in the cities. In the last two decades this has led to a rural exodus of unprecedented proportions (chapter 9). The massive transfer of people to metropolitan centers of the country has strained the urban economy's capacity to provide productive and well-paid employment to the growing number of job seekers, whose ranks are swelled by high rates of population growth in years past and by the recent infusion of migrants into urban labor markets. Caught between poorly remunerated jobs and the high cost of city life, the result for many migrant and native urbanites is poverty, inadequate housing and poor diet (chapter 11).

A national nutrition survey in 1975 showed that only 33 per cent of the Brazilian population met the FAO/WHO "Low" calorie requirement. Approximately 17 per cent experienced deficits of over 400 calories a day (averaging 543 calories consumed). Although experts disagree as to the proper way to represent nutritional standards, consumption deficits of this magnitude are unmistakable evidence of nutritional problems since they average 2.7 times a margin of error of 200 calories in deficit estimation. The National Household Expenditures Study (ENDEF) found that this degree of malnutrition afflicted 29 per cent of the population in the NORTHEAST and around 9 per cent in the SOUTHEAST. The total shortfall in consumption amounted to over 10 billion calories per day (World Bank 1979: 18).

Planners and politicians in Brazil have long endorsed the precepts of modernization theory that poverty and insufficient employment are transitory features of the development process. To speed the transition to a fully modern society, the Brazilian government in recent decades adopted a range of aggressive policies designed to streamline the economy, attract foreign investment and stimulate capital accumulation and reinvestment. Over the last twenty years or so these initiatives have suffered setbacks and revision. Nonetheless, the policies formulated during the military regime, in power from 1964 to 1985, were sufficiently consistent in substance and intent that they came to be called the "Brazilian model of development" (chapter 3).

Judged strictly on the basis of aggregate indicators, the Brazilian model was eminently successful, at least in the late 1960s and early 1970s, a period when the economy grew at an impressive rate of around 10 per cent a year. The rapid increase in GNP, dubbed the "economic miracle," was regarded the world over as one of the legendary accomplishments of development planning. Yet, even before the growth rate began to fall in 1974, the Brazilian model of development drew criticism on a number of counts (chapter 3). Critics singled out: the loss of individual rights and freedom of expression during the authoritarian regime (Soares 1979); the use of violence by the military to repress political activity and to limit the power of organized labor (Singer 1972); the fall in real wages from 1964 to 1974 and the consequent rise in infant mortality rates in some cities (Wood 1982); the deterioration in the distribution of income during the 1960s (Hoffman 1972; Fishlow 1972) and the failure to reduce income inequality in the 1970s (Denslow and Tyler 1984); the increase in foreign control over the most dynamic sectors of industry, and the "dependent" character of domestic growth

(Cardoso 1973); the development policies that favored capital-intensive investment and the failure of new production technology to generate sufficient jobs to employ the growing supply of urban labor (Lluch 1979); and, in rural areas, the relative decline in labor absorption caused by the combined effects of demographic increase, the concentration of landholdings and the expansion of capitalist social relations of production.

In the early 1980s, Brazil entered a period of economic crisis, caused in large part by a recession in the international economy. The annual rate of change in Gross Domestic Product turned negative in 1981 and again in 1983, a slowdown with far-reaching social and political consequences (chapter 5). The evidence for the first half of the decade, spotty as it is, shows a decline in real income, a rise in unemployment, an expansion of poorly paid informal jobs and a drop in the rate of labor absorbed in the formal sector (Pfeffermann 1985). The economic downturn was severely felt, especially among the urban poor.

In mid-1984 the global economy began to recover from its worst recession in forty years. Yet, it is unlikely that the current improvement will be enough, by itself, to restore Brazil to past growth rates. The lasting consequences of the world crisis, as well as the external debt and the legacy of deep-rooted socioeconomic and regional inequalities, challenge Brazil's future ability to achieve sustained and equitable economic growth. As we will show in this volume, whether or not this effort is successful will determine the life chances of millions of Brazilians.

Population, development and inequality

A population's demographic behavior is linked to social and economic inequalities, such as the ones noted above, because the material conditions that people confront in their daily lives, and the expectations that they have for themselves and their children, exert a strong impact on the pattern and level of births and deaths, and on the propensity to migrate from one place to another. If a privileged minority enjoys access to a disproportionate share of wealth and other amenities – a characteristic not unique to Brazil – we can expect to find sharp variation in the demographic behavior of population subgroups. Similarly, a change in income or education, or a change in the degree to which people have access to public services, or any transformation in socioeconomic and political organization that improves or erodes the quality of life of one group relative to another, modifies the pattern of differences by social strata in births, deaths and geographic movement.

It is the composite of these changes among strata of the population that accounts for demographic shifts observed in the aggregate. If we note, say, a drop in the national mortality rate, we can be sure that, underlying this overall decline changes have taken place that are more or less specific to different regions of the country and to different socioeconomic strata of the population. The fall in the overall death rate may be due to a large decline among middle income households, while mortality rates for the rest of the population remain the same. Or the aggregate outcome may be the (unlikely) result of a sharp reduction in deaths solely among the poorest stratum of society. National-level changes in the transition from high to low death rates generally occur as a consequence of a combination of events, such as a rapid shift in mortality among the middle class, and a slower rate of change among the poor. Yet other patterns are possible, including the offsetting effects of opposite trends among different social strata. A moderate decline at the aggregate level, for example, could be the result of a rapid drop in the death rate among middle and upper strata of the population, the national-level effect of which is blunted by a mortality rise among low-income groups.

Which demographic trajectory a country follows tells us a great deal about the kind of social change underway. Other things being equal, a development model that raises aggregate economic output, and which equitably distributes the benefits of growth, will have different demographic consequences compared to a highly concentrationist development strategy the results of which favor a small elite, or cause an absolute deterioration in living standards among particular social groups or geographic areas. Fertility, mortality and migration rates are thus closely tied to the structure of inequality which itself changes in the course of development.

That subgroup demographic rates can serve as a kind of barometer or yardstick with which to investigate the distributional consequences of transformations in socioeconomic and political structure is an idea that calls for a particular research agenda. The methodological task is to decompose aggregate measures of fertility, mortality and migration into estimates that correspond to key dimensions of geographic and socioeconomic stratification in Brazil. The conceptual challenge is to situate the interpretation of these disaggregated estimates of demographic performance within a broader model of social, economic and political organization.

As a technique, decomposition of aggregate rates is hardly new to the field of demography. Yet, recently developed methods have greatly enhanced our ability to disaggregate demographic estimates. Traditional measures of mortality and fertility rely primarily on vital registration statistics. In developing countries this limitation meant that demographic indicators were often of dubious quality and nearly always restricted to aggregate rates for large geographic units. The newer approach, developed mainly by William Brass (Brass et al. 1968) in the 1960s, uses indirect methods to measure vital rates from surveys and census data. As a consequence, more accurate estimates at the national and regional level are now available even in those countries where the record of vital events is precarious. So significant are the implications of the improved accuracy and flexibility of these methods that the availability of new estimates has led to what one observer (Escudero 1980) called the "silent revolution" in population studies.

Indirect estimation procedures have another important advantage, especially for the objectives of this volume. Unlike the vital registration system, census data contain a wide range of information about individuals, such as their income, educational attainment, family organization and place of residence. This means that we can make use of individual-level sample data drawn from the 1970 and 1980 censuses to generate demographic rates specific to different socioeconomic strata of the population. Although the information included in the census questionnaires is not always ideal for operationalizing concepts such as social class, samples of census data, because of their coverage and large number of cases, nonetheless represent a significant advance over other sources.

How we interpret disaggregated estimates of demographic behavior is primarily a conceptual matter. Given that fertility, mortality and migration rates are closely associated with numerous aspects of socioeconomic and political structure, a narrow approach that pays exclusive attention to demographic variables and their immediate determinants will not suffice. Birth and death rates, and the propensity to move from one place to another, are behaviors inextricably embedded in the very economic and institutional arrangements transformed by the process of socioeconomic development. Demographic change, as McNicoll (1978: 80) put it, "cannot properly be isolated from the overall style of the development process."

In Latin America, each country's "development style" is the outcome of the complex interplay of geography, history, economics, population and public policy. These factors are more or less unique to every national context. Yet, beyond the specifics of each case, commonalities remain. For our purposes, the most important is the "combined and uneven" character of the expansion of capitalist production and trade (de Janvry 1981: chapter 1). Capitalist development is combined, because it forms a system on a world scale, with the result that its components – regions, nation-states and regions within nation-states – are organically interrelated. Capitalist development is uneven, in that the process is neither linear nor homogeneous. On the contrary, it is marked by inequalities over time (periods of expansion and stagnation), space (inequalities between and within countries) and individuals (social differentiation into classes and strata).

If development favors certain geographic areas and social groups over others, and if these differences have demographic consequences because of their impact on fertility, mortality and migration, then neither development nor population studies can proceed very far if we insist, as much work in both fields has done, on treating the economy and the population as undifferentiated aggregates. It follows that our conceptualization of population and social change must encompass a country's class structure, its system of socioeconomic stratification and the various mechanisms, both domestic and international, that determine how the benefits and costs of development are distributed, both spatially and socially.

These observations suggest the need to formulate a conceptual framework that incorporates the prominent issues in development studies as well as the conceptual and technical advances achieved in demographic research. The proposed framework, which we present in the next chapter, views a society's eco-demographic and sociopolitical organization as interacting dimensions of a single whole. In subsequent chapters we will draw on the framework as a guide to selecting and ordering a wide range of data relevant to our interpretation of disaggregated estimates of fertility, mortality and migration. The framework thus serves primarily as a heuristic device with which to conceptualize demographic behavior in terms of a broader model of developing society.

Social inequality, and the reciprocal relationship between inequality and demographic behavior, is the thread that ties together the various themes pursued here. By social inequality we refer to the distribution within a society of scarce material and non-material goods and services. The term encompasses the distribution of income, housing, education, nutrition, public services (water, sewage) as well as access to jobs and productive resources, such as the access to land in the countryside. Spatial distinctions, such as rural and urban residence and region of the country, play a central role inasmuch as geography is associated with differences in the distribution of quality of life indicators. The origin of these inequalities, in turn, can be traced to the structure of social, economic and political organization which is itself conditioned by a country's position in the world economic system.

Analyses of social indicators, disaggregated by socio-spatial criteria, focus on two aspects of inequality. One deals with relative differences at a point in time. An example is the proportion of households with running water by level of household income. The ratio of rich to poor households gives an indicator of the magnitude of the difference that separates the two social groups. Comparing the results for 1970 and 1980 may show a rise or fall in relative access to this public service. The second approach is to focus, not on relative differences, but on absolute changes over time. The poorest strata of the population, for example, may benefit from increased access to running water (an improvement in absolute terms), yet may do so at a slower rate compared to middle income groups (which implies a deterioration in relative terms).

Both approaches are relevant to the demography of inequality, but for different reasons. An improvement or a decline in the absolute value of the various social indicators has a more or less direct consequence for fertility, mortality and migration. Here the concern is for the processes (both social and biological) that take place within households such that access to, say, income or running water lead to patterned outcomes in demographic behavior. On the other hand, changes in relative inequality (whether or not the absolute values are rising or falling) are the distributional outcomes of the structures and processes that characterize the overall style of development underway in a country during a given period. The former approach addresses "micro" environment within which demographic behavior occurs. The latter approach addresses the "macro" changes that determine the characteristics of the household decision-making environment. Clearly both perspectives, and the relationships between the findings at each level, are essential to a full understanding of population and social change.

Stated in its broadest terms, the objective of this volume is to investigate the mechanisms by which transformations in Brazil's social, economic and political structure affect, and in turn are affected by, the demographic behavior of people who live in different regions of the country, and who occupy different positions in the social system. Explanations for the empirical findings draw on economic and political history, and on a range of insights from development and population studies.

2

Framework for the study of population, development and inequality[1]

The proposition that changes in fertility, mortality and migration rates can only be understood with reference to the broader social system in which demographic change occurs is by now little more than conventional wisdom. Yet despite the considerable theoretical and empirical attention given to these relationships, no central paradigm has emerged that systematically links structural change and demographic behavior in developing countries.

Many accounts of population change amount to an eclectic listing of empirical generalizations. An example is Notestein's (1953) explanation of the demographic transition. In his well-known discussion of fertility, Notestein mentioned no fewer than fifteen different phenomena associated with the decline in the birth rate, ranging from changes in women's consciousness to the impact of the rise of urban–industrial production on the cost of children (see chapter 7). Each element of the argument can be supported by "hard" data. Yet the various fragments hardly add up to an understanding of structural change, nor to a coherent picture of how demographic behavior is embedded in the process of economic growth and development.

Attempts in contemporary demography to model the relationship between population and development are often deficient because they are, unsurprisingly, overly demographic: population variables and the relationships that immediately affect fertility, mortality and migration upstage economic and political concerns, which are typically relegated to the category of background contingencies (Bulatao and Lee 1983; Bongaarts and Potter 1983; Stokes and Schutjer 1984: 197). Researchers have devoted attention to examining, say, the impact of urbanization on fertility rates. Yet urbanization itself is treated as a given rather than as something to be explained. Similarly, demographers have made significant headway in identifying the "proximate determinants" of fertility, such as age at marriage, postpartum infecundity and contraceptive use. Yet the development-related transformations in social, economic and political organization that induce a change in the proximate determinants are either left unexamined or are addressed unsystematically in the form of *post hoc* generalizations.

Similar limitations apply to economic demography, albeit for different reasons. In the tradition of Malthus's classic study of how population growth and economic development affect one another, one branch of economic research is cast at the macro level. A prominent and still influential example is Coale and Hoover's classic analysis of the negative impact of high fertility on savings, investment and economic growth. In this tradition, population and economy are treated as aggregates, the former acting on the latter independently of class structure, institutional setting and historical context. A separate strand of neoclassical economic research is cast in terms of individual decision-making rather than the macro properties of the economy and population (see chapter 7). Examples include the cost/benefit models of the decision to migrate, supply/demand models of the decision to bear children and to use contraception, and the use of household time allocation theory to study women's economic and reproductive behavior.

Important as both micro and macro contributions have been, neither individual-level demographic research nor studies framed at the aggregate level systematically account for the concepts and the relationships that concern students of Third World development. Even a casual review of contemporary development literature reveals the considerable attention given to such concepts as social class and conflict, the concentration of income and land ownership, the role of ideology, the function of the state and its relation to dominant interest groups, the expansion of capitalist social relations and the global constraints on national development. With some notable exceptions (both in the US, but especially in Latin America), these issues, if they enter demographic research at all, generally do so in an *ad hoc* manner, external to an explicitly elaborated analytic framework.

Social scientists in Latin America have made considerable progress in better integrating demographic and development concerns. Significant empirical and theoretical advances have come from researchers associated with the Latin American Demographic Center (CELADE), the Latin American Faculty of Social Sciences (FLACSO), the Commission on Population and Development in Latin America (CLACSO). CLACSO's working groups on migration and reproduction, as well as its regional program on population and development (PISPAL), have also been especially important. The Latin American perspective is characterized primarily by attempts to explain the relation between demographic behavior and structural phenomena, such as a country's overall style of development, the organization of the labor market, and the institutional arrangements that influence the process of economic change and that govern the exercise of political power.

These contributions notwithstanding, there remains a tendency to concentrate on variation in a level of a single index, such as total fertility or net rural–urban migration, giving less attention to how changes in the overall index break down into its components parts, and how such changes vary by social class and socioeconomic strata (Miró and Potter, 1980). Moreover, the problem of conceptualizing the relationship between structural change and demographic behavior is far from resolved. Finally, many of the theoretical and conceptual advances in the economics and sociology of development have yet to make their way into the study of differential fertility, mortality and migration.

A fruitful way to proceed is to place the concept of inequality at the center of the conceptualization of population and development. The concept is useful because of its potential to bridge two areas of research. On the one hand, students of Latin America have long been concerned to show how the structure of social change has led to unequal outcomes in regional development, income distribution and land ownership, as well as other dimensions of stratification, including gender and racial–ethnic distinctions. Demographers, on the other hand, have developed a number of techniques to generate disaggregated estimates of fertility, mortality and migration. In principle it is not hard to see that the two research traditions can be joined for a better understanding of the relationships between structural change and demographic behavior. Before introducing such a framework, it is useful to summarize the evolution of recent perspectives on development and inequality.

Perspectives on development and inequality

In the 1950s and 1960s, influential analysts in the modernization school endorsed a development model which predicted that a rapid increase in Gross National Product would translate into significant welfare gains among the poor. An improvement in the living standards of low-income groups would result from the anticipated "trickle down" effect of economic growth on employment and wages, and from the transfer, through migration, of people from marginal activities in the country-side to productive employment in the city. The pyramidal social structure of the past, with few at the top and the vast majority at the bottom, would give way to a diamond-shaped class structure in which most people would be in the middle. The rise of a strong middle class, they argued, meant the emergence of democratic political institutions from the despotism of pre-industrial society. Factory jobs and urban life-styles further implied the triumph of modern over traditional values and attitudes – a new cognitive orientation that would lead to greater equality between men and women, and a decline in the fertility rate as couples increasingly endorsed the small family size norm and adopted efficient means of reproductive control. For modernization theorists, expanded industrial production was thus the necessary if not sufficient condition for egalitarian socioeconomic and political organization, and for the transition from high to low rates of population growth. The abundant literature in this tradition emphasized such topics as the sources of achievement among urban entrepreneurs and the psycho-logical obstacles to innovation among small farmers in the countryside. The perspective implicitly regarded underdevelopment as a "social problem" on a par, say, with crime or urban sprawl, only located in other countries (Portes and Walton 1981: 3).

Proponents of modernization theory regarded social and economic "backwardness" as an original pathology, one that could be attributed exclusively to lack of contact with the modern world. The diagnosis implied an unambiguous cure: the infusion of massive doses of capital, technology and modern attitudes imported from developed countries. Once the developing economy moved from the "take off" stage into a period of sustained growth, indicators of modernity would spread "outward" from city to countryside, and "downward" from the upper and middle classes to all of society.

The diffusion of modern traits implied, not only that social in-equality would decline, but also that fertility rates, and hence the rate of population growth, would drop, just as it once had in the now devel-oped countries. By sharing the same assumptions and causal reasoning as the modernization school, the "theory of the demographic tran-sition" was, in effect, little more than the diffusion model applied to the study of population change.

During the transition to modernity, before the diffusion process was completed, modern and traditional traits would exist side by side. The dual economy phase, which modernizationists conceived in different and sometimes contradictory ways, would last until growth in the pro-ductive modern sector absorbed the labor once employed by the less productive traditional sector (Lewis 1954). Where economic growth failed to alleviate poverty, analysts argued either that growth was not rapid enough (see de Janvry 1981: 258), or that persistent and increasing poverty is the necessary cost of the early stages of development (Ahluwalia 1976; Kuznets 1955). Widespread poverty and unemployment, and the sharp disparities in wealth between an affluent elite and the rest of the population, were thus treated as inevitable, yet transitory, features of the onset of the development process. Movement toward a homogenous modern society was to be achieved by further industrial expansion and a continued influx of foreign capital and technology. By regarding the distortions of a dual society as an impermanent stage in a linear development trajectory, the diffusion model provided appealing "scientific" support for advocates of *laissez-faire* philosophy. And it is primarily this feature of the perspective which accounts for the essentially conservative message of the modernization paradigm.

Events in recent decades steadily eroded the deep-seated optimism of the modernization paradigm. The conclusion derived from data in the 1960s and 1970s that aggregate economic output and social equity were not necessarily linked ran counter to the predictions of the modernization paradigm, and fundamentally challenged the accepted wisdom of the "Development Decade" (Adelman and Morris 1973; Felix 1983; Fishlow 1972). The discordance between theory and data sparked a worldwide debate as to the relationship between growth and distribution in contemporary developing societies. Although far from settled, the controversy nonetheless provoked important revisions in mainstream development economics. Old assumptions about the necessary conditions and determinants of development have been replaced by a more cautious agnosticism in these matters (Todaro 1977). Likewise, simple formulas that emphasized capital accumulation, development planning and foreign aid gave way to a keener appreciation of the complexity of the development process. Among development assistance agencies and institutions, the faith accorded free market principles was supplanted in the 1970s by the "basic needs" approach – a strategy that (ineffectually) called for the direct redistribution of income and resources toward the rural and urban poor.

In the sociology of development, a new round of theoretical critique, begun in the 1960s, adopted a less sanguine assessment of both the prospects for and the consequences of achieving rapid economic growth in less developed countries. According to the new perspective, regions and states relegated to the periphery of the global system were underdeveloped because of, not in spite of, their historic relationship to metropolitan centers (Amin 1976; Cardoso 1972, 1973; Dos Santos 1970;

Frank 1969; Wallerstein 1974). With this postulate as a starting point, researchers invoked different mechanisms to explain the dynamics of uneven world development.

Raul Prebisch (1950) of the Economic Commission for Latin America (ECLA) anticipated many of the arguments later advanced by dependency and world-systems theorists. His work documented the progressive deterioration in the terms of trade experienced by countries that export raw materials and agricultural commodities in exchange for finished goods. To escape the pernicious effects of unequal trade, ECLA recommended a restructuring of the international division of labor through import substitution industrialization (ISI) in the periphery of the international economy. In the 1950s and 1960s, ISI became the cornerstone of development policy in the larger countries in Latin America, but the desired result – autonomous national development – was never fully achieved (Booth 1975).

Prebisch (1950) used orthodox economic analysis of trade data to discover the inadequacy of the classical Ricardian theory of the mutual benefits expected of international specialization and exchange. Research in the Marxist tradition came to the same conclusion, yet found the basis for unequal exchange, not in trade relations but, rather, in the production process itself. For Emmanuel (1972) the exploitation of the periphery could be traced to wage differences between advanced and developing countries. Other things being equal, the exchange of commodities at the single world price is detrimental to countries with low returns to labor since the rate of surplus value extraction is greater compared to a high wage country. Amin's (1976) explanation for unequal exchange rested on differences in productivity and wages, and on the global division of labor imposed on the periphery, which relegates developing countries to a role that limits their future development.

ECLA's distinction between center and periphery found expression (although in different terms) in Gunder Frank's radical critique of modernization theory and import substitution policy. Frank (1967:6) envisioned the "development of underdevelopment" caused by a single chain of exploitation which extended from metropolitan centers of the world system to the farthest outpost in the Latin American countryside. The bold metaphor drove home the idea that underdevelopment, far from being a passive state caused by being left behind in the transition to modernity, was the outcome of an active process determined and modified by capital accumulation and expansion in metropolitan centers of the global economy.

The debate stimulated by Frank's crude model of exploitation advanced development studies in several important directions. Some critics faulted Frank for his inattention to the internal structure of the periphery. They advocated a class analysis of developing countries which focused on capitalist and non-capitalist modes of production and their articulation in urban and rural settings (e.g. Chilcote and Johnson 1983; Laclau 1971). Other critics objected to the overly determinist portrait of metropolitan dominance of an acquiescent periphery (Portes and Walton 1981). The static and unidirectional vision of surplus transfer, as Booth (1971) correctly notes, could hardly account for the clear evidence of economic growth, at least in the larger countries of the developing world.

In light of the shortcomings of Frank's model, Fernando Henrique Cardoso (1972, 1973) pointed to the dynamic, yet at the same time "dependent," character of Latin American capitalism. Politically weaker, and with a lower level of technology, Latin American economies could not function autonomously. They were exploited as sources of cheap labor and raw materials, while the center specialized in advanced technology. Dependency, moreover, was not a purely economic concept. It described, among its many manifestations, cultural dependencies as well (Worsley 1984).

Dependency meant that accelerated economic expansion did not, as the modernization paradigm would have it, produce the same social, economic or political results manifested in developed countries. Instead of the local entrepreneurial class being strengthened, the subsidiaries of transnational corporations (often bolstered by the policy of import substitution industrialization) took over the more dynamic industrial activities and larger scale enterprises. With foreign control of industry, capital-intensive technologies were continuously introduced, oriented to the conspicuous consumption of an affluent elite at the expense of the employment and consumption needs of the majority of the population. The need to control inflation, to limit imports and expand exports, and the need to repress urban and rural uprisings led authoritarian regimes in several countries to introduce deflationary economic policies. Rather than easing tensions and promoting democracy, dependent development aggravated economic, class and political polarization (Cardoso 1973).

World systems theorists took the dependency framework a step further. For Wallerstein (1974), as well as other writers in the ECLA tradition such as Osvaldo Sunkel, the world system itself became the unit of analysis. The parts which make up the world system are countries which are classified into three types: a core of advanced and dominant states (the United States, Western Europe, Japan and other developed countries), a periphery of dependent states, and a semi-periphery of buffer states such as Brazil. The center, or core, exploits the periphery by direct extraction of profit or tribute, or by unequal exchange of commodities. It does so with the active participation of the state in the commanding metropolitan economies. In the periphery, ruling classes emerge which, owing to their position as intermediaries in the system of exploitation, have vested interests in preserving the prevailing patterns of production and unequal distribution.

In the tradition of Kondratief's search for long swings in the capitalist system, Wallerstein and his associates have been joined by both Marxist (e.g., Mandel 1975) and conservative economists (e.g., Rostow 1978), as well as historians (e.g., Stavrianos 1981) and anthropologists (Wolf 1982), in sweeping analyses of secular trends and cycles in the world system since its beginning in the sixteenth century.[2] Older visions of time and place saw world history in terms of battles, kings and cabinets, or as a mere succession of events with no particular pattern or meaning. The appeal of the global view was how it clarified the commonalities between such seemingly different regions as Africa and Latin America, finding likenesses among them in terms of comparable functions within an evolving world system.

Critique

Conceptual approaches to the study of development and inequality have come a long way since the heyday of modernization theory. Even if they are not entirely satisfactory, contemporary views are a welcome corrective to the nation-centric premises of the once-dominant modernization school, and to the naive evolutionary assumptions upon which the paradigm rested. Dependency and world-systems perspectives have significantly advanced a more global understanding of the interrelated character of development and underdevelopment on a world scale. Yet these efforts remain deficient in two important respects.

Analyses that deal exclusively at the world level, as well as studies that find the causes of underdevelopment in the exploitative relationships imposed from the outside, do not by themselves tell us much about the internal process of social and economic change within countries in the periphery or semi-periphery. Moreover, speculations about the long cycles of expansion and retraction in the global economy forget that it was insights developed in the study of specific historical processes that informed and gave rise to the original theories (Portes and Walton 1979: 13–18). The nation-centrism of the modernization school has given way to the global-centrism of the world-systems perspective – a model in which the parts, whether countries or regions, are analyzed solely in terms of their relationship to the global economy. Theories of underdevelopment, Worsley (1984: 41) contends, have become "bogged down in a seemingly endless multiplication of exercises in mode-of-production and world-systematics in which distinctive features of each country simply disappear and all become look alikes, only distinguished from one another insofar as some are central, others peripheral or semiperipheral."

Events and relationships at the world-systems level condition the course of development and change within the periphery. Yet global properties do not represent the full range of country-specific causal forces, nor do they predict the form such transformations take within a country. Indeed, even if we assume, along with neo-Marxian theorists, that the basic laws of capital accumulation and expansion remain essentially constant, the actual manner in which such intrinsic "tendencies" play themselves out in developing countries will vary under different institutional arrangements, historical epochs and cultural traditions (Sunkel 1979: 28). What is needed are analyses of concrete development experiences, such as this study of Brazil, which bring empirical evidence to bear on the process of social change in a particular setting and during a given time period.

Case studies of this kind must give closer and more systematic attention to population variables than current theoretical and empirical researches on development and inequality are wont to do. As Cassen (1976: 812) notes in his extensive review of the literature, it is a "sad reflection" on the separation of demographic from mainstream economic studies that few of the recent estimates of changing personal income distribution in developing countries have considered the influence of demographic variables, and that the prolonged debate on "growth versus distribution" has rarely incorporated possible feedback effects via changes in population growth and structure (exceptions, for Brazil, include Fishlow 1972; Langoni 1973; and Merrick and Graham 1979).

The result is a profound, perhaps growing, disjuncture between the fields of development and population studies. Much of the demographic literature on Third World populations is divorced from new directions in development theory.[3] By the same token, the lively debate about the global properties of development and inequality is blind to the significance of population. It follows that we must strive for a more holistic, less fragmented view of demography and development. To do so requires a framework that assembles into a single model the theoretical and conceptual advances achieved in both fields.

Conceptual framework

The framework proposed in this chapter views Brazil's political, socioeconomic and demographic organization as interacting dimensions of a geopolitical unit that is itself part of a larger world system. We contend that the demographic phenomena which take place within families or households – such as births, deaths and decisions to migrate – can be understood as behaviors that are embedded in, and that interact with, a set of extra-household structures and processes, some of which extend beyond the boundaries of the country itself. We further maintain that the multiple structures and processes involved in the study of population, development and inequality can be grouped into a smaller number of concepts and relationships. Finally, we argue that these limited sets of concepts and relationships can be loosely arranged in terms of causal priority, thereby constituting a model of society that can be used to guide the process of selecting, conceptualizing and interpreting data.

In its most general form, the proposed framework identifies three tiers, or levels of conceptualization. The primary level is the "eco-demographic infrastructure." The central components of infrastructure are "modes of production" and "modes of reproduction." These two components are closley related to each other, and, in their interaction, have a profound influence on the way other dimensions of society are organized. Specifically, the manner in which goods and services are produced (i.e., modes of production), and the way in which population is reproduced (i.e., reproduction), involve a set of interrelated institutions and processes – called infrastructure – upon which is erected a society's "stratification system" and its "politico–ideological super-structure." A simplified version of the model is shown in Figure 2.1.

The scheme endorses the precepts of materialist reasoning in that it

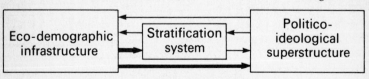

Figure 2.1 General model of proposed framework

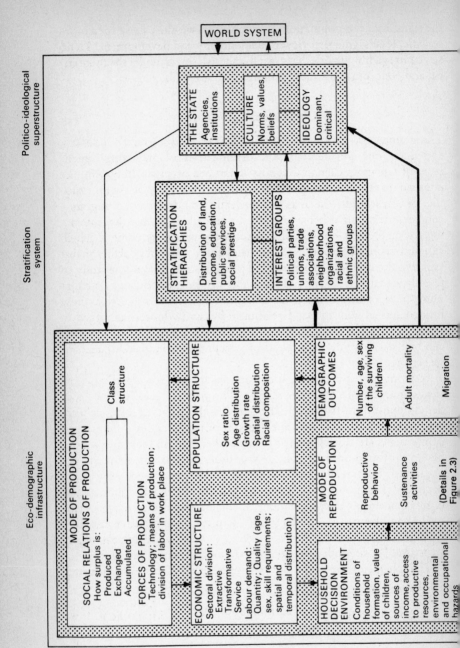

Figure 2.2 Conceptual framework for the study of population, development and inequality

attributes causal priority to infrastructure. The priority accorded infrastructure is depicted by the thicker left-to-right arrows, which imply a particular form of causal association. The type of causality invoked – the notion of structural limitation – is adapted from Eric Olin Wright's (1979; 1985) work on class structure. By this we mean that eco-demographic institutions and relationships impose limits of possible variation on, and probabilistically determine, the stratification system and superstructure.

The model does not endorse a one-way determinism, however. To the contrary, superstructure and the stratification system, although essentially derivative of infrastructure, have reciprocal, at times overriding, influences on eco-demographic processes and relationships. Drawing, again, on Wright's "model of determination," the thinner right-to-left arrows between the major elements of the framework refer to a process of "transformation" in which the practices of social actors (individuals and organizations of various sorts, including the state apparatus) transform a given element within the constraints established by infrastructure.

To put it more concretely, the eco-demographic infrastructure imposes broad limits on possible variation in, say, the form and the actions of the state (one element of superstructure). At the same time, the initiatives of the state, as well as actions of interest groups endowed with different degrees of social and economic power (stratification), actively influence the course of history in ways that cannot be explained by a crude infrastructural determinism. In this way the very structures that set limits on stratification and superstructure are simultaneously transformed by the practices of individuals, interest groups and state policy. The notion of transformation thus establishes the "conceptual space" that permits us to take seriously historical contingencies, social movements and state practices that lead to diverse development experiences. The arrows of varying thickness thus refer to special types of causality (limitation, transformation) between infrastructure, stratification and superstructure. They do not represent, as in other diagrams, flows of goods or energy.

In the pages that follow we will elaborate on this basic scheme. We first explain what we mean by mode of production and reproduction, and show how these parts of the model interact to comprise the eco-demographic infrastructure. Subsequent sections define, and posit the relationships between, the remaining two tiers of the conceptual framework: stratification system and politico-ideological superstructure.

Figure 2.2 provides a more complete picture of the concepts and relationships involved. In later chapters, we will rely on the model as a guide to the processes of formulating a research strategy and interpreting empirical findings. For present purposes, the diagram serves as an organizational tool and as a reference point for the discussion of the model's concepts and relationships.

Population structure

A familiar set of variables describe a population's structure: sex ratio, age profile, birth and death rates, geographic distribution, migration flows and rate of increase, to name those most often used. These variables are summary measures in that they represent the aggregate characteristics of a population, or population subgroup. An age-specific fertility rate, for example, measures the frequency of births among women in a particular age category. It is not difficult to see that the fertility rate, like many other population measures, is the aggregate outcome of events that take place at an individual level. Hence, a fertility rate is the cumulative result of the reproductive behavior that transpires between couples, men and women who are generally members of a household.

This rather obvious point immediately leads us into complex conceptual terrain. Suppose we use standard techniques of demographic analysis to demonstrate that a change in population structure has taken place – say, a decline in the birth rate. With appropriate data we may ascertain that lower fertility was caused by an increase in contraceptive use. If we wish, in turn, to find out why women adopted contraception, we enter the realm of decision-making, the changing costs and benefits of children, and so on. In effect, we must descend from an aggregate observation (lower fertility rate) to examine events that take place inside the household (why couples postpone or forego having another child). The processes that condition a couple's reproductive behavior are biological, social, economic, cultural and ideological in origin, and they interact with one another and with the extra-household environment in complex ways. We can summarize the principal relationships involved in the shift in reproductive behavior by conceptualizing what we henceforth refer to as a "mode of reproduction."

Mode of reproduction

Figure 2.2 shows the concept MODE OF REPRODUCTION in capitals to emphasize its importance within the eco-demographic base. We do so as well to distinguish mode of reproduction from derivative concepts, such as "population structure." The latter is derivative in the sense that, as noted above, population structure is the cumulative, or aggregate result of the demographic outcomes that take place at the level of individual households. Within households we can, in turn, draw a conceptual distinction between reproductive behavior, the result of which is a certain number of surviving children, and sustenance activities that determine seasonal or permanent migration.

Reproductive behavior

The dynamics of household behavior do not take place in a vacuum. As shown in Figure 2.2, reproduction is influenced by a wide range of variables whose origins lie outside the household unit: the value of children, the rules and conditions of household formation, the sexual division of labor, and access to income, education and employment opportunities, to name only the most important ones. It is widely recognized, for example, that households in rural areas engaged in subsistence agricultural production exhibit markedly different organizational patterns compared to households whose members are engaged in wage-labor in an urban–industrial environment, and that such differences translate into rural–urban variation in fertility rates. But the central question is conceptual. How do we identify the mechanisms by which the "household decision environment" (in this example, a rural and urban setting) lead to particular demographic outcomes?

To address this issue we formulate a household model that draws a conceptual distinction between reproductive behavior on the one hand, and household sustenance activities on the other. The former refers to the various processes that lead to a given number of surviving children; the latter refers to the productive activities that meet the maintenance requirements of child and adult members of the domestic unit. Reproductive and sustenance activities, which in reality are inextricably intertwined, sustain and reproduce the household on a daily and generational basis.

Within a population, every household is, in some sense, unique. Yet, abstracting from particular household units, we should be able to identify patterns of behavior that are more or less common to groups of households located in the same ecological or socioeconomic circumstance. Hence, we expect to find systematic differences between, say, urban middle-income households and rural small-farmer households in reproductive and sustenance activities. Viewed in this manner we can identify a limited number of "modes of reproduction." The concept is empirically derived from analyses of the way in which couples organize their reproductive and sustenance activities as the household interacts with the background characteristics that constitute the domestic unit's decision-making environment. Inasmuch as the environment changes – for example, comparing urban and rural contexts, or landless and landed households in the countryside – we can expect to find different reproductive modes.

The concept of reproduction has been used in different ways by demographers and social scientists. Demographers generally adopt a narrow definition of the term. Reproduction refers to biological procreation, measured by the number of children born to a woman, or by a fertility rate among a group of women. At the other end of the continuum is the Marxist definition of reproduction which encompasses, not only the biological dimension (as in the reproduction of labor), but the social and economic system generally. Hence, Marxists speak of the reproduction of the class structure, the reproduction of the conditions of existence of capital and the reproduction of ideology as processes essential to a given social formation. Feminists, concerned about the many household activities that women perform, take a middle position. Reproduction, for them, refers "not merely to the bearing of children...but also to their care and socialization, and the maintenance of adult individuals through their lives, processes which create individuals to fit more or less into the social structure of society and so ensure the continuation of that society in the next generation" (McKintosh 1981: 9). The feminist view of reproduction, which is broader than the biological definition yet more restricted than Marxist usage, is the definition that conforms to what we mean when we identify a mode of reproduction.

Figure 2.3 schematically presents a model of household sustenance and reproductive behavior. Let us first trace the various mechanisms that determine the number of surviving children. For clarity of exposition it is convenient to begin with the demographic outcome, and then work backwards through each of the relevant steps. As noted to the right of Figure 2.3, the sex and age of surviving children are the result of a decision process to either enhance or reduce family size. Following Easterlin (1975) and others (e.g., Bongaarts and Menken 1983) we can conceptualize reproductive decisions in terms of a supply/demand

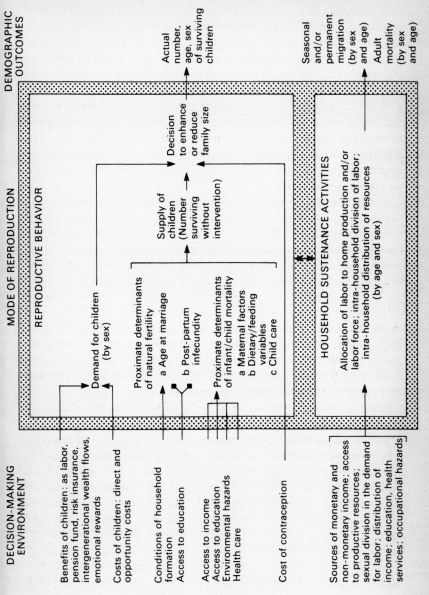

Figure 2.3 Mode of reproduction

model. According to this approach, three considerations enter into the decision process. One is the demand for offspring. Demand is determined by weighing the benefits against the costs of children. Benefits are associated with the value of children (as labor, pension fund, risk insurance), net intergenerational wealth flows and emotional returns to childrearing. Costs can be measured in terms of the direct expenditures involved, and the opportunity costs of child care. Population studies generally conclude that socioeconomic improvement leads to a rise in the net direct costs and the opportunity costs of children, thereby reducing the number of children desired (demand) (Leibenstein 1954). Rising income also appears to be expressed in terms of a preference for higher quality children (Schultz 1981), a factor that further contributes to lowering family size.

In the rational calculus that couples perform, the demand for children is weighed against the supply. Supply refers to the number of offspring a couple would have in the absence of any form of contraception (natural fertility). If the demand for surviving children exceeds supply, parents will be motivated to have additional births, and they will not use contraception. Conversely, when the number of surviving children exceeds (or is expected to exceed) the number desired, parents will be motivated to limit family size. Whether they actually do will depend on the third element of the decision model – the perceived costs (emotional and material) of contraception. Hence, decisions regarding family size are a function of the demand for children, the supply of offspring in the absence of reproductive regulation and the costs of contraception or other forms of control, such as infanticide.

Moving another step backward in the causal chain, we are now in a position to ask: What determines the supply of children? Figure 2.3 specifies the proximate determinants of fertility and of child mortality. The proximate determinants of fertility refer to the biological and behavioral factors through which social, economic and environmental variables affect the birth rate. The principle characteristic of a proximate determinant is its direct influence on fertility. If one proximate variable changes, such as a rise in contraceptive use or an increase in the age at marriage, then fertility also changes (assuming the other determinants remain constant). Hence, differences in the levels of fertility can always be traced to variations in one or more of the seven proximate determinants: marriage (and marital disruptions); the onset of permanent sterility; postpartum infecundity; frequency of intercourse; use and effectiveness of contraception; intrauterine mortality; and abortion.

The first two establish the duration of the reproductive period; the other five determine the rate of childbearing and the duration of birth intervals. Empirical studies show that four of the seven proximate determinants (marriage pattern, contraceptive use, abortion and lactational infecundity) account for nearly all of the variations in fertility, when reproduction is subject to deliberate control. Only two variables – age at marriage and postpartum infecundity – account for most of the variation in natural fertility (Bongaarts and Potter 1983).

In his study of child survival, Lincoln Chen (1983) borrowed the conceptual approach developed in fertility research to identify four sets of proximate determinants of infant and child mortality. The first is parental factors, including age and parity, the interval between births, and maternal nutritional status. The second set includes diet and feeding variables during pregnancy and following birth. A third set of variables is infections and infestations, which may affect the child both during pregnancy and in the first five years of life. The last set of variables is childcare, particularly health care service availability and childcare behavior in response to illness.

The proximate variables are fundamental to the study of the relationship between social and economic structure and demographic behavior. Socioeconomic and environmental factors at the national, community and family levels affect a population's birth and death rate only through their impact on one or more of the proximate determinants, which operate at the individual level. From the point of view of comparative sociology and development studies, the important aspect of the scheme is that differences in birth and death rates between, say, developed and less developed countries, or between upper and lower income strata within the same population, can be traced to differences in the proximate variables (see Davis and Blake 1956). A list of the proximate determinants and their values therefore gives us a portrait of the individual-level factors that directly affect fertility and mortality, and, as a consequence, the rate of population growth.

Depicting a mode of reproduction on the basis of proximate determinants is an important yet preliminary step. Knowing the proximate reasons for a fertility change is undoubtedly a major analytical clarification that can narrow the search for explanation. But a full account of a change in vital rates must go beyond an inventory of changes in proximate variables. In effect, we must ask: What are the determinants of the proximate determinants of fertility and mortality?

To the left of Figure 2.3 we present a partial list of the most important socioeconomic factors that comprise the household decision-making environment, showing how they operate through the various proximate determinants to affect the number of surviving children. The conditions of household formation, for example, affect age at marriage in a population. In a rural setting, where access to land is a prerequisite to establishing a new household, marriage may be delayed – and fertility reduced – if land is in short supply. The mean age at marriage is also influenced by economic conditions. Other things being equal, recession induces young people to postpone marriage; prosperity fosters early unions. Finally, greater educational attainment by women may reduce fertility by delaying the entry into unions, and by raising the opportunity costs of children.

Socioeconomic conditions also affect the length of postpartum infecundity, the second proximate determinant of natural fertility. Postpartum infecundity is determined by the duration of amenorrhea which, in turn, is sensitive to breastfeeding practices. Although research on the determinants of lactation is far from complete, it is generally accepted that breastfeeding is initiated less frequently and decreases in duration as education rises. Length of lactation is also reduced by the economic pressures that push women into the labor force (Lesthaege 1981). Evidence for Latin America shows a decline in both the initiation and the duration of breastfeeding, a trend that increases the supply of children (Keller et al. 1981, cited in Bongaarts and Menken 1983: 50–1).

Turning to the proximate determinants of infant and child mortality, it is clear that maternal factors, dietary and feeding variables, the control of infections and infestations, and child care practices are closely associated with a couple's access to income, its education endowments and the environmental risks to which their children are subjected.

Three major points summarize the argument we have presented in this section: (1) The supply of children that would survive without deliberate attempts to limit family size is established by the proximate determinants of natural fertility and of child mortality. (2) Actual family size is the outcome of a rational calculus in which couples take into account three factors: the demand for offspring, the supply of children and the cost of contraception. (3) It is through the demand for children, and through the proximate determinants of natural fertility and child mortality, that socioeconomic background factors manifest their impact on the number of surviving children.

Household sustenance and migration

Models of rational choice have also been applied to the study of migration. In the neoclassical economic framework, population movement is conceptualized as the geographic mobility of workers who respond to imbalances in the spatial distribution of economic opportunities and other determinants of quality of life (see Rothenburg 1977; Spengler and Myers 1977). Migration flows are the cumulative result of individual decisions based on the rational evaluation of the benefits to be gained and the costs entailed in moving. The model has been extended to include variables such as the amount of knowledge available, the utility significance of the costs and benefits to the individual making the decision and "lifetime income" prospects, defined as the present value of expected income due to migration (Sjaastad 1962). The cost-benefit approach has been further modified to account for the highly segmented labor markets in urban areas of developing countries by including in the model the probability of obtaining desirable employment in the modern sector (Harris and Todaro 1970).

The neoclassical economic approach undoubtedly captures a central aspect of migration – the rational calculus involved. Yet the individual reductionism of the neoclassical model leaves us at a loss when it comes to explaining the macro-structural processes that are the historical origin of the profile of costs and benefits confronted by the potential migrant. To the extent that analysts search for the causes of migration by narrowing their focus to individual decision-making, the conclusions drawn are necessarily limited to the realm of secondary causes (Wood 1982). As in the case of fertility, the task is to conceptualize individual decision-making (which the neoclassical model does well) within the larger context of changing socioeconomic and political structures (such as the model we propose here).

The cost-benefit decision regarding migration is also mediated by events that take place within the household. The gains and losses entailed by moving from one place to another are conditioned by the compensatory activities households adopt in the face of changes in social and economic structure. Researchers have conceptualized such behavior in terms of a series of sustenance strategies by which the household actively strives to achieve a fit between its consumption necessities, the labor power at its disposal (both of which are determined by the age, sex, and skills of its members), and the alternatives for generating monetary and non-monetary income (Deere and de Janvry 1979; Wood 1981: 339; see also, Long 1984; Schmink 1984).

A household's standard of living can be thought of in terms of the effectiveness of its sustenance strategies formulated within the limitations imposed by the physical environment and by socioeconomic background variables (Wood 1981). The profile of available employment opportunities, or the means to carry out home production, may be such that the household is able to meet its maintenance requirements and to expand savings and the quality of consumption. These conditions are likely to be associated with a relatively stable population characterized by low rates of seasonal and permanent migration. Alternatively, the constraints on productive activity (for reasons internal or external to the household) may be such that the net sum of monetary and non-monetary resources falls below that required for the maintenance and the reproduction of the unit.

The way households respond to their environment is an important focus of data collection and analysis (Lerner 1980; Torrado 1980; Olivera 1982). The relevance of the domestic unit lies in the fact that household behavior mediates the individual-level impact of forces that lie beyond the unit itself. The literature on "household strategies" (see Schmink 1984) highlights the multiple initiatives members undertake to actively negotiate structurally imposed constraints. Households may send secondary workers such as wives and children into the labor force, intensify agricultural production (e.g., Chayanov 1966; Boserup 1965), engage in craftmaking or other forms of home production (Scott 1978), alter the sexual division of labor (Deere 1978), reallocate caloric consumption among its members (Gross and Underwood 1971), lower or postpone childbearing (Merrick 1985), permit a rise in infant mortality through the selective investment of scarce resources in older children (Scrimshaw 1978) or migrate (Wood 1981).[4]

The conceptual approach outlined here neither contradicts nor replaces the cost-benefit model. Instead we have retained the basic insight of the economic perspective – that people behave rationally in the allocation of scarce resources and in the face of changing opportunities and constraints. But we have also sought to complement the neoclassical economic approach by noting that migration decisions are mediated by intrahousehold processes, namely the sustenance initiatives undertaken as the domestic unit interacts with its socioeconomic, political and physical environment.

Economic structure

Thus far we have emphasized the idea that modes of reproduction can be understood in terms of the way in which households organize reproductive and sustenance activities in interaction with the extra-household environment. Hence, we have argued that a change in the decision-making environment, such as a shift in the economic value of children or the availability of income-generating jobs, will have an impact on the domestic economy, and that this impact will alter demographic outcomes, leading to a change in population structure.

In this section we investigate, not the demographic consequences of the household's socioeconomic environment, but, reasoning in the opposite direction, examine the origin of the factors that create that environment in the first place. If we ask, for example, why children have a high economic value in one society and not in another, the answer will surely lead us to an analysis of economic structure. To simplify our conceptualization of economic structure, we can focus on two aspects especially important to eco-demographic relationships: the sectoral division of the economy (what Marx called the social division of labor), and the associated quantity and quality of labor demand (as shown in Figure 2.2).

The standard sectoral classification, advanced by A. G. B. Fischer (1935) and Colin Clark (1940), posited a tripartite scheme: primary (agriculture, fishing, forestry, mining); secondary (manufacturing, construction, utilities) and service or tertiary sector (commerce, transport, communications, services). More recently, Browning and Singelmann (1978; see also Singelmann 1978) proposed a more detailed scheme made up of thirty-seven industry groups classified into six major categories; extractive, transformative and four types of service activities: distributive, producer, social and personal services.

The sectoral division of economic organization (i.e., the relative importance of the extractive, transformative and service sector) is associated with a particular profile of labor demand. To illustrate the point we need only contrast an agrarian and an industrial system. A rural extractive economy, based on primitive forms of technology, generates a demand for labor that is quite different compared to a predominantly urban industrial economy dominated by the transformative sector. The distinction between the two economies can be seen in terms of the differential selectivity by age and sex, by the skill levels required, and by the spatial and temporal distribution of the demand for workers.

The structure of the economy – which we have defined according to sectoral divisions, and in terms of the quantity and quality of labor demand determines central aspects of the household decision environment. And, as noted in Figure 2.2, it is the household's socioeconomic environment that influences mode of production and, hence, population structure.

Modes of production

In an earlier section, we argued that population structure (age distribution, birth rate, and so on) can be viewed as the aggregate result of reproductive behavior that takes place within individual households. Following similar reasoning, we can think of economic structure (sectoral division; labor demand) as the result of aggregating the many individual units of production that make up a society's economic system. For analytical purposes, we can group these multiple production units into a limited number of "MODES OF PRODUCTION." Figure 2.2 shows the term in bold type to emphasize its importance within the eco-demographic base, and to distinguish it from derivative concepts, such as "economic structure."

In our scheme, modes of production refer to the different ways people organize themselves to wrest sustenance from the natural environment. Modes of production refer, specifically, to the social relations people enter into in order to combine the biological capacity to work with the physical implements and mental skills of production to fulfill subsistence needs and to generate a surplus. Different modes of production can be identified in terms of (a) the social relations and (b) the level of technology that characterize a given economic activity. On the basis of these criteria, a broad distinction can be drawn between capitalist production, the signal characteristic of which is the wage relation and the recruitment of workers through a labor market, and non-capitalist modes, based on other means of labor recruitment and remuneration.

The mode of production that is dominant has far-reaching implications for other dimensions of social and political organization. If we ask, for example, how people produce, exchange and accumulate surplus product (i.e. if we identify the social relations of production), the answer is the basis for distinguishing between primitive communism, slavery, feudalism, capitalism and socialism. Beyond these "generic" modes of production, we can identify numerous subtypes within the capitalist and non-capitalist mode.

In the sociology of development there is longstanding debate as to the meaning and the theoretical status of mode of production. In the framework elaborated above, different modes of production are identified at the level of the labor process. The concept refers to the way in which labor power is deployed in the workplace, which, in combination with the means of production and technology, generates a surplus that is appropriated in a particular way. For our purposes, different modes of production can be empirically identified on the basis of varying types of social relations found within units of production. By virtue of situating our definition at the level of the forces and relations of production, and by treating mode of production as an empirical phenomenon, we apply the term in a way that departs from other usage.[5]

In Latin America, as in other developing areas, several modes of production are present simultaneously. A growing body of research shows that modes of production are not independent of one another, as dualist theories of development would have it. Instead, they are "articulated," often in novel ways (see Wolpe 1980). A times, different modes of production conflict with one another, as when industrial capitalism erodes the economic viability of small commodity producers. Yet different modes of production can also be functionally interdependent. One example is the peasant production of cheap wage goods, a phenomenon that operates in the interest of capital by lowering the reproduction cost of labor in urban areas. Another is the seasonal movement of migrant labor from the peasant mode to the capitalist plantation. Seasonal wages provide needed cash supplements to small farmers, and thereby contribute, contrary to the proletarianization thesis, to the persistence rather than the demise of the peasantry. At the same time, so the argument goes, employers benefit from a ready supply of cheap workers.

The theoretical and conceptual debates about the articulation of modes of production (see Wolpe 1980) need not detain us here. For our purposes it is sufficient to note that we have at hand the analytical tools to identify the various modes of production that characterize a given research site. And that, in contrast to dualist perspectives on development and social change, it is useful to think of modes of production as closely interrelated phenomena, and to keep in mind that the nature of the relationships between them is historically and geographically variable.

Class structure

To describe a society's modes of production is also to identify its class structure. So long as the productivity of labor remains at or close to a subsistence level (as in the case of hunting and gathering groups), differentiation tends to be social in nature (along age, sex and kinship lines) rather than economic (as when one group appropriates the surplus produced by another). Once an increase in labor productivity makes a significant and sustained surplus possible, the conditions are set for a struggle over how this surplus will be distributed. We speak of a class society when one subgroup of the population relies on institutionalized rules and ideologies (as opposed to, say, simple plunder) to garner surplus they did not themselves produce. Social classes are thus defined primarily by the way in which labor is recruited and remunerated in the production process, and the manner in which surplus is exchanged and accumulated. Inasmuch as modes of production are historically variable, so too is class structure. Slavery, medieval feudalism and modern capitalism have in common the existence of surplus, yet, in each case, the social relations of production, and therefore the society's class system, are markedly different.

Early treatments of the class structure of capitalism posited a straightforward dichotomy between workers and the owners of the means of production. The classical Marxian perspective assumed a homogeneity of interests internal to each class and an opposition of interests between them: wage earners pressed for higher pay and improved conditions of employment; capitalists pressed for ever higher rates of surplus extraction. Class conflict, and the competition between capitals in a competitive marketplace, were the engines of constant technological change, the effects of which reverberated throughout sociopolitical organization.

Current analyses retain the all-important notion that materially determined conflicts of interest (rather than consensus) lie at the heart of socioeconomic structure, yet elaborate the conception of social class to better capture the complexities of contemporary industrial and semi-industrial society. In those instances where the capitalist class suffers divisions that arise from sectoral differentiation, such as between financial, industrial and commercial capital, Poulantzas (1973) speaks of "class fractions." Divisions may further arise within the working class between mental and manual labor, or between supervisory and direct labor (see also, Wright 1979, 1985).

Similar reasoning leads Portes (1985) to characterize Latin American class structure using three definitional criteria: ownership of the means of production, control over labor and the mode of remuneration. On the basis of this scheme, he identifies five major class categories: dominant, bureaucratic–technical, formal proletariat, informal petty bourgeoisie, and informal proletariat. Portes uses the framework to analyze trends in income distribution, to characterize the major structural changes underway in the region and to explain the origins of political movements in urban Latin American.

The assumption underlying the studies noted above is that class structures constitute the fundamental organizing principles of society. For theorists like Wright (1985: chapter 2), this general proposition implies two corollaries which, taken together, illustrate the centrality of class in analyses of social and demographic change. First, class structures define pivotal benchmarks in trajectories of social change. Critical junctures in the process of development – say, the transition from a rural–agrarian system to an urban–industrial economy – can be specified by changes in class structure (e.g., the demise of the peasantry; the emergence of an urban proletariat). Second, the antagonisms intrinsic to a class-divided society stimulate and shape the course of social change. Not all transformations can be traced to class conflict, as is the case, for example, of changes induced by warring religious groups or by the impact of cultural and technological diffusion. The thesis, rather, is that perspectives on development, such as modernization theory, which ignore classes and the conflictive relations between them present us with superficial and incomplete accounts of how and why social change occurs.

A class analysis, as this discussion is intended to illustrate, is more than a taxonomic exercise. The utility of the concept does not lie in classification but "in its capacity to underline strategic relationships involved in the deployment of social labor' (Wolf 1982: 76). Class categories thus provide the basic analytical tools for mapping the structure of economic production, and for identifying the constellation of interests associated with it. A class perspective is essential to understanding the genesis of economic and technological change. And, as discussed in a later section, analyses of class structure play a role in establishing the origins of dominant ideology, and in comprehending the nature of the ideological battles that form the content of political discourse within the planning and legislative branches of the state, and in society at large.

Production and reproduction: comment

Modes of production and reproduction, as numerous studies in economic and social demography have shown, stand in a relation of reciprocal causation within what we have labelled the eco-demographic infrastructure. Following Marvin Harris's (1979: chapter 3) lead, our intent is to expand the Marxian notion of "economic base" to explicitly incorporate demographic variables and processes. The framework in Figure 2.2 – which is an abstract conceptualization – privileges neither one nor the other. At certain moments in history, and under particular conditions of social and economic organization, population growth may be the primary determinant of the social relations of production and of change in economic structure. Under different circumstances – for example, when capitalism is dominant – the primary determinant of change is production. Which is the more important, production or reproduction, will depend on the case at hand.

Anthropologists have argued that demographic increase against fixed resources and technology is the cause of fissioning among certain hunting and gathering groups and that increased population size is associated with greater societal complexity (e.g., Carneiro 1967). Larger size of population may also induce changes in technology, as when Boserup (1965; 1981) attributes agricultural innovation and the diffusion of technology to population pressure. Analysts concerned with the transition from feudalism to capitalism in Western Europe also turn to population growth as contributing to the creation of the proletariat. Once a capitalist system is firmly entrenched, population-stimulated innovation in manufacturing may occur because of the relationship between population size, market demand and scale economies in production (Simon 1976). Alternatively, demographic increase may obstruct industrial growth because of its negative impact on savings and investment (Coale and Hoover 1958; Enke 1960; Leff 1969). On balance, current research suggests that population growth can, and often does move a country in a "modern" direction, although market-induced adjustments to growth do not appear to be large enough to offset negative effects on per capita income of higher ratios of labor to other factors of production (National Academy of Sciences 1986).

The shortage of population can stimulate the emergence of particular social relations of production. An example is slavery in the New World. Historian Eric Williams (1944) shows how the imbalance between the supply and demand for labor gave rise to the slave mode of production in the Caribbean. Both in the Caribbean and in North America efforts were first made to force Indians into service. When these efforts failed, landowners resorted, first, to white indentured servants, convicts and other temporarily unfree labor. But Indian slavery and white servitude were inferior forms of labor recruitment compared to slaves from Africa, who possessed the cheapest and best labor power.

Other studies, mostly in social demography, reverse the causal direction to show that changes in economic organization impose optimizing pressures on the population, thereby affecting reproductive behavior. The transition from high to low fertility and mortality regimes, for example, is attributed to the evolution of bureaucratic, commercial, technical and urban-based employment. In the theory of the demographic transition, such transformations in socioeconomic structure, by creating adverse economic balances for large families, induced a decline in the birth rate (Notestein 1953).

In drawing a conceptual distinction between mode of production and reproduction in the way that we have in Figure 2.2, should not disguise the essential inseparability of the two. Reproduction, in the sense in which we use the term (to include the socialization of children and the maintenance of adults), largely determines the productive needs of society and provides an essential means to their being met, namely, labor. This occurs, not merely because there are new mouths to feed, but also because the cultural level of socialization determines how much and what type of production is required. Production and reproduction function as limits on each other. Hence, it is less likely to mislead if we regard the eco-demographic infrastructure as a system that produces both people and things, often in the same process (as in the case of the peasant household), and which, of course, has its moments of reproduction, production and consumption (Jagger 1983: 158).

The concepts and relationships discussed thus far – how modes of production and reproduction are linked to economic and population structure – are conceptually situated at the level of eco-demographic infrastructure. Yet, these relationships are also influenced by other dimensions of social and political organization, which are themselves premised on the eco-demographic base. A clear example, to anticipate the presentation that follows, is the role of the state. The principal features of its structure and function are largely determined by the eco-demographic infrastructure. At the same time, state initiatives, such as development policies that stimulate certain forms of investment, or laws requiring children to attend school, can exert an important influence on modes of production and reproduction. To address issues such as these, and to complete our model of the social system, we introduce the two additional tiers in Figure 2.2: stratification system and politico-ideological superstructure.

Stratification hierarchies

The way in which a society organizes production and reproduction structurally limits and probabilistically determines the character of its stratification hierarchies. The eco-demographic infrastructure of a rural agricultural system, to take a straightforward example, generates occupational categories and patterns of land and income distribution that are quite different from the patterns associated with an urban–industrial base. The two systems are further differentiated in terms of prestige hierarchies, and with respect to the distribution of services and a broad range of amenities, such as access to education.

If the eco-demographic infrastructure establishes the fundamental attributes of the stratification system – as the above comparison of an agrarian and an industrial society suggests – it is also true that the actions of the state modify, often significantly, the form and the degree the various hierarchies assume at given historical moments. In a capitalist mode of production, for example, the increase in the concentration of income may be attenuated by minimum wage legislation or transfer payments in the form of welfare programs. Similarly, state-legislated educational policies that subsidize access to schooling, or agrarian reforms that turn agricultural lots over to rural workers, can profoundly affect the distribution of human capital and land ownership. Stratification hierarchies, therefore, can be conceptualized in terms of the interaction between the fundamental determinations of the eco-demographic infrastructure and the modifications induced by the actions of the state. What we have labelled "stratification system" in Figure 2.2 thus occupies an intermediate position between infrastructure and superstructure. The intent, which is difficult to represent in the figure given a diagram's inherently mechanistic depiction, is to underscore the multiple determinations that yield particular stratification hierarchies.

Social classes and social strata: comment

The distinction between social strata and social classes has significant methodological implications for the study of population. In a previous section we defined social classes at the level of infrastructure, in terms of the more or less discrete categories that characterize the social relations of a given mode of production. Socioeconomic strata, on the other hand, are descriptive concepts that depict gradations in income, education or social prestige. The former is firmly entrenched in the Marxian tradition, and situates its definitional criteria at the level of production, in terms of the division of labor and the form of surplus appropriation in the workplace. The latter is of Weberian vintage, defining social strata according to market or exchange relations, or in terms of ascribed characteristics such as racial and ethnic identities.

In population and development research, social classes and social strata each play important but different roles in data collection and interpretation. An example drawn from the study of infant mortality (see chapter 5) illustrates the nature and the significance of the distinction. In the initial phase of empirical research, the findings document the inverse relationship between the probability of death in the early years and level of household income. The analytical focus, at this point in the investigation, centers on the impact of one aspect of social stratification (quantity of income available to the household) and the probability of death in the first twelve months of life.

In subsequent stages of the investigation the inquiry can proceed in two directions. One is to explore, at a micro level, the various biological and behavioral mechanisms through which income (more properly, the lack of income) leads to a high death rate among infants. The other research avenue proceeds in the opposite direction, into the terrain of macro relationships that determine the distribution of income to begin with. To explain the high concentration of income we introduce a wage determination theory. It is based on the general proposition that, in addition to considerations of supply and demand, income levels are determined by the relative power of capital and labor in the workplace. In order to substantiate this general proposition, we turn to historical analyses of various periods in Brazilian history which illustrate the political and institutional mechanisms adopted by the state to control unions and to weaken the bargaining power of labor. In so doing we displace social strata as the central analytical axis with a concern for social class.

The point we wish to emphasize is that controversy as to whether social strata *or* social class is the appropriate dimension is a fruitless debate, and one that confuses levels of analysis (i.e., the distinction between infrastructure and structure). Insofar as the analysis of infant mortality is concerned, both strata and class are relevant (in addition to the behavioral and biological phenomena involved). Yet, each concept occupies a different "conceptual position" within the framework and, as a necessary consequence, enters the chain of reasoning at a different point in the argument.

Interest groups
Interest groups – or "class formations" in Wright's (1985: 28–9) ter-

minology – refer to collectivities such as unions, political parties and neighborhood organizations. Some interest groups have a clearly defined class base, such as labor unions. Other collectivities may coalesce along ethnic and racial lines (chapter 6), or in terms of place of residence (chapter 5), and therefore are not clearly associated with a particular social class. This is not to say that interest group formation is arbitrary, or independent of the other dimensions of social organization. Whatever their basis, interest groups nonetheless operate within the limits imposed by the eco-demographic infrastructure. Inasmuch as collectivities are successful in advocating their interests they can, depending on their objectives, influence production and reproduction, and/or shape the content of state policy.

Superstructure

The state

Farthest removed from the eco-demographic base, yet interacting with all levels of social organization, are the state and the cultural and ideological precepts that give subjective meaning to social action and political practice. The state is both a set of organizations (branches and agencies of government, including the army and the courts) possessing legitimate authority, and a set of institutionalized ways of conducting public business. Unlike classical liberalism, which treats the state as a neutral arbiter of competing interests, the materialist orientation conceives of the state (as well as culture and ideology) as a component of superstructure – those aspects of social organization which are "erected" on a society's infrastructure. The state institutionalizes the conflict between contending classes and social groups and intervenes at all levels of social structure to secure cohesion (not always successfully). The structure of economic production and the existing distribution of material goods and political power is thereby maintained (Poulantzas 1973).

Recent studies shun the strict determinism that tainted earlier materialist treatments of the state, yet continue to endorse its class-based character and the system-maintenance functions the state performs. If the "instrumentalists" once saw the state as a mere tool of the dominant class, analysts now speak of the state's "relative autonomy." Walton (1986: 189) summarizes the reasons why the state is more than simply an instrument of the dominant class: First, its own legitimacy depends upon the fact, or appearance, of serving all people. Second, in the attempt to find the least hazardous path through the thicket of conflicting interests, the state is bound to act in ways that do not represent a single class or group. Third, the state develops its own interests in legitimacy and political support. The notion of relative autonomy labels the indeterminacy between the economic and the political without abandoning the strong influence of the former over the latter.

Claus Offe (1985), drawing more from Weber than from Marx, comes to a similar conclusion. The state, Offe argues, is independent of any systematic class control, yet the bureaucracy, which depends on capital accumulation for its continued existence, must represent the interests of capital anyway. In the Latin American context, O'Donnell (1973) contends that the need to increase capital accumulation became increasingly difficult once the initial phase of import-substitution industrialization had run its course. The need to "deepen" industrialization through vertical integration could be achieved only by attracting foreign capital. To do this required increasing the rate of profit and guaranteeing a favorable long-term investment climate. The outcome in Brazil, as in Chile and Argentina, was, according to O'Donnell, the imposition of "bureaucratic-authoritarianism," the only regime type capable of contending with the structural imperative of later stages of post-World War II development in the larger countries of Latin America.

If the 1960s saw the exhaustion of import-substitution industrialization and an end to parliamentary systems, the 1980s, with the redemocratization of Brazil and Argentina, holds the promise of the exhaustion of bureaucratic-authoritarian regimes (Stepan 1985: 318). These political transformations have stimulated a renewed interest in the state as the subject of theoretical and empirical research (see Carnoy 1984; Evans, Rueschmeyer and Skocpol 1985). Whatever differences separate contemporary approaches, all endorse the conviction that, one way or another, the structure and the function of the state is intrinsically bound to the economy and its associated class structure and interest groups, and that the state, as a key participant in production and market exchange (Evans 1985), necessarily plays a central role in analyses of economic and demographic change.

Culture

Culture is a term in the social sciences that is used far more often than it is defined. For our purposes, culture refers to norms (and their associated sanctions), values, belief systems and language. Culture provides a set of rules and evaluative principles that guide behavior, and a cognitive orientation that supplies an ontology and cosmology. To acquire a culture – to be socialized – is to acquire a vision, or model, of the social and natural world, and of the relationship between the physical and metaphysical.

The cognitive orientations, as well as the behavioral rules that are appropriate to particular situations and which adhere to different social roles, pervade human interaction. In the realm of production, the status rank of particular jobs, like the normative expectations of a "fair day's work," are among the subjective criteria people routinely, often unconsciously, invoke in their daily lives. Similarly, the sphere of reproduction is, to one degree or another, structured by people's perception of what constitutes appropriate behavior, and by the patriarchal assumptions about a "woman's place," a man's role as "breadwinner," or a "mother's responsibility" to her husband and her children.

Yet, as the framework asserts, cultural traits do not exist in isolation of other dimensions of social structure. Rather, the cultural cognitions that subjectively inform human behavior at all levels of social organization are also, to one degree or another, derivative of the eco-demographic and stratification systems constructed by human action.[6]

Ideology

Within the broad spectrum of cognitions that comprise a culture, certain attitudes, values and beliefs morally justify existing socioeconomic, political and gender relationships. As such, they contribute to perpetuating a given social organization. Those aspects of culture that perform this function are what we refer to as "dominant ideology."

Because powerful economic groups control both the means of material and mental or ideological production, the ideas that become influential in a society at a given point in its history reflect only a narrow range of possibilities coincident with the material bases of existing power and privilege. This does not imply a one-to-one identity between economy and consciousness. The construction of ideology – what Eric Wolf (1982: 390) calls the "ecology of collective representations" – takes place in a field of ideological options in which groups delineate their position through selection among alternatives. If a society's economic organization gives rise to idea-systems that morally justify existing structures, such systems are also multiple and contradictory.

The production of ideology is not only cognitive. It also involves the exercise of power to maintain ideological hegemony. Calls for a more equitable distribution of land or income, or for smaller family size, or any ideas that run counter to the assumptions embedded in dominant ideology and which threaten the position of vested interest groups, at best receive little attention. At worst, such proposals are labelled "subversive" and their proponents are silenced by the repressive arm of the state. Ideas, therefore, are rarely "innocent." Mental conceptions, including belief systems, morality, philosophy and law, as well as patriarchal definitions of women's roles and their reproductive responsibilities, either reinforce (dominant ideology) or challenge (critical ideology) existing social and economic relations. And they do so actively, as biased participants in sociopolitical intercourse.

World system

Finally, none of the relationships depicted in Figure 2.2 operate in isolation from the larger global context. Latin America's present underdevelopment is partly the legacy of its colonial past, and of the peripheral role that the region has played in the world system. John Walton (1986: 3–5) identifies three critical periods in the international division of labor, each of which had different economic and demographic implications for developing countries.

The first involved the incorporation of colonial regions as new sources of raw materials and as (often grudging) consumers of manufactured goods produced in the center. In those regions where labor was in short supply, the burgeoning world demand for labor-intensive commodities such as cotton and sugar led to slavery. The forced migration of men and women from Africa forever changed the racial and cultural composition of New World populations.

The second international division of labor, which dates approximately from the 1930s, involves industrialization within the underdeveloped periphery by a national bourgeoisie, foreign enterprise, or the two together. Relying on a heavy share of capital goods from the advanced countries, the logic was to capture and deepen local markets and, later, to implement the policy of import substitution. The development policies adopted during the period often subsidized urban industrial growth at the expense of the agricultural sector. The demographic result was to stimulate rural-to-urban migration, a flow that reached tidal proportions by the late 1950s.

Today's third stage, begun in the 1960s, features the export of the production process itself from center to periphery, relocating in the hospitable confines of the Third World where assembly plants draw on abundant sources of cheap and highly tractable workers. The "new international division of labor" is based on globally integrated production, orchestrated by the multinational firm and executed with the active participation of state in both center and periphery. As a new stage in the international system, the results differ from the past, generating novel forms of uneven development. Internationally linked export sectors of Third World economies grow and profit in the midst of generalized poverty. Thriving 'offshore production" plants in such industries as electronics and textiles maximize returns from the high productivity afforded by sophisticated technology and the low cost of labor, often at the expense of employment in the advanced centers of the global system.

As a consequence of these transformations, fluctuations in international commodity and financial markets exert greater influence than before. Salient examples include the consequences of the oil price hike in 1974 and 1978, soaring interest rates in developed countries in the late 1970s and the world recession in the early 1980s. For developing countries these events have meant a decline in export revenues, reduced industrial investment, rising unemployment and a spiralling foreign debt. As we shall see in subsequent chapters, externally-imposed contingencies such as these have profound internal economic, political and demographic ramifications.

*   *   *

The framework developed here introduces population variables into a reformulated materialist model of socioeconomic, political and demographic interaction. The concepts and relationships identified serve to orient the analytic journey from population, to social structure and back again. Nowhere is the spirit of this approach more succinctly stated than in Marx's discussion of method in *The Grundrisse*. In the introduction to that volume, he cites population as an example of a category which should be treated as the outcome of multiple determinations. People are the basis of a society's productive activity. Yet, if we begin with undifferentiated population as the analytical unit, we do so with a chaotic vision of the whole. An understanding of population, therefore, depends on the prior elucidation of "simpler concepts," such as the social classes of which a population consists.

Yet, it is one thing to make the epistemological claim that explanations of the relationships between population, development and inequality require a more holistic approach than is traditionally used; it is quite another to develop a strategy for studying the social world which allows one to systematically link quantitative findings about demographic behavior with historical and qualitative data on socioeconomic and political structure. General propositions about moving from the concrete to the abstract and back to the concrete are not, in themselves, very helpful. The problem, Wright (1979: 12) notes, is *how* to move from the concrete to the abstract, and how to move back. And to this methodological problem we would add a theoretical one: how to anticipate causality in highly complex systems, which is after all a major objective of social science, without falling prey to rigid determinism, or to the teleological functionalism shared by such apparently diverse theoretical positions as that of Talcott Parsons and certain brands of Marxism.

The issue, in our view, is fundamentally a conceptual one. We can always make the familiar (and, in academia, the self-serving) claim that "more data are needed." Yet, in a country like Brazil at least, much of the key information either exists or can be generated. The mere accumulation of more data will not, in itself, get us very far. The challenge, rather, is to arrange the information into a coherent story. The job is complicated by the fact that available data are necessarily cast at different levels of analysis ranging from quantitative censuses and surveys, to anthropological ethnographies and historical accounts of institutional change. Indispensable to the task is some guide, or blueprint, which, if only in a preliminary way, serves to order and to direct the process of data collection and interpretation.

For a conceptual framework to perform this function, and for it to do so while embracing a holistic view of the socio-demographic system, requires that the model specify causal priorities, however tentative and subject to qualification. The kind of freewheeling holism one often finds in the literature, in which everything is causally connected to everything else, is singularly unhelpful in developing a strategy for studying the social world. A system of any kind, whether social or physical, by definition involves relationships between component elements such that change in one leads to changes in the rest. Yet, in the social world some relationships are essential to the entire structure; others are subsidiary. And even the latter are not wholly derivative since subsidiary structures can themselves modify the primary ones in ways that are essential to the course of change and development.

The framework outlined in previous pages defines eco-demographic base, stratification system and politico-ideological superstructure. It further posits a set of causal relationships, or determinations, that link the various components of social organization. It is worth repeating here that the framework itself should not be thought of as the end product of research. Rather it is a prelude to analysis. The conceptual framework does not provide answers, not does it represent an a priori conclusion. It is designed only to explicate the logic of the relations to be explored, and to chart the course of an investigation. The elements of the framework do not, in themselves, represent concrete phenomena. To apply the framework requires, therefore, that we "fill in" the institutional details and the contingent historical factors that enter into the story of a particular country – in this case Brazil.

The conceptual framework outlined in this chapter, like all frameworks, is not falsifiable in the same way that a null hypothesis can be rejected on the basis of a particular empirical finding. The framework can, and hopefully does, generate theories and hypotheses that, in turn, are subject to empirical verification. But the framework itself is more properly regarded as the conceptual map of the terms and relational principles that allow us systematically to join different types of data within a coherent model of the overall socio-demographic system. The framework posits a way of conceptualizing the social system such that the causes and the consequences of changes in purely demographic variables – fertility, mortality, migration, population growth, age structure – can be seen as integral components of a larger model of economic and political structure.

The model outlined in previous pages endorses, at least in a very general sense, essential features of historical materialism. The causal priority given to the economic sphere, as well as the importance accorded class, conflict and ideology in the study of change and development are among the insights appropriated from the longstanding materialist tradition. Contemporary versions of materialist thought further inspired us to abandon a nation-centric view in favor of a perspective that treats nation-states, and the regions within them, as elements of a world system of relationships.

Yet we have adhered dogmatically neither to the original materialist formulation, nor to its neo-Marxist successors. The most significant departure from the basic model and its modern variants was to expand the definitional scope of infrastructure (see Seccombe 1983). In our framework a society's mode of production and its mode of reproduction together comprise its eco-demographic base. By incorporating population into the conceptualization of infrastructure, we explicitly invite demographic variables into the core of the analytical framework. In this way we distance ourselves both from those perspectives, such as orthodox Marxism, that treat population structure and change as epiphenomena of economic organization, as well as neo-Malthusian approaches that advocate a crude demographic determinism. In our view, human reproduction is inextricably bound up with the structure of material production, forming, in their interaction, the infrastructural limitations within which the other dimensions of social and political organization emerge.

The idea of structural limitation is central to understanding the causal relationships between the various elements of the framework. As a general definition, the concept of structural limitation "constitutes a pattern of determination in which some social structure establishes limits within which some other structure or process can vary, and establishes probabilities for the specific structures or processes that are possible within those limits" (Wright 1979: 16–17). The concept of structural limitation retains the fundamental causality posited by the materialist position, yet avoids the pitfalls of vulgar determinism. Certain aspects of social organization, such as political institutions, are "determined by" other more basic structures and processes, such as the eco-demographic infrastructure, inasmuch as the latter probabilistically determines the former within a wide range of possible alternatives. Specifically, the eco-demographic base (modes of production and reproduction) conditions, but does not uniquely determine, other aspects of social and political organization – namely, stratification hierarchies; interest groups; the form and action of the state; and the cultural and ideological elements of human consciousness.

These "determined" structures, moreover, are not simply passive outcomes, or reflections of infrastructural properties. On the contrary, social classes, interest groups of various sorts and indeed the state itself often take actions that transform modes of production and reproduction. If the forces of transformation overwhelm the forces for maintenance of the existing order, the base itself is changed. Hence, the very infrastructure that sets limits on the action of classes, interest groups and the state is at the same time transformed by the actions so limited. This is another way of making the point we have emphasized throughout: that economic and demographic institutions and processes both affect, and are affected by, the process of social change and development.

3

Growth and distribution in historical perspective

The first Portuguese to land in the New World in the sixteenth century settled the eastern seaboard of South America. The sparsely populated region they encountered stood in marked contrast to the densely inhabited Mexican *meseta* and Andean *altiplano* colonized by Spain. For the *conquistadores* in Spanish Latin America, the presence of long-established indigenous civilizations in Mexico and Peru meant the opportunity to appropriate vast quantities of gold and silver. The plunder of conquered territories provided Spain with a booty previously unknown to the world. As Spain consolidated the defense of its precious-metal-producing areas to the west, Portugal sought other ways to exploit its possessions in the Americas. The early colonists who settled the coastal regions turned to the export of brazilwood, a valuable dye product from which the country took its name. Within a few years of the initial expeditions, merchants obtained license from the crown to establish trading posts where logs were received from the local natives in exchange for tools and clothing. From these modest beginnings Brazil later grew into the largest and most economically powerful country in Latin America.

Economic cycles and the moving frontier

Sugar

The exploitation of hardwoods in the sixteenth century was only the first of many export cycles. By the mid-1500s the European population of the colony grew to about 100,000, and the once plentiful brazilwood forests were depleted (Simonsen 1969: 121). Sugar then became Brazil's principal export product. The rise of sugar production, in response to increased demand in Western Europe, illustrates the domestic consequences of international market forces associated with the emerging world economy in the sixteenth and seventeenth centuries. Before that time, few Europeans even knew of the existence of sugar. By 1650, the nobility and wealthy had become inveterate eaters of sugar, a commodity that figured prominently in their medicine, literary imagery and displays of privilege. By the late 1700s, the use of sugar had spread beyond the ranks of the aristocracy to become a necessity – albeit an expensive one – in diets generally. By 1900 sugar supplied nearly one fifth of the calories consumed in England (Mintz 1985: 5–6).

The first plantations in Brazil were located along the humid northeastern seaboard, in a band of rich soils called the *Zona da Mata*. Sugar production was highly labor-intensive, and required substantial capital investment. The practice of handing out large tracts of land, and the sizeable investment that sugar required laid the foundation for the emergence of a powerful landed elite. The establishment of large plantations, and the failure to develop a more diversified economy, meant that about 90 per cent of the income generated by the export trade remained concentrated in the hands of sugar mill and plantation owners (Furtado 1963: 48).

Once set in motion, the plantation system showed a remarkable resistance to fragmentation. The required linkages between growing and cutting cane, and the boiling and crystallization process, meant not only that labor had to be highly synchronized but also that the combination of land and mill be kept intact. Because of the indivisibility of land and mill, sugar-cane plantations have not usually been divided upon inheritance (Mintz 1985: 50). A major social consequence is that the degree of land concentration in the Northeast is, even today, among the highest in the country.

The demand for labor on the plantations far exceeded the available supply. Efforts to exploit the Indian populations were unsuccessful, and it was too costly to transport the necessary number of Europeans. Long before the colony of Brazil was founded, the Portuguese had participated in brigandage ventures. Drawing on this grim talent, slavery became the solution to the planters' labor shortage, a decision based less on racist grounds than the simple economic fact that black African slaves were the cheapest source of unfree labor. Slavery, moreover, was well-adapted to the technical needs of growing cane and converting it into sugar, a process that required careful scheduling at the top and iron discipline at the bottom of the labor process within the plantation (Mintz 1985). By the end of the seventeenth century about 70 per cent of the colonial population was of non-European origin.

The forced migration of Africans influenced the cultural and racial profile of Brazil's growing population. The slave mode of production also established racial inequalities that were not eliminated by the abolition of slavery in the late nineteenth century. Indeed, socioeconomic differences between racial groups continue to manifest themselves in contemporary Brazil. As the analysis in chapter 6 will show, the white–nonwhite distinction recorded in the 1980 census strongly correlates with differential life chances, as measured by success in the labor market, and in terms of child mortality patterns and other quality of life indicators.

While sugar dominated the economic and political life of Brazil during much of the colonial period, the growing supply of West Indian sugar in the second half of the eighteenth century led to a fall in the world price. The decline in the value of sugar, combined with the rising cost of slaves, sent the once prosperous Northeast into recession. To this day the Northeast remains the most populous and poverty stricken area of Brazil.

Sugar production generated few other economic activities. Of the total value of sugar ready for shipment at port, not more than 5 per cent came from the services rendered outside the mill. The expenditures that were made were largely limited to transportation and warehousing (Furtado 1968: 47). Other purchases included draft cattle, firewood for the furnaces, and beef, which formed part of the diet of even the slave population. Leather was in high demand for the boxes used to ship sugar to Europe. Cattle breeding was thus one of the few subsidiary activities stimulated by the sugar economy. Owing to the arid conditions in the interior of the Northeast, the low livestock density the pastures could support, and the availability of land, cattle raising quickly spread to the backlands, reaching as far as the present states of Maranhão and Piauí by the seventeenth century. When the sugar economy went into recession, the farmers and ranchers who supplied food and draft animals to the plantations reverted to subsistence production.

Gold, cotton and rubber

In the eighteenth century, sugar continued to be an important crop in terms of volume. But, as its profitability declined, the economic center of the country shifted away from the Northeast to central and southern Brazil. The discovery of gold in Minas Gerais in 1695 was a major stimulus for this movement. The feverish search for precious metals marked a new phase in the economic and demographic history of the country. Gold production, which reached a peak in the 1750s, mobilized great resources in the Northeast, mainly in the form of slave man-power. It also attracted migrants from southern Brazil and, for the first time, large contingents from Portugal. The heavy immigration from the mother country was due, in part, to the characteristics of the mining process. Unlike the large-scale operations in Mexico and Peru, the al-luvial deposits in Brazil afforded prospects even to persons of limited resources. The influx of population to central Brazil, in turn, was re-sponsible for the urbanization process that began with the appearance of numerous small towns and cities (Baer 1965). So great was the mi-gration to the gold areas that the government attempted to control population movement by requiring official permits and patrolling stra-tegic entry points. To regulate the shipping and trading of gold, Portu-gal moved the Captaincy General seat to Rio de Janeiro in 1763.

In the 1820s, cotton production for markets in the United States and Britain exceeded sugar's share of total exports. Cotton was the princi-pal crop grown in what was then the colony of Maranhão. After fluctu-ations in price, the cultivation of cotton fiber was intensified in the 1860s in response to the disruption in the international commodities trade caused by the Civil War in the United States. During the "world cotton famine," Brazil gained a larger proportion of the major world markets. This brought a degree of prosperity to the Northeast, especially in Ceará. But the gains were short-lived. In 1877 a drought struck the area with such devastating intensity that an estimated 200,000 people died of starvation (Furtado 1968).

Deteriorating economic conditions in the Northeast coincided with the rise in the industrialized countries' demand for rubber. The soaring price of natural latex, caused mainly by the development and increasing use of the pneumatic tire, initiated yet another cycle in Brazil's export economy. Thousands of workers abandoned the drought-stricken Northeast and migrated to the remote regions of the Amazon in search of rubber trees. But, as in the case of sugar production a century before, the high price of rubber attracted foreign competitors. Soon plantations were established in Southeast Asia that were based on a far more ef-ficient system of production compared to the primitive method of col-lecting rubber from trees widely dispersed throughout Amazônia. The increased supply of latex in the early twentieth century caused Brazil's rubber boom to collapse. In response to the rise and the fall in the price of rubber, the heavy migration to the Amazon was followed by an equally significant out-migration from the region in the 1920s.

Coffee

The exploitation of brazilwood, sugar, gold, cotton and rubber all played a role in the demographic and economic history of Brazil. But none of these commodities had a more lasting impact on the contemporary structure of agricultural and industrial production than did coffee. Coffee was introduced into Brazil around 1723 from French Guiana and was cultivated for local consumption in many parts of the country. It acquired commercial importance only at the end of the century. Prices rose as coffee grew more and more popular in the United States and in Europe. The disruption in the supply from what was then the French colony of Haiti further stimulated the demand for Brazilian coffee.

The spread of coffee cultivation occurred in three relatively distinct phases (Margolis 1979). Production for export began in the Paraíba Valley, north of the capital city of Rio de Janeiro. In the 1830s coffee was Brazil's largest and most lucrative export crop. By the 1870s, soil erosion and insect damage reduced crop yields in the valley, and cultivation spread westward into the interior of the state of São Paulo. So successful was coffee production that, by the end of the nineteenth century, Brazil accounted for three-quarters of the world's total supply. The expansion of coffee cultivation into the state of Paraná, which reached a peak in the mid-1950s, marked the latest phase in the movement of the coffee frontier.

Coffee was a highly labor-intensive crop like sugar, but it required less capital. Land was abundant and the expansion of coffee was limited only by the short supply of labor. The problem became serious in 1850 when the importation of slaves was suspended. The labor shortage threatened to become critical when slavery was abolished altogether in 1888. Between these two dates there was a dramatic increase in the trading of slaves within Brazil, yet this was insufficient to meet the growing demand for labor. As a solution, growers in southern Brazil looked to Europe for needed manpower. The imperial government and the state of São Paulo by this time were under the decisive influence of the rising class of wealthy coffee growers. The state subsidized the cost of transportation, and workers were actively recruited from Portugal, Spain and especially from Italy. There population pressure and economic depression had created a surplus of readily available labor. The influx of immigrants reached a peak in 1891–1900 when over one million people, mostly of Italian extraction, entered the country (Smith 1972).

Both rural and urban São Paulo were profoundly affected by the coffee boom. The great fortunes accumulated from the sale of coffee on the profitable international market provided capital for roads, railway and light industry. Although the plantation economy began modestly, with landholders proudly declaring that they depended on the outside world only for the purchase of gunpowder and salt (Dean 1969: 4), with the accumulation of capital, self-sufficiency gave way to a market economy and to the increased circulation of money. The prerequisites for an industrial system soon followed. As the value of the export crop rose, and the areas under cultivation expanded (made possible by the use of immigrant labor), banks and other credit institutions were established. A railroad system, though oriented to the needs of the export economy, provided the infrastructure that made domestic manufacturing profitable.[1] In the early twentieth century, São Paulo became the most advanced region of the country. "By the 1920s," Dean (1969: 13) notes, "it had replaced Rio de Janeiro and the federal capital in Brazil as the most important industrial center. By the 1940s the state undoubtedly possessed the largest agglomeration of manufacturing capacity in Latin America."

Contemporary frontier expansion

Coffee cultivation spread southward into Paraná in the middle of this century. This was soon followed by two additional phases in the expansion of the agricultural frontier. In the 1950s and the 1960s cattle ranches moved into the Central West region, the first frontier movement that was not directly associated with a particular export commodity. The westward expansion into the states of Mato Grosso and Goiás was stimulated in large measure by public investment in roads. Another significant factor was the decision to move the capital city from Rio de Janeiro to Brasília, in the inland state of Goiás. The inauguration of the new capital in April, 1960, and the completion of the Belém–Brasília Highway, ended the isolation of the west.

The agricultural frontier has continued to push northward in the 1970s and the 1980s into the humid tropical areas of the lower Amazon basin. While this process had been underway for some time, increased government intervention was decisive. In 1970, the President, General Médici, announced the Program for National Integration. This initiative called for the construction of the Transamazon and the Cuibá–Santarém Highways, and made a commitment to finance and administer the colonization of new lands made accessible by road. This gave frontier policy a more aggressive posture, manifested in elaborate colonization projects, road construction and tax incentive legislation designed to attract private investment to the region. We will explore the socioeconomic and demographic impact of these events in chapter 10. For now it is sufficient to note that state policy designed to bring this remote area of Brazil into the national economy is a key factor promoting the current occupation of Amazônia.

Political change and industrial growth

When Napoleon's armies swept through Europe and the Portuguese court sought refuge in its colonial possession in the New World, Brazil suddenly became the seat of the Portuguese Empire. For fourteen years Dom João VI ruled the empire from Rio de Janeiro. After Napoleon's abdication and the King's return to Portugal, pressure mounted to end Brazil's colonial status. In 1822, Dom Pedro, scion of the royal family, declared Brazil a sovereign nation under his leadership. Ruling as Emperor Dom Pedro I, he preserved the monarchical form of government.

In the second half of the nineteenth century there was a growing demand, both from abroad and from factions inside the country, to abolish slavery. Dom Pedro II, during whose reign the emancipation act was signed in 1888, lost the support of powerful landed groups. In 1889 the Crown fell without defenders, an event that marked the transition from monarchy to republic, which endured until 1930.

The First Republic, as it is now known, was a loose federation of states dominated by members of the ruling elite of São Paulo and Minas Gerais. During the Republican period the country's economy rested on the export of primary products. The mainstay was coffee, although other commodities played a part. In the first decade of the twentieth century rubber exports from Amazônia accounted for 40 per cent of all exports. But the boom proved to be short-lived and the spectacular rise in the rubber trade was soon followed by an equally dramatic decline. Other exports included sugar from the Northeast and cacao from Bahia.

Although agricultural commodities occupied center-stage, industrial production began to take hold. Light industries began first, mainly in textiles, clothing, shoes and food production which accounted for 57 per cent of industrial output in 1902, rising to 64 per cent in 1919. Workshops in the *colônias* and small towns in southern Brazil expanded to meet the growing needs of small farmers and a rising rural middle class. Much of the early industrial activity was pioneered by importers who found it profitable to produce what they had been buying abroad (Baer 1979: 33–7). The items included furniture, farm tools and equipment, grain mills, steam turbines, leather goods and foodstuffs such as cooking oil and lard. The flow of manufactured goods into Brazil was interrupted by World War I. This could have contributed to industrialization (Simonsen 1969), although there is disagreement about the relative importance of this factor (Baer 1979: 39).

Still, coffee remained the "hinge on which the Brazilian economy was to swing for several decades to come" (Merrick and Graham 1979: 15). Since coffee prices are most responsive to supply factors, the government attempted to control fluctuations by limiting the quantity of coffee reaching the market. The government developed a "valorization" plan designed not to curtail production but rather to withhold from sale coffee that was already grown and harvested. Artificaly high prices paid to domestic producers only encouraged new investments in the crop, thereby accentuating the need for further government intervention. Price defense policies thus had to be combined with measures to discourage further investment, an initiative that met with limited success. Coffee was protected at the expense of industry and other sectors of agriculture and increased Brazil's indebtedness to foreign banks that financed the stockpiling scheme. "The coffee ruling class," as Furtado (1963: 204) put it, " ... managed to transfer to the community as a whole the bulk of the burden of the cyclical price fall."

The protective actions taken by coffee growers eventually led to their political undoing. A decisive event was the onset of the world depression, a factor that mobilized new political coalitions in the country. But, even before the stock market crash in 1929, the export economy was in crisis. The second bumper crop in as many years sent unprecedented quantities of coffee onto the market. Prices fell, the valorization program failed and financial reserves were severely strained (Poppino 1968: 255). Reaction against the excessive power and dominance of coffee growers, especially in military and civilian administrative circles and among industrialists, culminated in the Revolution of 1930 that brought Getúlio Vargas to power (Furtado 1963: fn. 3). Vargas was a charismatic figure who ruled Brazil until the end of World War II.

The depression

Compared to the United States, Brazil weathered the Great Depression relatively well. Indeed, the 1930s proved to be an important decade for Brazilian industry. It is ironic that this is attributed, in part, to the government's continued support of the coffee sector. Since coffee accounted for the largest proportion of the country's exports, the support program was taken over by the federal government which bought all coffee, destroying what could not be sold or stored. This dampened the rise in unemployment, not only in the coffee sector, but also in other areas of the economy linked to it. Because the value of the product was less than the income created, coffee support was a type of anti-cyclical program that absorbed some of the shock of the depression. Furtado (1963: 211) notes: "Brazil was in fact constructing the famous pyramids which Keynes was to envisage some years later. Even though undertaken unconsciously, it implied an anti-cyclical policy of much broader scope than any practiced by industrialized countries."

A sharp devaluation of the currency in the 1930s increased the price of imports. Less income was spent abroad and domestic employment levels were maintained. This boosted internal demand for manufactured goods. The coffee support program thus sustained employment and internal demand at a time when imports fell. The consequent rise in the relative price of manufactured goods acted as a catalyst for a spurt of industrial production (Baer 1979: 43).

With the Revolution of 1930, a new coalition challenged the power of the dominant agricultural elite and significantly altered national political institutions. Vargas and his associates saw themselves as modernizing nation-builders who found the panacea for the country's economic ills in industrial expansion. Under Vargas, the federal government was no longer the mediator between contending regional groups. It now became a dominant factor in the political and economic arena and the once highly autonomous states were soon brought under firm central control. In a 1937 ceremony, Vargas burned the state flags as a dramatic symbol of the federal government's increased power. Vargas looked to labor for his political support and passed a wide range of policies that favored the working class while, at the same time, bringing the incipient labor movement under state control. A key element of Vargas's Estado Novo (1937–45) was an elaborate corporatist system of labor relations in which unions were formed under the tutelage of state administrative agencies (Erickson and Middlebrook 1982: 214–15). Centralized control over wages and labor continues to this day, a factor that has profound consequences for the distribution of income (discussed later in this chapter) and for the level and pattern of mortality rates in Brazil (chapters 4 and 5).

Postwar development

Vargas remained chief of state until 1945. After 1937, he ruled as dictator without the restraints of congress or elections. Following the defeat of the Axis powers, Vargas was deposed by the armed forces in a wave of postwar democratic enthusiasm. But Vargas did not disappear from the political scene, and in 1951 he returned to office by popular vote. Vargas remained in power for only three years, when he was again forced to resign. An attempt to assassinate an opposition leader resulted instead in the murder of an air force officer. The incident, and widespread accusations of corruption within the administration, brought a wave of anti-Vargas sentiment. Rather than accept an ultimatum from the military, Vargas took his own life.

There was then a succession of freely elected presidents. The most visible was Juscelino Kubitschek (1956–60). Promising "fifty years of growth in five" he stimulated an unprecedented rate of economic growth in steel and transportation, and established a national automobile industry. But these ambitious development schemes exacted a high price. A threefold increase in the cost of living, and a spiraling foreign debt, were among the legacies of the Kubitschek years.

These factors undermined the economic and political stability of subsequent administrations. Jânio Quadros was elected in 1960 but resigned after only seven months in office. His successor, João Goulart, described as a "labor-leftist" (Poppino 1968: 280) was deposed by the army in March, 1964. The military, which assumed power with the support of the middle class and the business community, continued to exercise ultimate political power in Brazil until 1985.

The period from 1945 to 1960 was one of rapid industrial growth. Domestically manufactured products began to replace imported consumer durables and intermediate goods. Industrialization brought sweeping changes in social structure, and modified the balance of power between urban and rural interest groups. New development ideologies that were to guide state economic policies in the postwar years accompanied these changes.

Old policies were based on orthodox theories of international trade that were grounded in the classical law of comparative economic costs. Here the ideal international division of labor was one where developing countries generated primary products in exchange for finished goods produced by developed ones. The ideological premises of such a view were thoroughly compatible with the interests of Brazil's traditional oligarchy. This affinity is clearly revealed in President Campos Salles's claim (in 1889) that Brazil's place was to export that which it could best produce and import from others what they are better suited to provide (cited in Dickenson 1978: 13).

The economic and political emergence of an urban bourgeoisie in the 1950s fundamentally changed all that. Development policy became "inward oriented," with an emphasis on "import substitution industrialization" (ISI) that would foster domestic production of imported manufactured products. To protect and stimulate domestic industry, various types of exchange controls and tariffs were applied, and the inflow of foreign capital was encouraged (Bergsman 1970).

The theoretical underpinnings of ISI came from the writings of Raul Prebisch, of the United Nations Economic Commission for Latin America (ECLA). Rejecting the orthodox view, Prebisch persuasively argued that the classic international division of labor widened rather than narrowed the income differentials between the industrial "centers" and the agricultural "periphery" of the global economy (reviewed in chapter 2). In retrospect, however, it appears that ISI did not do away with external dependence so much as change its nature. Despite the effort to break away, Brazil continued to rely on imported capital goods to run its industrial parks (Baer and Doellinger 1978: 155).

Brazil's ISI policies also worked to the detriment of the agricultural sector. In the 1950s the prevailing development framework was the "dualist" model that relegated agriculture to a secondary priority. In countries with a high rate of population growth, it assumed zero marginal productivity in the "traditional" sector. Under these circumstances the function of the state was to promote industrial accumulation by shifting resources from the agricultural export sector to the urban industrial economy. Involuntary transfers were accomplished through discriminatory trade and exchange policies. (The impact of these policies on agriculture and the consequences for rural to urban migration are discussed in chapter 9.) Import substitution industrialization, and the various mechanisms by which the state subsidized domestic industrial groups, contributed to, and were a reflection of, the profound changes in the socioeconomic and political structure of the country.

Military rule and economic "miracles"

Political and economic turmoil marked the years following Quadros's sudden resignation in August, 1961. Vice President Goulart was allowed to take office only on condition that he share power with a newly created parliamentary form of government, an arrangement that hampered the emergence of a strong executive. Even after a 1963 plebiscite restored full power to the presidency, Goulart found it difficult to chart a clear course through the many opposing pressures. Agitation for land and tax reform grew. Labor leaders demanded wage adjustments. The business community pressured for credit relief. Foreign suppliers expected cash for all sales to Brazil as the Goulart government seemed headed for a unilateral moratorium on the foreign debt (Skidmore 1978). Goulart appealed to nationalist sentiment and announced that the government would expropriate privately owned petroleum refineries and begin a partial agrarian reform. In the context of a severe economic crisis, and in a political climate increasingly permeated with cold war hysteria, these were catalysts that set off the 1964 military coup.

The end of civilian government was the beginning of aggressive economic policies designed to control inflation, attract foreign investment and stimulate capital accumulation. The unprecedented rise in aggregate output between 1968 and 1974, dubbed the Brazilian "miracle," was regarded a premier accomplishment of economic policy. Despite the allusion to divine intervention, the "miracle" was the consequence of a more or less distinct model of development planning.

The priority concerns in the first years after the coup were to stabilize and reform financial markets. On the advice of civilian technocrats, the military government curtailed expenditures, improved the tax-collection system, and tightened credit. Bonds and savings deposits were indexed to the rate of inflation. The Capital Market Law of 1965 strengthened and stimulated greater use of the stock market. Tax incentives were widely used to influence regional and sectoral imbalances (the impact of these on Amazônia is dealt with in chapter 10). The Brazilian National Development Bank (BNDE) financed the acquisition of capital goods produced in Brazil. To keep the exchange rate from becoming overvalued and to discourage speculation, the cruzeiro was devalued at frequent but unpredictable intervals. The wage sector was squeezed by policies that meant wages lagged behind inflation and increases in productivity.

The "inward oriented" development of the 1950s was replaced by tax incentive schemes designed to stimulate and diversify Brazil's exports into manufacturing products, thus reducing its dependence on agricultural commodities, especially coffee. Foreign capital policies encouraged both official and private loans and attracted substantial direct foreign investment.

Political repression was an essential ingredient in this development model. The powers of the legislature and the civilian judiciary were sharply reduced and elections and political parties were controlled by the military government. Backed by an authoritarian regime, technocrats had a free hand to adopt measures that would badly shake if not topple a democratic government (Skidmore 1978). Troublesome public figures were banished from political life (see Soares 1979), and censorship silenced opposition voices. Violence and torture were used to eliminate "subversives," especially in the late 1960s and the early 1970s. These drastic actions were justified with a heavy dose of cold war rhetoric. By linking internal political issues to the international ideological struggle, small problems and conflicts were elevated to the category of threats to the nation's security (Cardoso 1982).

Table 3.1 presents time series data on key indicators of economic growth. The stagnation in the Brazilian economy, which began around 1962, continued after the military takeover, lasting until 1968. Observers attribute this to the stabilization measures applied in the early years of the military regime, and to the necessary time lag it took before the reforms in the financial system could take hold. In 1968 Brazil entered a boom period that was to last until 1974. From 1968 to 1974 rates of annual growth averaged 11.3 per cent, nearly three times that recorded in the previous five-year period. Industry was the leading sector, expanding at 12.6 per cent a year. Within manufacturing, growth was concentrated in consumer durables and chemicals (Baer 1979: 94–5).

The economic downturn after 1973 coincided with the rise in the international price of oil. This was an event with severe repercussions in the domestic economy. Although researchers disagree as to the relative importance of the petroleum price rise in deflating the "economic miracle," (e.g., Faucher 1981), the fact remains that the country has been, and continues to be, highly dependent on foreign oil supplies.

After the oil crisis, economic planning deviated from the post-1964 orthodoxy. Sensitive to the victories of the opposition parties in the senatorial election of November, 1974, the government could hardly withstand a continued recession. To stimulate industrial production, planners took measures to expand aggregate demand. Rigid import controls and export promotion programs were adopted to fight the balance of payments deficit. But at the end of 1976 the economy was heating up too quickly. The rekindled inflation rate was attributed to excessive demand. Policy makers revised the ambitious investment programs begun in 1974 in an effort to curb inflation (Bacha 1980: 41–3).

Table 3.1. *Yearly growth rates of real Gross Domestic Product, industry and agriculture*
(percentage change)

Years	Real GDP	Industry	Agriculture
1956–61	7.8	10.3	5.7
1962–7	3.7	3.9	4.0
1968	11.2	13.3	4.4
1969	9.0	12.1	3.7
1970	8.8	10.3	1.0
1971	13.3	14.3	11.4
1972	11.7	13.3	4.1
1973	14.0	15.0	3.5
1974	9.8	9.9	8.5
1975	5.6	6.2	3.4
1976	9.2	12.9	4.2
1977	4.7	2.3	9.6
1978	1.7	5.9	−0.9
1979	6.4	6.4	5.1
1980	7.2	7.9	6.3
1981	−3.2	−10.2	6.4
1982	0.9	0.6	−2.5
1983	−3.2	−6.8	2.2

Sources: Baer (1979: 95); Tyler (1984: Table 2)

Throughout the 1970s macroeconomic policies followed this sort of stop-and-go pattern.

The economic path Brazil pursued has had far-reaching consequences. The distribution of personal income, already skewed in 1960, became even more concentrated following the coup. Similarly, transnational firms, already present in the country, assumed greater importance after 1964. Operating independently or through joint ventures with Brazilian firms, they now dominate the most dynamic sectors of the country's economy, even though foreign investment represents only 10 per cent of total investment (Baer and Doellinger 1978; Bacha 1980). Foreign trade has greatly diversified. Primary sector exports now include (in addition to coffee, sugar and other traditional items) soybeans, citrus concentrate and frozen poultry. In 1978 manufactured goods accounted for 50 per cent of total foreign trade with a significant proportion derived from the sale of armaments. In 1980, Brazil sold more than US$1 billion in weapons, ranging from flamethrowers to ships. Brazilian helicopters are being used in Paraguay and Bolivia, and submarines will soon be produced in collaboration with the West German navy (Levine 1982: 63).

Fettered to the international system

Nowhere is the interdependence of the modern world more evident than in international financial markets (Furtado 1982). And no single issue more clearly reflects the consequences of this interdependence on the prospects of Brazilian development than does the current debt crisis. In 1964 the Brazilian foreign debt totaled US$3 billion. By 1974, the first full year of the oil crisis, it had jumped to over US$17 billion, and it soared again after the "second shock" in 1979. By 1982 the debt was around US$80 to US$88 billion. In 1984 Brazil owed its creditors more than US$100 billion.

Interest rates oscillated between 4.4 and 5 per cent in the first half of the 1970s, but the floating rates more than trebled in 1981 and 1982 to between 15 and 19 per cent (Pang 1983). The jump in interest rates has had disastrous consequences. Each percentage point rise cost Brazil an extra $450 million a year. In 1983, Brazil was only able to close its books after a massive infusion of loans from the United States and European Banks and the International Monetary Fund. Brazil saw very little of the money, however, as most of it went to pay the $11 billion in interest. Repaying the principal was out of the question. But, so long as interest payments keep coming in, private banks continued to reap huge profits.

The financial house of cards could easily tumble, especially in a recessionary period such as that in the early 1980s. If Brazil, or any other major borrower, refused to pay, or if a US bank were to ignite a stampede by calling in a loan, it would have immediate and far-reaching international consequences. The biggest financial institutions in the United States would be among the first to feel the pinch. Citibank, to take one example, had more on loan to Brazil in 1984 than its entire shareholders' capital (Lernoux 1984).

Under the military regime, the political opposition in Brazil demanded a moratorium on the debt as the only way to save the failing economy. Spokesmen for the United States banking community contended that a borrower who declared a moratorium without the approval of creditors would impose on itself an even worse recession. According to *Business Week*, such action would "reduce the debtor country to little more than a barter economy and make its ships and air-craft vulnerable to seizure by the banks" (July 25, 1983: 59). "The re-lationship," as one analyst wrote, "is a little like that of two people on a see-saw: if one jumps off suddenly, both are likely to get hurt" (Kuczynski 1983: 27).

In the 1950s and 1960s the great bulk of loans came from public sources. This included aid from industrialized countries and long-term credit from institutions such as the World Bank and the Interamerican Development Bank (IDB). When private capital went south it was mostly in the form of direct investments of various kinds. In the 1970s, however, public funding sources failed to keep pace with the needs of developing countries. The IDB and the International Monetary Fund faced difficulties raising the cash for their own operations at a time when private international banking entered a new era of unprecedented growth. The primary stimulus was the fabulous influx of new liquidity caused by the first OPEC price hike in late 1973. The billions of "petro-dollars" that suddenly entered the coffers of the Western banking system made credit cheap and prompted big international lenders to ag-gressively and incautiously compete for new borrowers. Lending to the Third World was immensely profitable, and Latin America became the prime target of foreign loans. By the end of 1981 close to 80 per cent of Latin America's debt was private and most of it was short term with changing interest rates.

The world recession in 1980–1 turned the global money market on its head. Latin American countries suffered the combined blow of a con-traction in the demand for their exports, a deterioration of the terms of trade, a rise in interest rates, a drop in the supply of external financing and a noticeable increase in protectionism (CEPAL 1983: 55). Whether the result was insolvency (that borrowers can "never" pay) or illiquid-ity (that they cannot pay now) is largely a question of degree and defi-nition. One way or another events in the early 1980s spelled a financial crisis of unprecedented proportions.

In Brazil the spiraling debt scenario played itself out in a somewhat different way. Unlike many of its Latin American neighbors, the crisis did not originate with reduced exports since the growth of these speeded up and diversified. Nor did it lie in greater imports, as these remained stable or increased only slightly since 1975. Rather, the pri-mary cause of the debt crisis has been the unfavorable trend in the terms of trade and the resources needed to service the external debt. In 1981, the "repatriation" of profits and interest alone represented 3.2 per cent of total product, whereas in the 1950s and 1960s the corresponding proportion did not exceed 1 per cent. Moreover, since 1975 a change in the relative prices of imports and exports cost Brazil an amount equivalent to 3.7 per cent of the annual gross product in the year in question (CEPAL 1983: 64).

To a very large extent Brazil's present problem of indebtedness was caused by the drastic deterioration in its terms of trade since 1978 and, to a lesser degree, the upsurge in interest rates. According to José Serra (1982), if conditions on the world market were as favorable in the early 1980s as they were in 1978, Brazil would have no balance of payments problem. That is, if the country had traded the same volume of goods and services from 1978 to 1982, but at the favorable terms of trade operating in 1978, instead of the rapidly falling terms of trade it actually experienced, it would have accumulated a trade surplus of US$25.7 billion (1982 dollars), rather than the deficit of US$6.3 billion. The estimated cost to Brazil of the change in the terms of trade was US$32 billion. Similarly, if Brazil had paid the lower levels of interest charged in 1978 throughout the following five years, it would have saved US$15.5 billion. Taken together, these estimates suggest that Brazil paid out no less than US$47.5 billion as a result of the two conditions on the world economy.

Economic crisis in the early 1980s

To contend with the debt problem, Brazil followed the standard economic recipe, which prescribes three basic policies: contractionary measures to slow the economy in order to reduce imports; a reduction in the relative prices of exports (through the devaluation of the cruzeiro so as to boost international sales); and an increase in domestic interest rates to attract foreign capital (Serra 1982). In addition to these initiatives, government investment was frozen which, in an inflationary economy, represents a significant decline in real terms (World Bank 1983: 32).

The annual rates of change in the Gross Domestic Product (Table 3.1) reflect the magnitude of the economic crises. The indicator of economic output fell from +7.2 per cent in 1980 to −3.2 per cent in 1981. The industrial sector suffered a whopping −10.2 decline the same year. In 1982, growth in GDP climbed back to +0.9 per cent, only to drop again to −3.2 per cent the next year (Tyler 1984). From 1981 to 1983, Gross National Product per head fell by 14 per cent, the rate of growth in informal employment rose to 6.5 per cent per year (compared to the earlier rate of 3.2 per cent), and infant mortality rates in large metropolitan areas, such as São Paulo, began to climb (Pfeffer-mann 1985). Factories laid off workers in response to the crisis and the outflow of capital to meet debt service payments lowered the rate of in-ternal investment, a factor that seriously undermines the prospect of future gains in job creation. Middle and lower income groups were especially hard hit by the recession, and by yearly inflation rates in excess of 200 per cent.

The return to democracy: 1985

Unlike other dictatorships in Latin America, the Brazilian "political model" from 1964 to 1984 preserved rather than destroyed key liberal institutions (Fernando Henrique Cardoso 1982). Authoritarian rule did not spell the end of Congress or the Judiciary. Political parties con-tinued to exist, and even elections were held after the military coup in 1964. But the continued existence of these institutions was largely sym-bolic. If existing legislation did not meet the needs of the regime, it was created; if laws and institutions were inadequate, they were amended, often after the fact (Soares 1985). The Brazilian military, during its twenty-one year rule, seldom resorted to brute force or electoral she-nanigans without first establishing legal justification for its actions.

Institutional Act No. 2 was invoked in 1965 to abolish the old politi-cal party structure. The military regime then organized politicians into two parties: Arena, the majority party that supported the regime, and a minority opposition party, the Brazilian Democratic Movement (MDB). Limited political competition was permitted, but the regime did not hesitate to wield its considerable power whenever the military deemed it necessary. A confrontation between the Armed Forces and civilian politicians provoked the 1968 Institutional Act No. 5 (AI5), a tough law that initiated a period of exceptional repression that lasted until 1974. AI5 allowed President Médici a free hand to close Congress and to cancel the right of *habeas corpus*. The regime banished trouble-some public figures from political life, censored opposition voices, and used violence and torture to eliminate "subversive elements."

The military manipulated the electoral system through a series of *pacotes*, or packages of rules and regulations that were carefully de-signed to weaken the power of the opposition at the polls, yet still retain the image of democratic process. The government also controlled access to the media, deprived some MDB candidates of their political rights and, in 1978, directly appointed one-third of the senators. Despite these efforts, the MDB won resounding victories in the congressional election of 1974 and again in 1978 as each election became a kind of plebiscite against military rule. The regime nonetheless maintained control of Congress by winning in the more conservative rural areas and smaller states which have representation out of proportion to their population.

The government was conscious of the growing power of the opposition, especially in the urban centers of the largest and most important states. The solution was the Party Reform Law of 1979. The new law was designed to exploit the divisions within the MDB by allowing the party to split into factions. The objective was to retain as many "Arenistas" under the same roof as possible, yet divide the opposition into warring groups (Soares 1980). Under the new law, the divisive tendencies took their course, both with Arena and the MDB. The first party to emerge from the shuffle was the so-called Social Democratic Party (PDS), the successor to Arena. On the opposition side, the PMDB was heir to the MDB, both in name and composition. Other parties included the Labor Party (PT) headed by popular labor leaders, notably Luís Ignácio da Silva (known as Lula) and the Brazilian Worker's Party (PDT), the personal vehicle of Lionel Brizola, who later became Governor of Rio de Janeiro.

The resurgence of political competition in Brazil was a consequence of the economic crisis that began in the mid-1970s. Before then rapid economic growth was one of the major factors that legitimized Brazil's military rule. Justifications for authoritarian control were grounded on the doctrine of "developmentalism," which held that investment and production must reach a certain level before a self-propelled economic expansion causes the benefits of growth to "filter down" to the population (Portes and Walton 1981: chapter 4; Soares 1978). Inequalities were recognized but regarded as transitory. As Geisel's planning minister, Mário Henrique Simonsen, tersely stated: "There is no point in distributing misery before creating wealth."

But the very success of the growth process in the late 1960s also undermined the regime's political support. Among other things, economic orthodoxy lifted protectionist barriers and opened the door to foreign capital. This trade policy and the consequent denationalization of the economy worked to the detriment of some industries and hurt important sectors of the bourgeoisie. The destruction of small and relatively weak enterprises was encouraged through a policy of "positive insolvency" which consisted of cutting government credits to firms that failed to show an adequate level of profitability. In São Paulo alone bankruptcies rose from 838 in 1964 to 3,359 in 1967 (Munck

1980, cited in Kohl 1981: 100). The growth strategy pursued by the regime thus tended to fragment the solidarity of its own class base.

Matters grew worse with external shocks, particularly the quadrupling of petroleum prices in 1973 and the doubling again in 1979–80. The result was slower growth rates accompanied by accelerated inflation. For a regime that justified its existence on the expectation of continued economic expansion, the slowdown increasingly translated into a crisis in the legitimacy of authoritarian rule (Bacha 1980; Soares 1978; Souza and Lamounier 1981). Evidence from the 1970 census of a rise in the concentration of income further questioned the likelihood of a "trickle down" effect in Brazil. And, finally, the crushing of the urban guerilla groups during the Médici years undercut the argument that democracy could not be restored because of the threat of internal subversion (Knight 1981).

The convergence of these events in the 1970s fostered a new political climate in Brazil. Authoritarian rule, economic policy and social equity soon held center stage in a growing public debate that grew increasingly difficult to quell. Persistent criticism from the opposition party and widespread economic uncertainty put great pressure on the military. The result was a process of liberalization as the regime sought to broaden its support and sap the strength of its political enemies. In 1974, President Geisel launched his "decompression" policy, endorsing a commitment to an eventual return to complete democracy. His successor in 1979, President Figueiredo, followed with a step-by-step process of *abertura*, or political "opening."

The road back to democracy was fraught with twists and turns, some dramatic detours and no small measure of backroom dealings which intensified the closer the country came to the appointed transition year (see Soares 1985). In January, 1984, thousands of people demonstrated in São Paulo for an end to military rule. The public display prompted Figueiredo, in a nationwide address two months later, to rule out direct elections. But the movement for *diretas já* only gained momentum as nearly a million Brazilians demonstrated for direct elections in several cities in April. The military regime responded with a sixty-day ban on public gatherings and, on April 30, initiated a state of emergency to block protestors in Brasília and other cities. The *diretas já* campaign, although unsuccessful in introducing direct elections, nonetheless had important political implications. Among other things, mass mobilization split the government party as politicians within the PDS grew increasingly wary of tying their careers to the regime's candidate, Paulo Salim Maluf. In early July, Vice-President Antônio Aureliano Chaves, along with several other major political figures including José Sarney (then head of the PDS), walked out of the ruling party to join the opposition.

The Electoral College, with six delegates from each of Brazil's twenty-three states and all members of Congress, had been structured to favor the regime's candidate. The PDS, which was strong in the sparsely populated states, should have enjoyed a comfortable margin of around thirty-five votes. But, by the time of the election, the political tide had definitively turned against those in power. On January 25, 1985, Brazil's Electoral College, in proceedings unmarred by any of the feared eleventh-hour trickery, gave opposition leader Tancredo Neves a resounding victory: 480 votes against 180 for his adversary. Neves, unfortunately, did not live long enough to assume the presidency. Suffering from ill-health, he died on the eve of his inauguration. The vice-presidential candidate, José Sarney, became President of Brazil in a ceremony marked by somber irony. Before his last-minute defection to the PMDB, Sarney had at one time been head of the military-backed PDS party. If Neves chose Sarney as a running mate in the crucial 1985 election, it was surely to appease the conservative political factions within and outside of the military establishment. No one anticipated, and few people welcomed, the sudden turn of events that thrust Sarney into the presidency.

The road to economic recovery

Despite his inauspicious beginnings, Sarney initially proved to be a more effective political leader than many people anticipated. His success was much helped by the sudden and equally unexpected economic recovery in Brazil. At the time of the inauguration, the Sarney administration inherited a $100 billion dollar foreign debt and a 200 per cent inflation rate. Yet the deep recession during the early part of this decade gave way to a new period of economic growth. Gross Domestic Product began to rise in 1984, reaching 8.3 per cent in 1985, the world's highest growth rate that year. The increase in Gross Domestic Product was accompanied by an increase in trade surpluses of around $12 billion a year since 1985, more than enough to cover interest payments on its foreign debt and more than every nation except Japan and West Germany. In São Paulo, the country's industrial heartland, newspapers were suddenly fat with "jobs available" advertising (Riding 1986).

Other indicators suggest that Brazil has emerged from the recession on a more solid foundation for future growth. Over the past decade manufactured goods rose from 30 per cent of total exports to 50 per cent. Brazil has also become self-sufficient in steel, aluminum, plastic and rubber products, as well as in many capital goods once imported from abroad. The country has also reduced its oil import bill from $9.4 billion in 1980 to $2.4 billion in 1986. The reduction was partly due to a drop in world oil prices, but other factors also played a role. Brazil increased its domestic oil production and developed sugar-based alcohol fuel as a petrol substitute for vehicles (Riding 1986).

With the Brazilian economy recovering from deep crisis, and operating within the constraints imposed by the international system, the new democracy faces the awesome prospect of juggling a set of complex and often contradictory demands: meeting popular expectations of an improved living standard, getting the economy back on its feet, and forging a more egalitarian model of social and economic development. Longstanding regional inequalities, and a highly skewed distribution of income and land ownership, pose a formidable challenge to future development in Brazil.

Regional inequality

The growth and diversification of Brazil's economy have lessened but not eliminated sharp regional inequalities. Early in the country's history it was the export of sugar that concentrated wealth and population in the Northeast. In the late nineteenth and early twentieth centuries, it was the sale of coffee on the international market that led to the incipient industrialization of São Paulo. The creation of a manufacturing sector in São Paulo soon took on a momentum of its own. External economies made it rational in the initial stages of industrial growth to locate in an already-growing area. The emergence of a growth pole thus had cumulative effects. In this way, the regional economy of southeastern Brazil advanced, while the northeastern region lagged behind.

In the 1950s the Superintendency for the Development of the Northeast (SUDENE) was created in an attempt to counteract the trend toward greater concentration of productive resources in the south. Through a series of tax incentive programs SUDENE sought to redirect investments by reducing the relative cost of locating industries in the Northeast. These initiatives resulted in some notable industrial growth in that area. Most of the activity, however, was in highly capital-intensive industries that were largely concentrated in the cities of Salvador and Recife (Baer 1979: 107). The failure of locational planning policies was due, in part, to the stimulus given to the manufacturing

Table 3.2. *Regional distribution of population and national income for selected periods*

	% of population[a]		% of national income[b]	
	1940	1970	1949	1970
North	3.6	3.9	1.7	2.0
Northeast	35.0	30.3	14.1	12.2
Southeast	44.5	42.7	66.5	64.5
South	13.9	17.7	15.9	17.5
Central West	3.0	5.4	1.8	3.8
Total	100.0	100.0	100.0	100.0

[a]*Source:* Merrick and Graham 1979: 119
[b]*Source:* Baer 1979: 187

sector by the import substitution policies undertaken in the 1950s and 1960s. These policies, and the improvements in energy and transportation in São Paulo, coupled with the region's pre-existing advantages, perpetuated and intensified the preeminence of the Southeast in Brazil's industrial geography.

In 1970, the state of São Paulo alone accounted for 35.6 per cent of total domestic product and about 44 per cent of capital accumulation (Camargo et al. 1978: 19). Approximately 51 per cent of Brazil's total capital investment in machinery and equipment took place in the city in 1970. Similarly, the metropolitan area represented 44 per cent of all investments in transportation equipment. In the industrial sector, São Paulo's labor force earned 63.3 per cent of total wages paid to skilled workers. The concentration of industrial production is further evidenced by the fact that, by 1970, the metropolitan area consumed half of Brazil's total supply of electricity. Finally, data on the regional distribution of banking assets reflect the concentration of financial resources: commercial banks in São Paulo accounted for 45.7 per cent of all deposits in the country, and 48.7 per cent of the value of commercial loans in Brazil (FIBGE 1975).

A comparison of population distribution and the distribution of the country's national income provides a measure of regional inequality. As shown in Table 3.2, the SOUTHEAST was the leading population center of Brazil in 1940 and continued to be so in 1970. The next largest concentration is in the NORTHEAST. Although the NORTHEAST con-

Table 3.3. *Measures of wellbeing, 1970 and 1980, for selected regions*

	1970	1980	1980/1970
Average literacy rates			
A. NORTHEAST	39.2	47.7	1.2
B. SOUTHEAST	71.1	79.3	1.1
C. Ratio B/A	(1.8)	(1.7)	
Per cent enrolled in school (grades 9–12)			
A. NORTHEAST	6.0	17.0	2.8
B. SOUTHEAST	12.0	26.0	2.2
C. Ratio B/A	(2.0)	(1.5)	
Per cent of households with piped water			
A. NORTHEAST	12.4	30.1	2.4
B. SOUTHEAST	44.2	65.9	1.5
C. Ratio B/A	(3.6)	(2.2)	
Per cent of households with sewage or septic tank			
A. NORTHEAST	8.0	16.4	2.1
B. SOUTHEAST	37.2	56.2	1.5
C. Ratio B/A	(4.7)	(3.4)	
Per cent of households with electricity			
A. NORTHEAST	23.3	42.0	1.8
B. SOUTHEAST	61.6	81.3	1.3
C. Ratio B/A	(2.6)	(2.0)	

Source: Denslow and Tyler 1984

tained over a third of the population in 1940 and 1970, its share of national income declined from 14.1 per cent in 1949 to 12.2 per cent in 1970. The SOUTHEAST, in contrast, held 42.7 per cent of the population in 1970, yet accounted for 64.5 per cent of national income.

The geographic distribution of national income in Brazil provides a picture of regional inequality broadly consistent with a pattern displayed by other key social indicators. As shown in Table 3.3, the SOUTHEAST consistently exceeds the NORTHEAST in quality of life indicators. In 1970, for example, the average literacy rate was 1.8 times higher in southeastern Brazil, a difference that remained fairly constant over the decade (1.7 in 1980). Similarly, in 1970 the proportion of the school-aged population, the per cent of households with piped water and with sewage networks or septic tanks was higher in the SOUTHEAST by a factor of 2.0, 3.6 and 4.7, respectively. Between 1970 and 1980 both regions experienced substantial gains, as indicated by the ratio of

Table 3.4. *Selected social indicators for the Northeast and the state of São Paulo*

	Northeast[a]	State of São Paulo
% of children under 3 years of age in houses with:		
no running water	65.3	25.7
inadequate sewage[b]	83.9	39.9
% of women 15–49 years of age in households with less than the minimum wage (per capita)[c]	89.9	47.6
% of population covered by social security[d]	27.4	71.3
% of children 1–5 years old with:		
1st degree malnutrition	47.1	33.8
2nd degree malnutrition	16.6	5.3
3rd degree malnutrition[e]	3.0	0.4

[a]PNAD region V, includes the State of Maranhão, Piauí, Rio Grande do Norte, Paraíba, Pernambuco, Alagoas, Sergipe, Bahia.
[b]Source, FIBGE 1982: 63
[c]Source, FIBGE 1982: 39
[d]Source, FIBGE 1982: 152
[e]Source, FIBGE 1982: 111

the 1980 to the 1970 values for each social indicator (right-hand column). With the exception of average literacy rates, these changes narrowed regional disparities.

Selected indicators presented in Table 3.4 offer additional insight into the disparities that characterize these two principal areas of Brazil (circa 1974–7). In the NORTHEAST, for example, 65 per cent of all children under 3 years of age lived in houses with no running water. Nearly 84 per cent lived in places with inadequate sewage facilities. For the State of São Paulo, the comparable figures are less than half these values (25.7 and 39.9 per cent, respectively). Whereas 71.3 per cent of the residents in São Paulo were covered by social security, only 27.4 per cent of those in the NORTHEAST participated in the welfare program. Data on household income indicate that about 90 per cent of the women of childbearing age in the Northeast lived in households with less than one minimum wage per capita, compared to 48 per cent in São Paulo. The marked regional inequalities shown in Table 3.4 are especially relevant to geographic differences in infant and child mortality rates explored in Chapter 4.

Income inequality

No other aspect of the Brazilian experience has sparked greater debate than the relationship between rapid economic growth and the equitable distribution of income and quality of life indicators. Equity can be assessed in several ways. The first relies on measures of the absolute level of poverty. Absolute poverty is broadly defined to include the lack of a minimal level of income and/or basic need, such as health care, education and nutrition. The second way of assessing equity looks, not at absolute levels of resources and amenities, but at the distribution of income among population subgroups.

Absolute poverty is obviously important in an analysis of population and economic growth. However, relative inequality is also a valuable concept because income distribution is the outcome of structural processes. It is a kind of "scorecard" that reflects the result of competing claims on the economy's output (Weisskoff and Figueroa 1976). As Marx once wrote, "Any distribution whatever of the means of consumption is only a consequence of the distribution of the conditions of production" (cited in Gurley 1983: 26). Political and institutional factors play a decisive role in determining the weight given to claims by competing social groups. Hence, the unequal distribution of income cannot be reduced to market forces alone. The way shares of total output are distributed, and the way the distribution changes and the reasons for these changes reflect the structure of Brazilian development.

Measures of income inequality

Data on the relative distribution of income in 1960, 1970 and 1980 are presented in Table 3.5. The values correspond to the percentage of total income that is received by each decile of the economically active population. By far the most striking feature of Table 3.5 is the high concentration of income, regardless of the year in question. In 1960 the top two deciles received well over half of total income. The comparable figures for 1970 and 1980 are 61.9 and 65.3 per cent, respectively. The lower four deciles of the economically active population in 1960, 1970 and 1980 received only about 10 per cent of total income.

The last two decades were periods of rising income inequality,

Table 3.5. *Distribution of income for income deciles, economically active population, 1960, 1970 and 1980*

Income-earning population (Deciles)	Percentage total income			Percentage change	
	1960	1970	1980	1960–70	1970–80
1	1.9	1.2	1.2	−37	—
2	2.0	2.2	2.0	+10	− 9
3	3.0	2.9	3.0	− 3	+ 3
4	4.4	3.7	3.6	−16	− 3
5	6.1	4.9	4.4	−20	−10
6	7.5	6.0	5.6	−20	− 7
7	9.0	7.3	7.2	−19	− 1
8	11.3	9.9	9.9	−12	—
9	15.2	15.2	15.4	—	+ 1
10	39.6	46.7	47.9	+17.9	+ 3
Lowest 40%	11.3	10.0	9.8	−11.5	− 2.0
Highest 20%	54.8	61.9	63.3	+13.0	+ 2.3
Gini coefficient	.497	.565	.590		

Sources: 1960 and 1970 from FIBGE (1979: 196). The 1980 distribution is derived from the advanced tabulations of the 1980 census, by Denslow and Tyler 1984.

especially between 1960 and 1970. During the 1960s the share of income accruing to the upper two deciles rose 13 per cent, while that of the first four deciles dropped by 11.5 per cent. There are also substantial losses in the proportion of income in deciles 5, 6, and 7. The largest rise in the proportion of income took place among the richest 10 per cent of the population. These changes are reflected in the increase in the Gini coefficient from .497 in 1960 to .565 in 1970. As a summary measure that varies between 0 (perfect equality) and 1 (perfect inequality), the 13 per cent increase in the coefficient indicates a greater concentration of income over the period.

The evidence for 1980 suggests that the income distribution profile either remained stable or became slightly more concentrated between 1970 and 1980. The top 20 per cent of the population increased their share of total income by 1.4 percentage points; the proportion going to the lowest 40 per cent of the population dropped by 0.2 percentage points. The increase in inequality, modest by 1960–70 standards, can be seen in the small rise in the Gini coefficient.[2]

Table 3.6. *Average income for income deciles, economically active population, 1960, 1970 and 1980*[a]

Income-earning population (Deciles)	average income			Percentage change	
	1960	1970	1980	1960–70	1970–80
I	39	35	49	−10	+40
2	43	64	85	+49	+33
3	64	81	123	+27	+52
4	93	104	149	+12	+43
5	130	137	185	+ 5	+35
6	161	171	234	+ 6	+37
7	191	205	300	+ 7	+46
8	240	279	414	+16	+48
9	324	429	643	+32	+50
10	842	1,319	2,006	+57	+52
Average	213	283	419	+33	+48

[a]In 1970 cruzeiros.
Sources: 1960 and 1970 from FIBGE (1979: 196). The 1980 distribution is derived from the advanced tabulation of the 1980 census by Denslow and Tyler 1984.

Turning from relative to absolute measures, Table 3.6 presents average real income figures for the economically active population. In the aggregate, real income rose 33 per cent between 1960 and 1970 and increased around 48 per cent in the following decade. In both periods large gains were recorded among the top income deciles. For the poorest strata of the population the picture is unclear. The available evidence indicates a 10 per cent decline in real income in 1960–70 and a rise of 40 per cent in 1970–80. However, these findings should be regarded with caution. Because of coding limitations, and because of the rather arbitrary assumptions necessary to estimate the tails of the distribution, changes in the first and tenth deciles are unreliable.

These data limitations do not preclude some general, if cautious, conclusions. Whatever the year in question there is little doubt that income is highly concentrated in Brazil. Conclusions as to the direction, and especially the magnitude, of changes over time are more problematic. Whereas the concentration of income suffered a marked deterioration in the 1960s, the evidence for 1970–80 suggests a small increase in income inequality. With regard to absolute levels of poverty, real income of the economically active population rose in both decades, although the rate of change varied by decile. In the 1960s, deciles 4 through 7 experienced relatively low rates of improvement in real income. In the 1970s the pattern of change is different: growth in real income appears to be much more equally distributed, as indicated by the last column of Table 3.6.

Causes of income inequality

Neoclassical economic explanations of income inequality center on the relationship between the skill level of the work force and the changing demand profile for labor (Langoni 1973). The argument assumes that the wage structure is anchored at the bottom by the elastic supply of unskilled workers. On the higher rungs of the educational ladder elasticities are low and declining. When economic growth accelerates there is a rise in the demand for labor, especially for qualified workers in the "modern" sector. This skill bias in the expanding demand for labor, together with the short-term inelasticity of the supply of qualified workers, gives rise to increasing wage differentials and, hence, to a greater concentration of income. The rise in inequality, however, is transitory. Investment in education eventually bears fruit in the form of an enlarged supply of skilled labor. These forces bring the employment market back into equilibrium. Wage differentials, in this view, may end up smaller than before the accelerated growth phase.

A related hypothesis refers to changes in the structure of the employment that accompanies the intermediate state of economic growth. Kuznets (1955) argued that, as labor moves from rural to urban occupations, income distribution would deteriorate. For Brazil this explanation is favored by Langoni (1973) and Fields (1977). As in the "skill differential" argument, Kuznets held that the rise in inequality would be followed by a more equitable distribution of income with further economic growth. The inverted U-shaped relation between income concentration and per capita income is broadly consistent with the findings of cross-sectional analyses of international data across countries (Alhuwali 1976).

Other analysts attribute increased income inequality to the wage policies adopted after the military coup (Fishlow 1972; Hoffman 1972). The control over the minimum wage level and the repression of labor unions, cornerstones of the stabilization program in the 1960s, caused a decline in the relative share of income allocated to unskilled and semi-skilled workers. The fall in the proportion of income in the intermediate deciles (fifth through seventh) is cited as evidence in support of this view as urban workers are highly represented in these income strata. In a test of the various competing hypotheses (the skills differential and the Kuznets effect arguments), Bacha and Taylor (1980) conclude that the wage-squeeze policies had the most significant impact on the concentration of income. A more detailed discussion of the wage control mechanisms, and the effect on infant mortality in São Paulo, is presented in chapter 5.

Baer and Figueroa (1981) combine various lines of reasoning in a unique analysis of the distributional effects of state enterprises. The latter play a dominant role in capital-intensive sectors of the economy such as steel, petrochemicals and public utilities. State firms account for 37.5 per cent of net assets in manufacturing, but employ only 11.5 per cent of the labor force. A characteristic of state firms in the post-1964 period is the control by technocrats bent on maximizing the economic power, growth and efficiency of their operations. Since the 1960s there has been a threefold increase in the capital/labor ratio of state enterprises, and the average capital/output ratio rose from 2.3 in the mid-1960s to roughly 5.0 in the mid-1970s. According to this argument, state firms in Brazil contributed to the increase in income inequality by adopting highly capital-intensive technology and through their pricing, employment and wage policies.

Land tenure inequality

In urban settings, where the cost of housing, utilities, transport, food and other necessities is highly monetized, income is a telling measure of poverty. In the rural area the income of wage earners, although hardly irrelevant, is a less satisfactory index. For a variety of reasons, access to land is a more appropriate measure of inequality in the countryside. Land is the means to produce basic sustenance needs and its ownership goes hand in hand with social prestige and political power. Land is also the key to credit, tax incentives and other privileges. The contemporary profile of land ownership in Brazil can be traced to the policies adopted by the Portuguese Crown to distribute land during the early colonial period.

Sesmarias *and the distribution of land in colonial Brazil*

Between 1534 and 1536 King João III divided Portuguese possessions in America into fifteen captaincies distributed among twelve donees.

The donatary captaincy system, successfully used in the Atlantic islands, proved an efficient means of securing a hold over new territory. Each captaincy averaged fifty leagues wide and extended westward to the ill-defined Tordesillas line that separated Portuguese from Spanish claims to the New World. In return for the inalienable land grant, the donee was expected to colonize the captaincy at private expense. Among the rights granted to him was the authority to distribute land in *sesmarias*. The institution, first adopted in Portugal as early as 1375, was used to improve agricultural production by redistributing land that was not effectively cultivated. The original law envisioned relatively small grants, never to exceed the amount of land that could be worked by a man and his family. In Brazil, where land was plentiful and colonists were few, the restrictions on the size of the *sesmarias* remained a dead letter from the start (Guimarães 1963). Even after the creation of royal administrators in 1549, when the prerogative to grant *sesmarias* passed from the donataries to the Governors-General, the practice of handing out large tracts of land continued with lavish generosity.

In 1696, 1697 and 1699 the crown attempted to limit the size of the holdings, and in 1699 tried to expropriate uncultivated property. These efforts met with little success (Burns 1970). Small farmers sought their livelihood beyond the reach of the authorities, resorted to cultivating tenant plots within the estates, or worked unclaimed areas between the poorly defined boundaries that separated large landholdings. The "latifundio-minifundio complex" thus originated with the land grant institutions of the colonial period (Prado Júnior 1971). Since then it has been perpetuated by the political and legal initiatives of the agrarian-based elite and, more recently, by an expanding capitalist system of production.

Land, labor and the state

The colonial policy of distributing land in *sesmarias* set the stage for a high concentration of land ownership in Brazil. But this pattern was one that the landed elite had to struggle to maintain. In a changing market for labor and commodities this often called for innovative measures to protect the interests of the propertied class. The Land Law of 1850 is an intriguing example of one such maneuver. At a time when the manpower shortage was the principal obstacle to expanded coffee production in southern Brazil, the plantation owners took a keen interest in the immigration of Europeans. Senator Vergueiro, a wealthy merchant-planter in São Paulo, recruited workers from Europe on his own account but with financial assistance from the government. The workers brought to Brazil were obliged to sign a contract to repay transportation costs and other financial advances. Planters anticipated that it would take immigrant workers at least five years to pay off these debts and another ten to accumulate sufficient capital to purchase a farm. What Vergueiro envisaged, then, was a government-subsidized pool of indentured servants (Dean 1971).

Additional measures were required to guarantee a self-sustaining system with the introduction of European farm workers. If immigrants were permitted ready access to land, there would be little incentive for them to work for growers and planters. Several features of the Land Law of 1850 provided the solution: state lands could only be alienated through public auction; minimum prices were set above the going rate, the buyer was obliged to pay in cash, and the resources generated from land sales went to defray the cost of importing additional workers to Brazil. The law subsidized immigration yet severely restricted the ability of newcomers to acquire property, thus assuring growers a supply of labor.

The Brazilian experience strikingly resembled Gibbon Wakefield's proposal for the organized emigration of labor from England to Australia, a plan to which Marx devoted the final chaper of *Capital I*. Wakefield's scheme was designed to keep the price of land high to prevent settlers from purchasing their own agricultural plots. In Wakefield's view, an artificially high land price would prevent the fragmentation of property and stimulate development since, otherwise, an entrepreneur who went to the trouble and expense of transporting a mass of workers would only find his men abandoning him upon arrival. For Marx, Gibbon's plan – and, by extension, that which took place in Brazil – illustrated the nature of capitalism: namely, that money could only become capital when there was free labor for it to exploit. And, if a free labor force did not exist, the state could create one through immigration policies coordinated with institutional mechanisms to insure that workers remained separated from the means of production.

The vast quantity of land in the public domain made it exceptionally difficult to limit *de facto* occupation of land, however. As a result, squatting (*posse*) by smallholders has been common throughout Brazil's history. Cyclical changes in agricultural production at times caused the fragmentation of large estates which also permitted a place for the small farmer. For example, when the productivity of coffee trees in São Paulo suffered from soil depletion, the coffee frontier moved southward. Plantations were often broken up and sold to small farmers who cultivated for their own subsistence and for the sale of surpluses to the growing urban population of the state (Prado Júnior 1971).

But this historically and geographically spotty expansion of small holdings hardly implies the democratization of land ownership. Whenever it became profitable to invest in cattle or in capital-intensive crops, small farmers were almost always eliminated (Graziano da Silva 1978: 34). The expansion of soy bean production and cattle raising in Paraná (Margolis 1973) is a recent example. So too is the struggle for land in Amazônia that we will analyze in chapter 10.

Measure of land inequality

Today, the extreme concentration of land ownership is the most salient characteristic of Brazil's agrarian structure. The social and economic problems associated with this pattern of land distribution have long been recognized. In the late eighteenth century the Viceroy, Marqués de Lavradio, spoke out against the existence of huge estates that were poorly managed and only partially cultivated when, at the same time, landless peasants petitioned him for small plots to till (Burns 1970). The Viceroy's bitter complaint could easily be made today.

Table 3.7 provides current estimates of the degree of land concentration in Brazil. In 1975, well over half of agricultural establishments were less than ten hectares in size yet occupied only 2.7 per cent of the land. At the other end of the distribution, landholdings in excess of 1,000 hectares comprised 0.8 per cent of all farms but appropriated nearly half (42.9 per cent) of the occupied territory. As extreme as these figures appear, the data in Table 3.7 probably underestimate the magnitude of land concentration because the same person may own more than one establishment. As we will show in chapter 9, the monopoly of land in the countryside is a primary contributor to the out-migration of people from rural areas.

The degree of land concentration in Brazil is among the highest in Latin America. In recent years there is evidence that the distribution of landholdings has become even more skewed. Estimates derived from the agricultural censuses indicate that the Gini coefficient for the size distribution of land ownership remained fairly stable between 1950 and 1960 at about .842. The index rose to .844 in 1970 and, in the short span of five years, increased to .855 by 1975. Analyses of the preliminary tabulations of the last agricultural census indicate that the Gini coefficient reached .859 in 1980 (Hoffman, n.d.), a finding that confirms a trend toward an increasingly skewed distribution of land ownership in rural Brazil.

Table 3.7. *Size distribution of rural properties by number of establishments and total area, 1975 (percentage distribution)*

Size of properties (in hectares)	Number of establishments	Area
Less than 10	52.1	2.7
10–100	38.0	18.6
100–1,000	9.0	35.8
1,000–10,000	0.8	27.8
10,000–100,000	0.1	15.1

Source: FIBGE, Agricultural Census 1975.

* * *

It is impossible to do justice in a few pages to Brazil's rich and colorful history, or to capture in a single chapter the complexity of its present circumstance. We therefore limited the purpose of chapter 3 to a selective account of major historical events, focusing primarily on those features of Brazil's economic, political and demographic past that have shaped the current profile of socioeconomic and spatial inequality. Three topics were of special concern: the cycles that characterized the country's economic history; the growth of an urban–industrial sector, and the associated transformations in political organization; and a summary of the historical antecedents of the contemporary pattern of spatial inequality, and of the maldistribution of income and land ownership. The overview of Brazil's past, revealed in the discussion of these three themes, provides historical examples of the dynamic associations between eco-demographic infrastructure, stratification system and political–ideological superstructure.

From the colonial period onward, the connection between production and population has been influenced by Brazil's changing role in the world economy. Exports such as sugar, cotton, rubber and coffee rose and fell in importance in response to fluctuations in international commodity prices. Within Brazil, the onset of each new economic cycle shifted the direction of population movement and, hence, the geography of demographic density. If the seventeenth-century sugar economy concentrated wealth, power and population in northeastern Brazil, subsequent cycles (gold and especially the expansion of coffee production) redistributed jobs and people to central and southern regions of the country. Between 1930 and 1950, the internal migration assumed two different characteristics, each associated with changes in the structure of Brazil's economy (Martine 1986). One direction was centrifugal as the spread of coffee production drew population away from the traditional seaboard settlements of colonial times into new agricultural frontiers that lay inland and further to the south. The other was a centripetal movement that increasingly concentrated population in the urban centers of Rio and São Paulo in response to a growing demand for industrial labor. The rural-to-urban migration increased in intensity in the period 1950–65 due to import substitution industrialization, which made metropolitan areas in the center-south increasingly attractive, and because of the increase in population growth (due to falling death rates), which added to the "push" factors in rural areas. In recent decades (1960–80) the rural exodus assumed massive proportions as a consequence of the mechanization of agricultural production in the more developed regions of the country, and because of the inability of the rural economy to retain labor in the more backward areas. So significant has been the cityward movement since 1970 that the 1980 census data showed, for the first time in modern history, an absolute decline in the size of the rural population.

If changes in structure of production influenced population, the overview presented in previous pages shows that the opposite causal direction is also true. The most salient example is the effect of labor scarcity during Brazil's early history, a phenomenon that stimulated the rise of particular modes of production, and, as a consequence, exerted a profound influence on the associated social, political and cultural institutions of the day. In the early colonial period, when sugar was the primary export, the shortage of population in Brazil's northeastern region led to slavery on the plantations. In a similar fashion, it was labor scarcity in central and southern Brazil during the coffee boom in the late nineteenth century that compelled the rising export-oriented class of landowners to press for state-sponsored immigration schemes. The policy of importing labor from southern Europe, combined with legislation to restrict access to land, led to the *colono* system, a mode of labor recruitment and remuneration that permitted plantations to expand in response to the rising world demand for coffee. The *colono* system, in turn, defined a mode of reproduction on the coffee plantations that encouraged high fertility (see chapter 7). Hence, we find that population variables gave rise to a particular mode of production which, once set in motion, exerted reciprocal effects on reproduction and population structure.

Such eco-demographic relationships were inseparable from changes in class structure and in the organization of political power. As Brazil's exports changed over the course of the nineteenth and twentieth centuries, and as the primary locus of economic activity moved from one region to another, a series of local elites sprang into existence and maintained themselves as distinct fractions of the dominant class (Roxborough 1979: 108). The result was a form of patrimonial politics in which there was considerable local autonomy and an absence of a strong centralized authority, a situation that characterized Brazil until the 1930s. The industrialization process, stimulated by the wealth accumulated from the export of coffee from plantations in São Paulo and later fostered by the interruption of international trade during the Great Depression, saw the emergence of an urban proletariat and a class of industrialists who soon attempted to wrest political control from the landed oligarchy. Indeed, the rise of such figures as Getúlio Vargas, and the emergence of populist political rhetoric in Brazil as well as other countries in Latin America from the 1930s through the 1960s, cannot be explained without reference to the political repercussions of fundamental changes in economic infrastructure and social stratification.

If the disruptions in international trade caused by the Depression and World War II provided the insulation from foreign competition that domestic industry needed to expand, development policies in the postwar period deliberately endorsed protective tariff and exchange controls to accomplish the same end. Import Substitution Industrialization (ISI) was a development policy deemed essential to meet the demands of the increasingly urban population, and to bring greater economic independence by achieving self-sufficiency in manufactured goods. ISI policy, and a host of other initiatives designed to bolster the industrial sector, were political manifestations of a new "developmentalist" ideology which would have been impossible to conceive under the former reign of landed oligarchs.

As these summary observations illustrate, a long-term view of Brazil's history provides concrete examples of the relationships set forth by the conceptual framework presented in chapter 2. In subsequent pages, our objective is to explore these associations in greater detail, examining, in particular, the manner in which spatial inequality and the concentration of income and landownership play into the relationships between population, economic change and development policy in Brazil.

4

Income inequality and length of life

Mortality occupies a special place in demographic inventories of socio-economic change. As a relatively sensitive indicator of the level and the distribution of living conditions, mortality bears a direct and obvious relationship to human welfare (United Nations 1980: 71). The mortality rate is the result of the interaction of three sets of factors that affect a population's wellbeing: public health services which influence mortality regardless of individual behavior (such as spraying insecticides that control malaria); health and environmental services that reduce the costs of health, but require some individual response (e.g., the availability of clean water); and an array of individual characteristics such as income, which affects health through nutrition and housing, and education, associated with the speed and the efficiency with which individuals respond to health services and environmental threats (Birdsall 1980: 16). Because the level of mortality is determined by the combined effect of all these factors, the death rate provides a summary measure of the quality of life that prevails in a population.

Newly developed demographic methods have greatly expanded the scope and the accuracy of mortality research. Traditional estimates of the death rate rely on vital registration statistics. The newer approach, developed by William Brass, measures mortality indirectly from survey or census data. In the Brass method, the proportion of children surviving to mothers in different age groups (20–4; 25–9 and 30–4), multiplied by the appropriate correction factor, yields estimates of the probability of death by exact ages 2, 3 and 5. These three childhood mortality values can then be combined to derive a summary measure of the average number of years of life expected at birth.

The Brass method has been of particular value in Brazil. In a country where the coverage of vital events is precarious, more accurate estimates of national and regional mortality levels are now available. Brass techniques also have a second advantage. Census data contain a wide

86

Table 4.1. *Life expectancy at birth, 1930/40 to 1970/80*

	1930/40	1940/50	1950/60	1960/70	1970/80
Life expectancy	41.2	43.6	50.0	53.4	61.6
Number of years of increase		2.4	6.4	3.4	8.2

range of information about individuals such as income, education and place of residence. This means that, for the first time, measures of differential mortality can be related to socioeconomic characteristics of the population. The Appendix presents a more complete discussion of the Brass method.

The mortality decline

The average number of years of life expected at birth (e_0^o) is a familiar measure of mortality. Because life expectancy is stated in years, the concept is readily interpretable. The measure can also be used for comparative purposes since life expectancy rates are unaffected by the age composition of a population, a factor that contaminates other indicators, such as the crude death rate. In the Brass method as we have applied it here, the estimates of expectation of life are derived from retrospective information on the mortality experience of children born to women 20 to 34 years of age. As a result, each value corresponds to the average mortality level during (approximately) the decade prior to the census.

Rates of life expectancy in Brazil, presented in Table 4.1, show that there has been a substantial decline in the death rate over the last forty years. In 1930/40 the average number of years of life expected at birth was around 41. In 1940/50 it rose slightly to 43.6. In the following decade life expectancy rose by over six years. By 1960/70 the average expectation of life at birth increased to 53.4 years, reaching a high of nearly 62 years by 1970/80. Although erratic in pace, the decline in mortality since the 1930s added an average of 20.4 years of life to Brazil's population.

When the mortality decline took place, and how fast it occurred, are two considerations that have important implications for understanding the causes of reduced mortality. Two schools of thought figure prominently in the literature devoted to this topic. One school finds the primary cause of lower mortality, not in the advances in medical technology, but rather in a higher standard of living (improvements in nutrition, housing and clothing, in cleanliness and personal hygiene and the creation of water supply and refuse disposal systems) (McKeown 1976; McKeown and Record 1962; McKeown, Record and Turner 1975). McKeown and his collaborators contend that it was only after 1900, perhaps as late as the First World War, that the application of new and existing medical knowledge had an appreciable impact on life expectancy in England.

The second line of reasoning emphasizes technological advances in methods of death control. This argument is especially relevant to decline in the death rate in developing countries, a trend that advocates of the diffusion model attribute to the importation of medical and public health measures from the more developed countries (Davis 1956; Stolintz 1965; Preston 1975). The diffusion perspective has important implications for the study of population and social change. Among other things, the model predicts that substantial mortality declines can occur in Third World countries more or less independently of sociostructural changes that accompany economic growth and development.

The diffusion model, which shares many of the underlying assumptions of the modernization paradigm (see chapter 2), places primary emphasis on the transfer of death control technology from developed to developing countries in the immediate post-World War II period, implying a rapid decline in the death rate in the late 1940s and during the 1950s and slowing thereafter. The estimates of life expectancy shown in Table 4.1 partly conform to this pattern. Whereas the increase in expectation of life was only 2.4 years between 1930/40 and 1940/50, the pace of the mortality decline accelerated considerably in the following decade, adding 6.4 years to life expectancy between 1940/50 and 1950/60. This was followed in the 1950/60–1960/70 period by a slower rate of increase in life expectancy, much as the diffusion model predicts. Yet contrary to expectations, the highest gain was achieved in the most recent period (1960/70–1970/80), when the average expectation of life rose 8.2 years.

The sharp mortality decline between 1960/70 and 1970/80 was undoubtedly associated with the substantial improvements in socioeconomic conditions that took place in the 1970s (see Table 3.3 and Table 3.6). The pace and the timing of mortality change over the last forty years therefore suggest that both the diffusion of death control technology and better standards of living played a role. Unfortunately, research on the relations between Brazilian mortality patterns and economic conditions, as well as on the impact of imported medical technology, has been limited, making it impossible to know with certainty the relative importance of the two.

Social and economic determinants of child mortality

Household income

In the 1970s per capita income in Brazil rose at an average annual rate of 4.9 per cent, reaching about US$1,800 in 1981. As we noted in chapter 3, analysis of the 1970 and 1980 censuses show that average real income rose approximately 48 per cent during the period, with gains recorded in all deciles of the economically active population (Denslow and Tyler 1984).

Income is a major determinant of the level of mortality (Cravioto and de Licardie 1973; Russell and Burke 1975). Low purchasing power is associated with poor diet and variety of other factors that comprise the standard of living of a population. Insufficient monetary resources limit investments in sanitation, reduce the reserves that serve as a buffer in times of sickness or emergency, and relegate families to substandard housing in high risk areas. In the absence of a fully socialized health service system, income also determines the access to health care and other social services that affect an individual's condition.[1]

Education

The standard of living of a population cannot be measured by income alone. Other relevant factors include literacy, education and access to social services. Table 3.3, presented in the previous chapter, shows substantial improvements along these dimensions between 1970 and 1980. The literacy rate rose, as did the rate of school enrollment. The largest gains in educational attainment occurred in ages 9 through 12.

Literacy, and the number of years of schooling, are inversely associated with mortality. The relationship is especially strong between a mother's educational achievement and the probability that her children will live to see their fifth birthday. Caldwell (1980) suggests three links by which the probability of death in early childhood is related to mother's education: (1) Mothers with more years of completed schooling tend to be less fatalistic about illness and more prone to seek assistance. (2) Educated mothers are likely to adopt improved child care practices. And (3) education may change intrafamily relationships in a way that has a positive impact on child health.

While Caldwell (1980) emphasizes education's independent effect on mortality via the three behavioral mechanisms, education can also be regarded as an index of other factors that potentially impinge on child as well as more general mortality regimes. Stable employment patterns, social prestige and a greater ability to manipulate the sociopolitical system are directly associated with educational attainment. Each of these factors contributes to a family's ability to reduce environmental health risks and to mobilize resources to cure sickness or recover from injury. More generally, the proportion of literate people in a population may reflect not only the abilities of individuals, but also society's capacity to provide social services (Palloni 1981: 642–3).

Infectious disease and environmental risk

Table 3.3 shows that, between 1970 and 1980, substantial gains were also achieved in terms of indicators of exposure to infectious disease and environmental risk. The percentage of households with piped water and with modern sewage or septic tanks increased by 62.2 and 56.0 per cent, respectively. The proportion of households with electricity rose from 47.8 per cent in 1970 to 67.4 per cent ten years later. The proportion of the population owning consumer durables, such as radios, televisions, refrigerators, stoves and automobiles showed similar increases during the period.

The availability of water, sewage and electricity facilitates the attainment of higher standards of cleanliness, provided that the basic principles of hygiene are known and applied. Piped water reduces the risks from well water and from improper home storage. Running water also reduces the cost of cleanliness. The washing of clothes, dishes and personal hygiene is greatly facilitated by access to piped water as compared to hauling it from a well, stream or public spigot. Sewage networks, in addition to serving as efficient waste disposal, may also reduce the contamination of well water used by the entire community. Similarly, electricity makes it easier to boil water, sterilize milk and heat food.

In Brazil, analyses of census and survey data find a strong association between the presence of water and sewage facilities in the home, and the level of child mortality (Sawyer and Soares, 1982). Merrick (1956), using an index of child mortality for urban Brazil and controlling for mother's education, concluded that the mortality of children living in houses with no running water was significantly higher (1.9 times greater in 1970; 2.5 times in 1976) compared to the mortality of children in places with piped water. Similarly, estimates of the level of life expectancy at birth for the metropolitan area of São Paulo in 1970 confirm the importance of sewage services in reducing the death rate. The average expectation of life at birth for children living in houses with adequate sanitation (65.2 years) was estimated to exceed by over a decade the life expectancy of those living in dwellings with no sewage facilities (FIBGE 1982; Vetter and Simões 1980).

The relative impact of determinants of mortality

It is easy to see that the determinants of mortality form a web of relationships such that the numerous variables involved interact with one another in complex ways. There is little reason to assume that, to take one example, the availability of piped water, in and of itself, would reduce mortality. Rather, running water is assumed to improve hygienic conditions. But this can be achieved only with knowledge of the basic principles of good health. Such information, in turn, is correlated with educational achievement. And education is a variable that may reduce mortality through mechanisms other than its direct relationship to health-related behavior. Moreover, educational attainment is closely correlated with income and, hence, with the likelihood of having water, sewage and electricity in the first place.

Merrick's analysis of data from the 1 per cent sample of 1970 population census and from the 1976 national household survey provides a rare insight into the relative importance of the various determinants of child mortality in urban Brazil in the early 1970s. The findings are of special interest because they provide estimates of the degree to which changes in several key socioeconomic indicators over the six-year period contributed to the overall decline in the death rate among children. Merrick found that educational gains by men and women jointly accounted for about 54 per cent of the drop in child mortality. The next most important factor, the provision of piped water, accounted for approximately 19 per cent of the decline (Merrick 1985b: Table 10).

The study also noted a statistical interaction between piped water and family income. Access to running water had a greater effect on reducing mortality among children born to low-income mothers compared to the effect of piped water on the probability of death among children in more affluent households. A statistically significant interaction term indicates that the provision of water facilities narrowed the income-related differences in the probability of death among infants and children in urban Brazil. Thus, an expanded city water supply partly compensated for the adverse effects of inequality in the distribution of income (Merrick 1985).

Regional inequality and length of life

Spatial differences in social and economic development documented in chapter 3 are reflected in sharp regional disparities in life expectancy, as shown in Table 4.2. In the 1930s the average length of life in the Central Northeast (34.7) was 16.2 years less than that recorded for the more developed South region (51.0 years). The overall mortality decline that took place in later decades has not eliminated these spatial inequalities. Between 1930/40 and 1940/50 the Central and Southern Northeast experienced relatively little change. Life expectancy in São Paulo, on the other hand, rose from 42.7 to 49.4 years, a rate of increase of 1.5 per cent a year. Because the Central and Southern Northeast lagged behind the mortality gains in central and southern Brazil (Rio, São Paulo and the South Regions), the range in life expectancy by region rose from 16.2 years in 1930/40 to 21.3 years in 1940/50.

The following decade was a period of rapid mortality decline for the country as a whole. Life expectancy in Brazil rose from 43.6 years in 1940/50 to 50.0 years in 1950/60, an increase of 15 per cent. As shown in the lower portion of Table 4.2 marked gains were recorded in Amazônia (+19 per cent), as well as in other high mortality areas, such as the Central and Southern Northeast. Increases in excess of 10 per cent also took place in Minas, Rio, São Paulo and Paraná.

Similar gains in life expectancy continued in Central and Southern Northeast between 1950/60 and 1960/70, although the rate of improvement slowed in all other regions of the country. As a result of improved mortality conditions in places with low life expectancy, and the slowed improvement in other areas, the range of geographic disparities in the average expectation of life at birth fell to 17.7 years in 1960/70 (panel A).

Between 1960/70 and 1970/80 the pace of the mortality decline accelerated once again, with fairly uniform improvements taking place among the ten geographic areas of the country. By 1970/80 life expectancy for Brazil reached nearly sixty-two years. Despite this increase, marked regional differences in mortality remained. In the most recent period, life expectancy in the Central Northeast was forty-nine, a level that is 18.8 years below the estimate for the South region (67.8 years).

Table 4.2. *Life expectancy at birth, by region, 1930/40 to 1970/80*

Region	1930/40 (1)	1940/50 (2)	1950/60 (3)	1960/70 (4)	1970/80 (5)
A					
Amazônia	39.8	42.7	51.0	54.2	63.1
N. Northeast	40.0	43.7	47.8	50.4	55.5
C. Northeast	34.7	34.0	39.4	44.2	49.0
S. Northeast	38.3	39.2	44.8	49.7	56.5
Minas	43.0	46.1	51.7	55.4	60.2
Rio	44.5	48.7	56.1	57.0	64.1
São Paulo	42.7	49.4	55.1	58.2	63.9
Paraná	43.9	45.9	53.4	56.6	63.2
South	51.0	55.3	60.4	61.9	67.8
Central West	46.9	49.8	54.0	57.5	62.6
BRAZIL	41.2	43.6	50.0	53.4	61.6
Range	16.2	21.3	20.0	17.7	18.8
B	(2)/(1)		(3)/(2)	(4)/(3)	(5)/(4)
Amazônia	1.07		1.19	1.06	1.16
N. Northeast	1.09		1.09	1.05	1.10
C. Northeast	.98		1.16	1.12	1.11
S. Northeast	1.02		1.14	1.11	1.15
Minas	1.07		1.12	1.07	1.09
Rio	1.09		1.15	1.02	1.12
São Paulo	1.16		1.12	1.06	1.10
Paraná	1.05		1.16	1.06	1.12
South	1.08		1.09	1.02	1.10
Central West	1.06		1.08	1.06	1.09
BRAZIL	1.06		1.15	1.07	1.12

Sources: 1930/40, 1940/50, 1960/70 from Carvalho and Wood 1978; 1970/80 estimated from advanced tabulation of the 1980 census.

Household income and length of life

Regional disparities in length of life are considerably wider when we further disaggregate them by the level of household income. The positive association between household income and life expectancy is evident in Table 4.3. For the country as a whole, people in the highest household income bracket in 1970 had a life expectancy of sixty-two years. This represents an average length of life that is over twelve years longer than for people in the lowest income category.[2]

There is an important distinction between the distribution of income among households and the distribution of household income among individuals. Larger households tend to have larger total income because of the greater number of earners, but small incomes per household member (Repetto 1977). As a result, the identity of the poor tends to be masked when the criteria is household income by virtue of including most of the poor in households that are larger and that have a greater total income. Were the analysis here based on strata of per capita household income, differential mortality would be even greater. The differences in average length of life presented in this study (based on total rather than per capita household income) are therefore conservative estimates of differential mortality in Brazil.

There is considerable regional variation in the relationship between household income and mortality. The lowest life expectancy rate in 1970 in the country (42.8 years) was found among the poorest households in the Central Northeast. This stands in sharp contrast to the expectation of life in the most affluent strata in the South. With an average life expectancy of 66.9 years, the highest in the country, the rich in the more developed region of southern Brazil outlived the poorest group in the least developed area by nearly a quarter of a century (24.1 years).

The differences in length of life between the lowest and the highest income group within each region are presented in column 5. The gap is largest in the Central Northeast (11.6 years) and is smallest in Amazônia (4.8 years). Between these two extremes, the differences in the remaining eight regions average 7.4 years and vary within a range of five to about nine years.

The relatively small mortality differential between the rich and the poor in Amazônia may be related to environmental factors. Prior to the penetration of the roads into the interior of the region, which took place after the 1970 census, the population was located primarily in small communities along the banks of the many rivers that fan out across the vast tropical basin. The area is subject to infectious diseases, especially malaria. Yet, in contrast to the Central Northeast, the river system provides a ready source of food and fresh water. The availability of these resources in the Amazon may account for the fact that mortality is less sensitive to income than in other regions of Brazil.

The significance of these mortality differentials are underscored if we place them in world perspective. The life expectancy rate among the poor in the Central Northeast, for example, is equivalent to that recorded in Africa in 1965/70. It roughly corresponds to the expectation

Table 4.3. *Regional life expectancy at birth by monthly household income, 1970*

Region	Overall average	Household income (in Cr$) 1–150 (1)	151–300 (2)	301–500 (3)	501+ (4)	Difference between highest & lowest income (5)
Amazônia	54.2	53.4	53.9	54.8	58.2	4.8
N. Northeast	50.4	50.0	50.8	52.7	55.7	5.7
C. Northeast	44.2	42.8	46.1	50.3	54.4	11.6
S. Northeast	49.7	48.9	50.3	51.9	54.9	6.0
Minas	55.4	53.8	55.4	55.6	62.3	8.5
Rio	57.0	54.1	54.8	57.6	62.1	8.0
São Paulo	58.2	54.7	56.1	58.7	63.9	9.2
Paraná	56.6	54.8	56.5	59.3	63.7	8.9
South	61.9	60.5	61.2	63.4	66.9	6.4
Central West	57.5	56.5	57.1	58.2	63.3	6.8
BRAZIL	53.4	49.9	54.5	57.6	62.0	12.1

Source: Carvalho and Wood 1978.

of life at birth in Western Europe in the 1860s. At the other end of the continuum, the average length of life among the most affluent households in the South approximates the relatively low mortality achieved in Western European countries between 1940 and 1950 (United Nations 1973: 110–11).

Mortality and the distribution of income

The highly skewed distribution of household income, noted in chapter 2, tends to depress the mortality rate for Brazil as a whole. This is because the aggregate life expectancy rate of a population is a weighted average of the rates that correspond to the subgroups within the population. In this case the weights are the proportion of households found in each category of household income. The aggregate mortality rate at one point in time is therefore sensitive to a skewed distribution of income since the high mortality of the poor receives a greater weight by virtue of their greater numbers. Similarly, a change in the distribution of the population across income strata would influence the mortality rate for the population as a whole since it would alter the relative weights that comprise the aggregate measure.

We can use the Central Northeast as an example to illustrate the impact of income distribution on the aggregate mortality rate within a particular region. If the population were equally distributed among the four categories of family income presented in Table 4.3, the life expectancy rate for the region would be the arithmetic mean of the four sub-groups – or 48.4 years. The actual life expectancy in the Central Northeast, however, is 44.2 years, considerably below the arithmetic mean. It is lower because a full 65.3 per cent of the households in the region is found in the lowest income strata (Cr$1–150). The effect is to depress the overall average by 4.2 years. Similar calculations for all ten regions indicate that because of the large proportion of low-income households, the estimated life expectancy rate (the weighted average) is consistently lower than the arithmetic mean.

Mortality and the geographic distribution of population

Just as a skewed distribution of income depresses the aggregate mortality rate within a region, so too does the concentration of population in high mortality areas influence the level of life expectancy for the country as a whole. About 32 per cent of all households in Brazil are located in the first four regions shown in Table 4.3 (Amazônia; Northern, Central and Southern Northeast). With an expectation of life below 55 years, these regions can be considered high risk areas. More striking, however, is the spatial distribution of the poor population of the country. Of the total number of households that earn less than Cr$150, half (49.5 per cent) are located in the NORTHEAST.

As in the case of income, the spatial distribution of the population affects the aggregate level of mortality. Reading down the column, the arithmetic mean of life expectancy for households with monthly earnings between Cr$1 and Cr$150 is 53.0 years. This is 3.1 years higher than the actual weighted mean of 49.9 years for the population in that income stratum. Among low-income households, the aggregate length of life is reduced because of the concentration of the population in the NORTHEAST

Within the upper income brackets the impact of the regional distribution of the population works in the opposite direction. In the highest strata of household income, a greater proportion of families is located in the more developed areas of the country. Well over half (54 per cent)

of all households that earn more than Cr$500 a month reside in southern Brazil. In São Paulo, Paraná and the South region the average length of life at birth is longer compared to families residing in the NORTHEAST who have the same monthly earnings. As a result of the concentration of affluent households in low mortality areas, the actual weighted mean of the life expectancy rates for the highest income strata is sixty-two years, 1.5 years above its arithmetic mean (60.5 years).

The overall level of life expectancy for Brazil is thus influenced by both the distribution of household income (row effects) and the spatial distribution of the population (column effects). It is the combined influence of these two factors that explains an otherwise puzzling feature of Table 4.3: the difference in length of life between the lowest and the highest category of household income for the country as a whole is 12.1 years, a figure that is greater than a comparable difference in any of the ten geographic regions (column 5).

Rural–urban residence

Observing the congested and unsanitary conditions characteristic of the cities of his day, Max Weber held that death rates varied directly with the degree of agglomeration of population (cited in United Nations 1973). Historical analyses of mortality rates prior to the twentieth century suggest that death rates were generally higher in urban than in rural areas. In the United States in 1930 conditions were far worse in the large cities than in smaller ones or in rural areas. Similarly, the average life expectancy for England and Wales in 1841 is estimated to have been about forty years, while the corresponding figures for the industrial cities of Manchester and Liverpool were about 24–5 years (United Nations 1973). The decline in mortality rates in developed countries, however, led to a progressive narrowing of the rural–urban differential. Recent estimates show less than a half-year's difference in life expectancy at birth between urban and rural residents in the United States and in a number of European countries (Davis 1973).

But in developing countries today, cities may have an advantage over the rural hinterland. The dangers of urban life are apparently offset by imported methods of reducing mortality and by the concentration of medical facilities and public health services in cities. According to Kingsley Davis (1973: 276–7), "cities in developing countries have been outposts of the advanced nations." Since they are the first to benefit

Table 4.4. *Regional life expectancy at birth by place of residence,*
1960/70, 1970/80

Region	1960–70 Rural	1960–70 Urban	1970–80 Rural	1970–80 Urban	Ratio U/R 1960/70	Ratio U/R 1970/80
Amazônia	53.7	54.9	62.5	63.7	1.02	1.02
N. Northeast	50.8	49.2	55.9	54.9	0.97	0.98
C. Northeast	44.6	43.8	47.8	50.0	0.98	1.05
S. Northeast	50.7	48.2	55.4	57.8	0.95	1.04
Minas	55.9	54.7	61.4	59.6	0.98	0.97
Rio	56.6	57.1	67.3	63.9	1.01	0.95
São Paulo	57.1	58.5	63.5	64.0	1.02	1.01
Paraná	56.4	57.0	62.5	63.8	1.01	1.02
South	63.0	60.9	68.9	62.4	0.97	0.98
Central West	57.7	57.2	61.4	63.3	0.99	1.03
BRAZIL	52.9	53.9	57.2	61.0	1.02	1.07

from technological and medical advances, their mortality rates dropped below those of rural areas.

Estimates of life expectancy by place of residence in Brazil are given in Table 4.4. To facilitate comparison, the ratio of urban to rural areas is presented in the right-hand columns. In 1960/70 the level of life expectancy in the rural area exceeds the urban rate in six regions of the country (ratios less than one). The reverse is true in the remaining four geographic areas. With only minor changes, the same general pattern holds in the following decade.

In both 1960/70 and 1970/80 the ratio of the rural to urban rates in all regions is close to 1.00. Whether the ratio is greater or less than unity also appears unrelated to the level of mortality across regions. In Amazônia, for example, the overall expectation of life is more than ten years below that found in the South yet, in both cases, the urban rate exceeds the rural rate.

That the mortality differentials between rural and urban areas are minimal and that they follow no apparent pattern may be due to lack of controls for other variables (Sawyer and Soares 1982) and/or to problems associated with the categories used by the census bureau in defining place of residence. The official definition of urban areas is seriously flawed as it classifies as urban all political-administrative centers of *municípios* (roughly equivalent to counties in the United States) and *distritos* (subdivisions of *municípios*). Many of these localities contain fewer than 1,000 people and are hardly characterized by those features conventionally understood as urban.

However, we find systematic differences between rural and urban areas when the mortality rates for each region are disaggregated by four categories of household income (Table 4.5). The ratio of urban to rural rates in the last column follows a consistent pattern. Urban life expectancy is below that of rural areas for low-income households, but the reverse is true for families in the highest income class. Thus, city dwellers have a higher probability of a longer life compared to those who live in rural areas *provided they have greater economic resources*. This pattern holds true in all ten geographic regions, although there is variation in the "threshold point," or the income category in which the urban rate exceeds the rural one.

Despite the consistency of these findings, several factors should be kept in mind. It is important to note that the census only includes data on monetary income. As a result, the income categories used in this analysis may not permit unbiased urban–rural comparisons. Because they are more likely to produce goods for their own consumption, households in the countryside undoubtedly have higher levels of real income compared to those in cities. Similarly, city dwellers may have lower real incomes because they face higher prices in urban areas, and because they are more likely to need a broader range of services that they must purchase. Because they live in areas of high population density, urban residents may require water and sewage facilities and have a greater demand for medical services. They also face higher costs to the extent that they must pay for rent, transportation and other necessities associated with city life. The higher levels of life expectancy among the poorest rural households may therefore be due to higher levels of real income compared to urban families in the same category of monetary income.

Nonetheless, focusing on the highest income groups (where the contribution to real income from home production is proportionately much less), one cannot reject the hypothesis that urban areas may have an advantage over rural places because of the greater concentration of medical facilities and better living conditions. The critical issue appears to be whether or not one can afford access to these benefits. The fact that life expectancy rates for upper-income households are higher in urban areas suggests that cities may indeed be better places to live, but only for those who can pay for adequate protection against the hardships that otherwise beset those with fewer financial resources.

It is not surprising, therefore, that both the lowest and the highest

Table 4.5. *Regional life expectancy at birth, by household income and place of residence, 1970*

Region	Household income	Overall average	Rural	Urban	Urban–rural ratio
Amazônia	1	53.4	53.8	52.6	0.98
	2	53.9	53.6	54.3	1.01
	3	54.8	53.2	55.8	1.05
	4	58.2	54.5	59.3	1.09
N.Northeast	1	50.0	50.7	47.0	0.93
	2	50.8	51.2	50.2	0.98
	3	52.7	51.9	53.3	1.03
	4	55.7	49.8	57.7	1.16
C. Northeast	1	43.8	44.3	40.0	0.90
	2	46.1	46.6	45.9	0.98
	3	50.3	48.2	50.8	1.05
	4	54.4	53.4	54.4	1.02
S. Northeast	1	48.9	50.4	45.1	0.89
	2	50.3	52.4	48.8	0.93
	3	51.9	52.3	51.8	0.99
	4	54.9	52.6	55.3	1.05
Minas	1	53.8	55.3	49.6	0.90
	2	55.4	57.2	54.5	0.95
	3	58.6	59.2	58.4	0.99
	4	62.3	61.9	62.4	1.01
Rio	1	54.1	56.8	51.2	0.90
	2	54.8	55.9	54.6	0.98
	3	57.6	56.9	57.6	1.01
	4	62.1	61.1	62.1	1.02
São Paulo	1	54.7	56.4	51.9	0.92
	2	56.1	57.5	55.7	0.97
	3	58.7	58.3	58.8	1.08
	4	63.9	61.4	64.0	1.04
Paraná	1	54.8	55.3	51.2	0.93
	2	56.5	57.1	55.5	0.97
	3	59.3	60.0	59.0	0.98
	4	63.7	62.3	64.1	1.03
South	1	60.5	62.0	54.6	0.88
	2	61.2	63.4	59.3	0.94
	3	63.4	65.2	62.6	0.96
	4	66.9	66.2	67.1	1.01
Central West	1	56.5	57.1	54.8	0.96
	2	57.1	58.7	55.6	0.95
	3	58.2	57.6	58.5	1.02
	4	63.3	62.5	63.4	1.01
Brazil	1	49.9	51.4	46.0	0.89
	2	54.5	55.9	53.7	0.96
	3	57.6	57.6	57.6	1.00
	4	62.0	60.0	62.2	1.04

Source: Carvalho & Wood (1978).

life expectancy rates are found in urban settings. The poorest people in urban Central Northeast had a life expectancy of forty years in 1970. This was more than twenty-five years lower than the average length of life for members of the highest income group in the urban South (67.1).

Who benefitted from the mortality decline?

The central topic that has concerned development analysts is whether or not the character of economic growth in Brazil has reduced or increased relative inequality between different socioeconomic strata of the population. The debate in the early 1970s largely revolved around the issue of income distribution. Evidence of a deterioration in the real income of the poor, and of an increase in the concentration of income between 1960 and 1970, raised serious doubts about the social consequences of the "Brazilian model of development." More recent data from the 1980 census, discussed in chapter 3, indicate that, although measures of relative inequality remained about the same from 1970 to 1980, real income rose among all population subgroups.

From a demographic standpoint, we can address the inequality issue by comparing the 1970 and 1980 mortality differentials by strata of household income. On the basis of the previous findings we know that the aggregate mortality rate fell substantially during the 1970s. The crucial question is which group benefitted most from the decline in the death rate? Since disaggregated life expectancy rates are a summary indicator of the overall standard of living that prevails within a given population subgroup, evidence of a change over time in mortality differentials offers a more accurate assessment of relative changes in living standards than does the conventional focus on income alone.

The estimates presented in Table 4.6 indicate that the gains in life expectancy from 1960/70 to 1970/80 were fairly evenly distributed across income strata. For the country as a whole, shown in the upper portion of panel A, the average life expectancy rose approximately four years for all income groups. In rural areas, the improvement was somewhat higher within the highest income category (5.3 years, compared to 4.2 and 3.9 years for households with earnings of Cr$1–150 and Cr$151–300). The reverse seems to be true in urban Brazil, where we find the largest gain among the poorest households. The more disaggregated rates presented in panel B suggest the increases in life expectancy averaged about 3.5 years in all strata except the lowest and the highest income groups, which experienced above average gains. Conclusions drawn from panel B should be regarded as tentative, however, due to

Table 4.6. *Changes in life expectancy, 1960/70–1970/80, by household income and place of residence*

	Household income (1)	1960/70 (2)	1970/80 (3)	(3)–(2) (4)
A Total	1–150	49.9	53.9	4.0
	151–300	54.5	58.3	3.8
	301–500	57.6	61.7	4.1
	501+	62.0	66.3	4.3
Rural	1–150	51.4	55.6	4.2
	151–300	55.9	59.8	3.9
	301–500	57.6	62.3	4.7
	501+	60.0	65.3	5.3
Urban	1–150	46.0	50.7	4.7
	151–300	53.7	58.2	4.5
	301–500	57.6	61.6	4.0
	501+	62.2	66.4	4.2
B Total	1–50	46.7	53.8	7.1
	51–100	49.6	51.0	1.4
	101–150	51.6	56.0	4.4
	151–200	54.0	58.2	4.2
	201–250	54.4	58.2	3.8
	251–300	56.1	58.8	2.7
	301–400	56.8	61.6	5.5
	401–500	58.8	62.0	3.2
	501–1,000	60.9	64.9	3.6
	1,001–1,500	64.0	68.3	4.5
	1,501–2,000	65.5	66.3	0.8
	2,001+	63.9	70.1	6.2

Note: Household income strata are expressed in 1970 cruzeiros.

the instability of highly disaggregated estimates, and because income data is often least reliable at the tail ends of a distribution. Despite these caveats, we can draw the general conclusion that between 1960/70 and 1970/80, improvements in life expectancy rates were more or less evenly distributed across income strata for Brazil as a whole, and within rural and urban areas of the country.

* * *

The average expectation of life in Brazil has increased by twenty years since the 1930s. The decline in the level of mortality is associated with both the importation of public health and medical technologies as well as factors endogenous to Brazil's social and economic development. The mortality decline has not occurred at an even pace. Rapid gains occurred in the immediate post-World War II years, and between 1960/70 and 1970/80. The substantial gains recorded in the most recent period can be attributed to the improvements in the overall quality of life as measured by economic and other social indicators. These include: a rise in real income; an increase in educational attainment; and a reduction in environmental risks associated with the increase in the proportion of households with water and sewage facilities and with electric power.

The decline in the aggregate death rate over the years has not eliminated the marked differences in mortality by region and by socio-economic strata. The geographic inequalities in social and economic development are reflected in the high mortality rates for the north-eastern part of the country relative to the more developed central and southern regions of Brazil. Although the average length of life has increased in all areas, life expectancy in the Central Northeast in 1970/80 remained around eighteen years below that found in the South (67.8 years).

Mortality differentials are also evident when the estimates of length of life are disaggregated by the level of monthly household income. People in the highest household income bracket in 1970 enjoyed a life expectancy that was over twelve years longer than people in households in the lowest income category. Between 1960/70 and 1970/80, life expectancy rates rose approximately four years within every income group in the country. Hence, the life expectancy gap between the poor and the rich remained about as large in 1970/80 as it was a decade earlier.

5

Wage policy, infant mortality and collective social action in São Paulo

The military coup in 1964 marked a new era of economic planning in Brazil. In an effort to contain inflation and attract foreign investment, the regime forged a development strategy that included, as a central component, a wage containment policy. The power of labor unions to act as effective bargaining units, already undermined by the corporatist legacy of the Vargas period, was further curtailed by legislative fiat, political repression and the occasional use of force. To achieve the labor peace required of a sound "investment climate," the direct negotiation between capital and labor was replaced by a bureaucratic method to establish salary levels. The procedure was putatively intended to adjust the minimum wage so as to recover income eroded by inflation. In practice the components of the formula designed to adjust for inflation were deliberately understated during certain periods. From 1964 to about 1975 the real value of the minimum wage deteriorated. In the latter half of the decade, a time of widespread labor unrest, the downward trend was reversed and the minimum salary gained in purchasing power.

Intervention in factor markets to promote development is a popular theme in neoclassical economics. Proponents of wage containment policy point to market distortions that understate the relative price of capital and overstate labor costs. Measures designed to reduce the price of labor are intended to correct this imbalance. In a two-factor neoclassical world with unemployed labor, lower wages are expected to produce an increase in employment and output, since more workers are hired with the same amount of capital. By increasing the rate of profit and investment, the model predicts favorable long-run effects on growth and employment. In an effusive endorsement of this thesis, *The Economist* (December 24, 1983) claimed that "Falling real wages, like falling oil prices, ... could herald a new age of low unemployment and low inflation ... When that happens," the editorial continued, "the world will enjoy many happy New Years."

According to defenders of wage-squeeze policy, the costs involved must be incurred in order to correct what they consider excesses brought about by the exaggerated claims of the trade unions. In fact, as Prebisch (1984: 162) notes, "neoclassical economists generally accept with resignation (and not without a measure of complacency in some cases) the economic and social costs in question for the sake of remedying the consequences of the violation of market laws by the labour force, as well as by abusive exercise of the power of the State." The argument rests on the assumption that the free play of market forces disseminates throughout society the fruits of technical progress which find expression in rising productivity.

The model disregards certain structural phenomena, especially changes in the workplace. The latter is crucially important since the presumed benefits of wage reduction are conditioned by the type of technology introduced. Technology determines not only the level of total output but also the substitutability between capital and labor. When the elasticity of substitution is less than unity, as in São Paulo, wage reductions benefit capitalists – both relatively and absolutely – due to a rise in total output but a decline in the wage share. Wage-squeeze policies under adverse technological circumstances also worsen the position of employed labor and only marginally improve that of the presently unemployed (Ahluwalia, 1976: 74–5). Hence, under certain conditions, the outcome of wage containment is a more unequal distribution of income, with little or no employment gain.

The debate about the distributional outcome of wage-lowering development policy should not be restricted to macroeconomic issues. Indeed, as we contend in this chapter, its arguable benefits must also be assessed in terms of the considerable social costs such policies impose on the working class. A cavalier faith in "the long run," without regard for the human consequences of wage compression, is shortsighted, especially in light of serious doubts as to whether or not current income sacrifices actually result in future rewards.

An analysis of wages, social costs and development policy must necessarily take a broad structural perspective. At the heart of the matter is the very process by which surplus is produced and retained, and how social groups struggle, in the workplace and through institutionalized state channels, to share in the fruits of technical progress. In Brazil, contemporary mechanisms of labor control and wage determination can be traced to early stages of industrialization in the 1930s, and to the political repercussions of an emerging urban proletariat. These issues, briefly summarized in the next section, provide the background for a detailed discussion of recent wage policies since the military coup in 1964. The analysis focuses on their effect on the purchasing power of low-income groups in the metropolitan area of São Paulo, Brazil's largest and most industrialized city.[1] Trends over time in infant mortality levels measure the social impact of wage-squeeze policies on the urban population.

The last section of this chapter pays attention to a different aspect of São Paulo as a social and economic system. In contrast to the previous "top-down" approach, which examines how social structure impinges on different classes of the urban population, here we explore the way conscious social action, on the part of individuals, households and collectivities of people, effects social change. The analysis focuses on the various ways the urban poor actively negotiate, and struggle against, the conditions of underdevelopment imposed on them. For this purpose, we investigate three types of action: the sustenance strategies households pursue, the initiatives undertaken by community organizations and occasional outbursts of collective violence.

We regard these forms of behavior as intrinsic to the system of relationships that define the urban complex. On the one hand they represent a response to structurally determined conditions (outlined in the first sections of the chapter); on the other, they constitute a set of initiatives which themselves alter the city's socioeconomic and political profile. In this manner our analytical focus gives concrete meaning to the abstract argument presented in chapter 2: that classes and social groups are not passive outcomes of infrastructural processes, as a dogmatic materialist view might suggest. On the contrary, the initiatives undertaken by people, acting to protect or to further their interests, constitute sources of pressure to transform the very structures that gave rise to social action. In keeping with Castells (1983: xvi), our perspective endorses the view that cities and citizens should not be seen in isolation from one another. Instead, the features of the urban economy which determine the constraints people confront, as well as the actions individuals or households adopt to contend with these conditions, are understood as integral parts of a single whole.

Corporatism and organized labor in Brazil

Following the coup in 1964, the wage policies adopted by the government relied on institutions that had been in existence long before the military took power. Of particular importance was the elaborate system of state–labor relations that was established during Getúlio Vargas's regime in the 1930s. The Estado Novo (1937–45) adhered to a corporatist philosophy whereby every social and economic sector was to be brought into a government-directed network of councils. The compulsory, hierarchically ordered, functionally specific *sindicato* (trade union) system established the framework by which the government reduced the political participation of labor organizations and weakened the bargaining power and the autonomy of unions (Erickson and Middlebrook 1982). The control, exercised through a set of legal and fiscal arrangements, gave the government a relatively free hand in union affairs.

Vargas's rise to power coincided with, and represented a reflection of, Brazil's early industrialization, and the emergence of an urban working class in the major cities in the center-south. As the head of a reformist civilian–military coalition, Vargas opposed the rule of the rural-based oligarchy in the *coup d'état* that brought him to power. The economic and political project Vargas launched aimed to establish a strong and highly centralized state apparatus that could foster the conditions for industrial expansion. His challenge to the power of the traditional elite required the backing of urban workers. Vargas's strategy was to enlist their support yet, at the same time, gain control of the incipient working-class movement. In early 1931, the government withdrew recognition of the few existing organizations and forced them to reapply for certification, a concession granted only to "safe" unions. Once he broke the power of independent trade associations, Vargas courted workers by creating the first national Ministry of Labor, raising wages and decreeing basic labor legislation and social benefits. In this way, Vargas, first in the early 1930s and later under the Estado Novo, constructed the institutional framework that to this day enables the state to retain a firm grip on organized labor.

Under the Estado Novo, Vargas created a complex system of labor courts in which the representatives of workers and employers shared the bench with professional magistrates. Rather than resolving conflicts through strikes, the court was designed to adjudicate disputes. Possessing the power to impose its decision on both parties, the labor court transformed the conflict between capital and labor into an administrative problem, resolved within a bureaucratic institution headed by judges appointed by, and responsive to the interests of, the federal government (Skidmore 1978).

In the *sindicato* system, only one syndicate is permitted for each occupational category. Those employed in a particular industry pay annual compulsory dues (*imposto sindical*). This is deducted from the worker's pay, and deposited in the bank of Brazil by the employer. Active union membership, however, is conferred only after paying a second fee, the amount of which is established by the individual union. The centralization of union resources gave great leverage to the Ministry of Labor. With the power to approve budgets and to release or withhold funds, the Ministry ensured that unions could resist neither the government-set wage levels, nor the other conditions of employment established by the labor courts.

The Ministry of Labor holds further power in terms of union organization and administration. Not only must elections of syndicate officials be "validated," but the Ministry can also "intervene" in internal union affairs whenever it deems that the interests of the workers are violated by elected officials. When this occurs, the union enters a kind of receivership in which the federal government is entitled to appoint new representatives until new elections are permitted (Skidmore 1973). Thus, the Ministry of Labor, with a firm grip on the union's purse strings, and with a legal right to directly interfere with the internal organization of the syndicate, wields substantial control over organized labor.

The major aspects of the institutional framework created under the Vargas dictatorship remained pretty much unchanged during the democratic era between 1945 and 1964. Following the coup, the corporatist labor system served the interests of the military regimes quite well. In the first two years after the takeover the government removed radical nationalists from elected public office and from a broad range of interest groups, including labor unions. The government intervened in at least 532 syndicates, concentrating its efforts on the larger, more important sectors of industry. In 1964 and 1965 the Ministry of Labor intervened in 70 per cent of those unions with more than 5,000 members, 38 per cent of those with 1,000 to 5,000 members and in 19 per cent of unions with fewer than 1,000 members (Erickson and Middlebrook 1982: 237).

Militant labor leaders were replaced by *pelegos* loyal to the military regime. The term, which literally refers to the sheep-skin blanket that protects the horse from the irritation of the saddle, is commonly used to describe any labor representative who supports the government, or who does not strongly oppose it. In the first two years of rule, the military placed *pelegos* in the leadership of over 500 unions and trade federations. Many of these individuals had been trained for their new role by the American Institute for Free Labor Development (AIFLD), an organization set up in response to the Cuban revolution by the US government and some elements of the AFL-CIO to promote pro-US business-type unionism in Latin America.

Installing *pelegos* in key posts within the union structure was only a variation on the state's longstanding effort to control and manipulate working-class organizations to its own political agenda, a task that became increasingly difficult in the face of the profound structural changes in Brazil's economy. Whereas 45 per cent of its people lived in cities in 1960, twenty years later about three-quarters of the population resided in urban areas. In addition, the process of industrialization radically transformed the workplace, leading to fundamental changes in social organization. In 1968 the largest factories employed no more than around 5,000 workers. By 1978, Volkswagen alone hired 38,000; Ford, 25,000 (Kucinski 1982). The "Brazilian Miracle" concentrated unprecedented numbers of people, not only in the confines of the factory gates, but also in residential neighborhoods (see "Responses to urban underdevelopment" in this chapter). Union membership soared, and the rank and file, sensing the power of numbers, grew more confident.

The tension between labor and management intensified in the late 1970s. These developments were triggered in August 1977 by the startling disclosure that the manipulation of wage data for industrial workers in the years 1973 and 1974 may have caused a 34.1 per cent loss in the real income of the Brazilian working class. The way this disclosure came about, as José Álvaro Moisés (1979: 51) notes, was at once curious and illustrative. Since the early 1970s the consulting agency supported by the São Paulo unions (DIEESE) repeatedly claimed that the official inflation data was falsified. This charge was ignored by the federal government until economists of the International Monetary Fund conducted an investigation. When DIEESE claims were confirmed, there was an immediate reaction, starting with the most important unions in the greater São Paulo area. Leaders of some 250,000 workers in automobile, electrical and chemical industries sought retroactive compensation for their union members (Moisés, 1979: 52).

These demands soon spread to other parts of Brazil. In 1979 alone about ninety organized work stoppages took place in São Paulo, Rio de Janeiro, Rio Grande do Sul and Pernambuco in an eruption of labor resistance that involved over 1.2 million people (Souza and Lamounier 1981). These initiatives were undertaken by a broad spectrum of workers, including laborers in heavy industry, teachers, bankers, doctors, civil servants, drivers, and journalists. The re-emergence of labor militancy marked the return of the working class to the political scene for the first time since the harsh repression of the major strikes in Contagem and Osasco in 1968.

Many of the work stoppages in the late 1970s were declared in violation of the 1964 Law 4.330, an updated and much more severe version of the old anti-strike provision (Decree 9.070). Others were presumably illegal by Law 1.632 of 1978, which prohibits work stoppages in the public sector and in industries considered essential to the national interest (Conjuntura Econômica 1980: 40).

The strategies pursued by organized labor in the later 1970s mark a new era of union activity. Compared to previous periods, the difference lies primarily in the scope of the demands proposed by what came to be called the "new labor movement" (Souza and Lamounier 1981; Almeida 1981). Going beyond the conventional concern for wages and working conditions, unions challenged the very structure of the corporatist framework. At the outset of the strikes, which began among metal workers in São Paulo, these broader aims were not explicitly recognized. It was only in the course of mobilizing workers for higher wages that union demands expanded to include three larger objectives: to replace the centrally controlled wage policy by a system of free and direct collective bargaining between workers and management; to remove unions from the tutelage of the Ministry of Labor; and, finally, to obtain an unrestricted right to strike, a condition deemed indispensable to union freedom (Almeida 1981).

The military regime never acquiesced to union pressure to rescind the anti-strike statutes. However, in order to move ahead with the plan to liberalize the political process in Brazil, authorities simply left unenforced laws that remained on the books. Similarly, the Ministry of Labor responded to the wave of labor unrest in a flexible manner, granting concessions on certain issues while resisting attempts to change others. Law 6.708/79, for example, preserves the essentials of the salary policy in effect since 1965. Yet, it permits unions greater leeway with regard to the salary adjustments associated with increases in productivity.

For a time at least, such measures defused the wide-ranging demands of the labor movement. According to one observer (Almeida 1981), the strikes between 1978 and 1980 indicated that labor was sufficiently powerful to disrupt production, yet not strong enough to forge a new institutional structure, free of state mediation. This weakness permitted the government to advance minor reforms while leaving the basic character of the system unchanged.

The world recession in the 1980s dealt a severe blow to organized labor's growing momentum. Hard hit by the economic downturn were the very industrial suburbs that spawned the new labor movement in the late 1970s. Bankruptcies reached epidemic proportions and many automobile manufacturers and firms producing parts sought to salvage their declining profit rates by sacking workers. From 1978 to 1983, some 40,000 people lost their jobs in the ABC district alone (San André; São Bernardo; São Clemente) (Latin America Regional Report: Brazil 1983: 6). Militant unionism, which blossomed during a boom period, proved ill-adapted to economic recession. Having learned to fight for higher wages, organized labor found it difficult to mount an effective means to defend their jobs. As elsewhere in the world, they discovered that, once wages become a secondary concern, a different defensive strategy was required.

It remains to be seen how the return to a democratic system will affect organized labor and its attempt to break away from the subordination to the state. One the eve of Tancredo Neves's inauguration, unions represented by the Central Único dos Trabalhadores (CUT) – linked to the Partido dos Trabalhadores (PT), community Church circles and militants of some clandestine parties – refused to hold a dialogue with the President-elect. But others, represented by the Confederação Nacional das Classes Trabalhadoras (CONCLAT), tied to the PMDB, did meet with Neves. According to some reports (Latin America Weekly Report 1985: 10), Neves agreed to several of CONCLAT's demands, including: the participation of union representatives in the management of state enterprises and pension funds; participation in the sub-committee which will set out the new government's economic program; freedom of activity for unions; and the commitment not to meddle in union affairs.

Wage policy

To sustain the growth of new industries, the expansionist Kubitschek administration (1956–60) relaxed the restrictive monetary policies that had been in effect earlier in the decade, unleashing massive inflation rates. In mid-1963, before the military takeover, President Goulart created the National Board on Wage Policy (Conselho Nacional de Política Salarial), an agency with authority to set wages in the public sector, and in private firms licensed to provide public facilities (Skidmore 1978). The goal was to contain the rising price of water, electricity, transportation and other services.

After the 1964 coup, the reduction and control of inflation became a primary goal of the Castelo Branco regime. This was accomplished in several ways. The most important was a centrally administered method of determining wage levels, a policy based on the Goulart precedent. Since 1964, an index of economic indicators sets the minimum wage level. This technique, according to the former Minister of Planning, Mário Simonsen, had the advantage of "pacifying" collective bargaining negotiations between capital and labor. The system avoided the disruption associated with strikes and other forms of labor unrest, and limited the rise in costs which led to higher inflation. The success of these policies, in Simonsen's view, created the economic and political stability required to attract foreign investment necessary to achieve rapid economic growth in Brazil.

The technocratic solution was neither as objective nor apolitical as its proponents claimed. The initial formula used to derive the minimum wage was based on a correction factor determined by the average rate of inflation during the previous 24 months, plus a small increase pegged to the rise in productivity. A third variable was added to account for the expected rise in inflation in the subsequent twelve-month period during which the minimum salary would apply. The latter, referred to as "residual inflation," proved to be a key aspect of the salary formula. When forecasts of inflation were unrealistically low (as they often were), the underestimation of future inflation reduced the real value of the minimum wage. In 1966, for example, residual inflation, which comprised a major part of the wage correction formula, was estimated to be about 10 per cent. The actual figure was closer to 40 per cent, causing a substantial drop in purchasing power.

This method was used with only minor modification (e.g., Law no. 5.451, June 12, 1968) until the oil crisis in 1974 led to exceptionally high inflation. The logic of the old formula led to such drastic declines in the real wage that a new solution was required. In accordance with Law 6.147 of 1974, the minimum wage was calculated on the basis of the inflation rate in the previous twelve months, multiplied by three coefficients: (1) an estimate of residual inflation; (2) an index of productivity; and (3) a correction factor designed to recuperate income eroded by previous underestimation of residual inflation. Unlike the earlier calculation, the rate of increase in productivity was multiplied by the average real wage (which itself was multiplied by the preceding residual inflation), hence leading to larger adjustments compared to before.

Despite these adjustments, real wages still declined when inflation was unexpectedly high. In December of 1974, at the end of the first year in which the new formula was adopted, a 10 per cent emergency bonus was required to offset the drop in real wages caused by the underestimation of residual inflation in the first semester of the year (DIEESE, 1975).

Wage determination procedures were again revised in October of 1979 in an effort to undermine labor's gathering momentum. Under the new system, salaries are adjusted every six months on the basis of a Consumer Price Index (CPI) calculated by the census bureau. The CPI is used as the base number for a set of adjustments factors intended to favor low-income recipients. For individuals who earn up to three times the minimum wage, the salary increase is 110 per cent of the CPI. The adjustment is equal to the CPI for those who earn seven to ten times the minimum wage, and is 0.8 per cent of the index in the case of individuals whose income exceeds ten times the minimum. In addition to semi-annual increases based on changes in consumer prices, the new procedure allows for annual salary increases according to a productivity index.

The method, which privileges the lower income brackets, was aimed at ending the tendency for real wages to fall without, at the same time, fueling inflation. The measure was assumed not to be inflationary since the cost of indexing salaries up to three minimum wages at 10 per cent above the CPI would be taken out of the upper wage groups. This, presumably, would keep constant total labor costs as well as a company's overall cost structure (Carvalho 1984).

Unlike previous methods, the government calculated the index for each industrial sector, but the figure can be disputed in a bargaining process between labor and management (Correa do Lago 1980). By making them subject to collective bargaining agreements, differences could be established between sectors and companies without affecting inflation since this part of the raise could not be passed on to the consumer in the form of increased prices. Unions contend that the procedure makes outright manipulation of the adjustment possible. They also claim that the method is flawed because it uses a single index for whole sectors of the economy. Ideally every firm would have its own index so as to avoid penalizing highly efficient workers and rewarding those in less productive establishments.

Questions remain as to the redistributive consequences of the wage adjustment mechanism. Other things being equal, the larger correction factor applied to the lower income stratum unambiguously favors a more equitable distribution of income over time. Yet two related factors suggest that the matter is far more complex than the simple procedure implies. One issue concerns the fact that the weights used to calculate the CPI were established years ago and are now out of date. The cost of living index does not, therefore, reflect significant changes that have recently taken place in the economy's price structure, especially the disproportionate increases in transportation and food prices. The latter are especially relevant since food weighs far more heavily in the budgets of lower income households. The National Family Spending Study (ENDEF), carried out in 1974/75, showed that food accounted for 50 per cent of total spending for families earning up to 3.5 minimum wages. This item accounted for about 20 per cent of total expenses for families with an income equivalent to ten to fifteen minimum wages, falling to 6 per cent among the wealthy (over thirty minimum wages). If food habits remain constant, this means that a 30 per cent hike in food prices in general translates into a 15 per cent increase in food expenses for the first group, 6 per cent for the second and a mere 1.8 per cent for the highest income stratum. Moreover, the rise in the price of food and public services has systematically outpaced the increase in the CPI. On the basis of these observations, Carvalho (1984: 121) concludes that wage adjustments at rates higher than the Consumer Price Index are simply compensatory and do not represent an actual 10 per cent increase in real income.

Workers in the service sector are at a special disadvantage. They are rarely unionized, and therefore have reduced power to bargain for wage increases. Even if service workers were organized, there remains the problem of how to quantify their productivity in the absence of a physical product that can serve as a unit of measure. The estimates that do exist (based on indirect techniques) do not bode well for service sector workers. The annual growth in productivity for industry and services were about the same in the 1940s (2.6 and 2.1 per cent, respectively). In the 1960s the annual increase in productivity in industry was 5.5 per cent, compared to only 0.6 per cent in services (Almeida 1980).

Compared to the United States, a change in the level of the minimum wage has far greater implications in Brazil. For one thing, a much larger proportion of the population earns salaries at, or close to, the legislated minimum. Although some observers claim that the importance of the minimum wage has been overestimated (e.g., Macedo 1981), others note that a change in the nominal value of the minimum wage affects a much wider spectrum of workers than those who actually earn the legislated minimum. Occupational salary levels, for example, are established using the minimum wage as a reference point. For Souza and

Baltar (1975), " ... it is the wage floor in the capitalist sector (determined by the minimum wage) that workers used as a 'lighthouse' that guides the earnings of the unskilled people working outside the sector, including those occupied in petty trade or production." Similarly, rents and numerous other prices are pegged to the minimum wage level. This practice is technically illegal, but it is widely used nonetheless. A change in the level of the minimum wage thus has ripple effects throughout the economy, affecting many aspects of daily life.

Real wages and infant mortality, 1963–79

Modifications in the method of determining the legal minimum wage described above, together with the high rates of inflation, caused the real value of the minimum salary to fluctuate over time. We estimate the

Table 5.1. *Infant mortality rate and real minimum wage index,*
São Paulo, 1963–79

Year	Real minimum wage index[a]	Infant mortality rate[b]
1963	93	69.9
1964	99	67.6
1965	96	69.4
1966	83	73.8
1967	80	74.4
1968	80	75.1
1969	78	83.8
1970	79	90.9
1971	78	94.6
1972	79	93.4
1973	80	94.6
1974	77	88.6
1975	83	88.2
1976	89	82.6
1977	91	72.6
1978	93	70.6
1979	96	64.6

[a] Real minimum wage index = $(X_i/Y_i)\,100$, where X_i is nominal wage in year i and Y_i is cost of living index. Minimum wage data from *Anuário Estatístico*, various years. Cost of living index from *Conjuntura Econômica*, various years.
[b] Deaths under the age of 1 per 1,000 live births. Source, *Anuário Estatístico*, 1963, 1964; Yunes and Ronchezel (16); Fundação Sistema Estadual de Análise de Dados (SEADE), various years.

real minimum wage in São Paulo by deflating the nominal wage level by a cost of living index for the corresponding year. The values, shown in the first column of Table 5.1, indicate a rapid decline in purchasing power from 1964 through the early 1970s, reaching a low in 1974. Thereafter, the real value of minimum wage began to rise. By 1978–9 the index approximated the levels recorded in 1963–4.

The conventional infant mortality rate is defined as the number of deaths under one year of age per 1,000 live births during the year. The rates for São Paulo are presented in the second column of Table 5.1. The infant death rate was just under seventy per thousand in the early 1960s. In 1965, when real wages began to fall, the infant mortality rate began to rise. In 1971, 1972 and 1973 the infant mortality rate reached a high of just under 95 per thousand. When the real wage index began to increase after 1974, the death rate dropped off. By the end of the decade infant mortality declined to a low 64.6 per thousand live births.

Figure 5.1 shows the relationship between fluctuations in real wages and the infant mortality rate from 1963 to 1979. The trends are nearly mirror images of one another, indicating a strong inverse relationship between the two. The decline in the real value of the minimum wage from 1964 through the early 1970s is associated with a rise in infant mortality. The upward trend in the death rate, however, was reversed in the late 1970s, when the minimum wage regained purchasing power.

Arguments for a causal relationship

Figure 5.1 leaves little doubt that fluctuations in the infant death rate coincide with changes in the real value of the minimum wage in São Paulo. An empirical association is not in itself evidence of a causal relationship, however. In analyses of infant mortality trends over time, this point is of particular importance because the death rate is subject to the effect of a host of variables other than income. If we are to conclude that changes in real wages cause the infant mortality rate to change, we must critically examine, and ultimately be in a position to reject, alternative explanations for the association.

The factors that influence the actual mortality rate include the pattern and the magnitude of rural to urban migration, changes in the distribution of income, increased investment in public health measures and improvements in other aspects of the urban infrastructure such as the expansion of water and sewage services. Moreover, the mortality level estimated from the registration of vital events is subject to error.

Figure 5.1 Real wage index and infant mortality rate, São Paulo, 1963–1979

Improved vital statistics, and the recording of non-resident deaths in the metropolitan area, can alter the mortality rate reported by the vital registration system without necessarily implying a real change in the death rate. In the following sections we examine each of these issues.

Vital statistics
Demographers are justifiably wary of drawing firm conclusions from mortality estimates derived from vital registration systems in developing countries. It is impossible to determine exactly the extent to which changes in data collection procedures affect estimates of infant mortality. The issue is further complicated by the fact that the numerator (infant deaths in a year) and the denominator (total live births in the same year) are subject to different sources and degrees of error. For Brazil, Yunes and Ronchezel (1974) conclude that the under-enumeration of live births is more serious than the under-reporting of infant deaths. A study of vital statistics in São Paulo found that 9.5 per cent of the children dying in the first year of life between 1968 and 1970 had not been previously counted in the city's birth records (Laurenti 1975).

In the last decade or two there has been improvement in both the registration of infant deaths and live births. But the effects of more accurate birth and death records on the infant mortality trend tend to offset one another. If reforms in data collection procedures correct for previous under-enumeration in the number of children born, the effect, by increasing the denominator of the ratio, is to reduce the estimated level of mortality. A more accurate register of deaths would have the opposite effect.

From this standpoint alone, it is implausible to attribute the infant mortality trend solely to changes in the quality of the vital registration records from 1964 to 1973. The argument implies an improvement in birth records by a factor sufficient to produce a 40 per cent increase in the infant mortality rate over the period. Similarly, from 1973 to 1979, one would have to attribute the drop in the death rate, either to a sudden deterioration in the quality of death statistics, or to a relative improvement in birth records of sufficient magnitude to produce a 33 per cent decline in the infant mortality rate. In view of attempts to improve the registration of *both* births and deaths in recent years, it is reasonable to conclude that changes in data collection procedures cannot fully account for the pattern shown in Figure 5.1.

Vital statistics for the metropolitan area of São Paulo are also subject to a source of error associated with the geographic allocation of deaths. By law (Decree 4.857 of 1939) all deaths are assigned to the location of occurrence rather than to the decedent's place of residence. In Brazil, medical facilities are concentrated in metropolitan centers, and rural medical facilities are relatively inadequate. Under these circumstances the facilities located in cities are used by people in surrounding areas. If a child is sick and is taken to an urban hospital where he or she dies, the death is recorded in the city. Mortality statistics in urban centers are therefore inflated by what has been graphically called the "invasion of deaths" (Berquó and Gonçalves 1974).

Berquó and Gonçalves (1974) investigated the degree to which the registration of non-resident deaths has contributed to infant mortality rates in São Paulo. On the basis of a detailed study of the original certificates, they separated deaths by place of residence, and the mortality level for the metropolitan area was corrected accordingly. Non-residents accounted for about 9.4 per cent of all infant deaths in São Paulo in 1960. The comparable figure for 1968 was 10.8 per cent (Berquó and Gonçalves, 1974, Table 20).

These findings indicate that the infant mortality estimates for São Paulo are indeed affected by the invasion of deaths. However, the bias appears to be relatively stable. It cannot, therefore, account for fluctuations in the infant mortality rate over time. More importantly, once non-resident deaths were removed, the death rate for São Paulo still increased between 1960 and 1968 (Berquó and Gonçalves, 1974).

Migration
We must also consider other factors that affect the actual proportion of deaths among live births. The rise in infant deaths in São Paulo, for

example, has been attributed to the flow of migrants to the city. This argument follows two lines of reasoning. One is an ecological explanation, based on the effect of migration on changes in the population at risk; the other is a cultural argument, premised on the attributes of the migrants themselves.

Leser (1974) maintains that the population growth of São Paulo due to migration has exceeded the city's capacity to extend water, sewage and electrical facilities. The result is substandard living conditions, particularly for new arrivals to the city who are relegated, for the most part, to the urban periphery where services are minimal. Since the death rate is sensitive to housing conditions and environmental hazards, families in the urban perimeter are exposed to a higher risk. By enlarging the size of the population in high risk zones, migration could lead to higher infant death rates independently of changes in the purchasing power of the minimum wage.

The second argument stresses the cultural and behavioral characteristics of the incoming migrants. The movement of people from rural to urban areas affects the infant mortality rate by altering the composition of the city's population. In the case of São Paulo, the influx of northeasterners, who presumably bring with them the low health and nutritional standards that prevail in the place of their origin, is said to raise the city's mortality rate (Knight et al. 1979).

There is little doubt that migration to São Paulo has profoundly affected the socioeconomic and cultural composition of the city's population. In 1970 migrants comprised 46.7 per cent of the total. About half (48.2 per cent) of these came from surrounding areas of the state. About one quarter of the migrant flow (26.2 per cent) originated in the NORTHEAST (Wood and McCracken 1984). Generally speaking, migrants tend to be employed in low-paid, unstable and less skilled occupations relative to people born in the city. The average income for natives was Cr$575 in 1970, compared to Cr$387 for migrants (MINTER 1976). The migrant labor force is primarily employed in two major job categories: construction and personal services. Personal services is especially important for women. Nearly half of the female migrants to São Paulo (45.6 per cent) were employed as domestic servants. The comparable figure for native women was 22.6 per cent. Of the total population that received less than one minimum salary in construction and personal services, 19.1 percent were natives while 80.9 per cent were migrants (MINTER 1976).

These data suggest that population movement affected the city's social and economic profile and, by extension, the overall level of child mortality. Yet, it is difficult to see how the rise and the subsequent fall in the infant death rate can be attributed solely to migration. For one thing, migration to São Paulo slackened during the 1960s (Graham and Hollanda 1972). This suggests a decline rather than an increase in the hypothesized migration effect on infant mortality. Since reduced migration occurred at a time when mortality rates were on the rise, migration cannot account for the upward trend in the death rate in the 1960s. The decline in infant mortality from 1975 to 1979 presents additional problems for the migration hypothesis. To attribute the downward trend to population movement implies that peripheral areas of the city experienced heavy (and necessarily increasing) out-migration (presumably of northeasterners). This interpretation, although logically possible, is implausible and empirically unsupported.

The distribution of income

The fall in the infant mortality rate could have occurred as a result of an improved distribution of income. Quite apart from a change in the purchasing power of the real minimum wage, a shift in the proportion of the population from low to higher income brackets would lead to a reduction in the level of the city's infant mortality. A shift in the composition of the population could lead to a drop in the aggregate rate because the overall mortality level is a weighted average of the rates for all subgroups, the weights being the number of live births in each income strata. The high mortality of the low-income groups (because of changes in composition) would receive a smaller weight by virtue of the reduced size of the population in the low-income strata, causing the aggregate rate to fall.

Unfortunately, we cannot examine this explanation because of the lack of appropriate date for the metropolitan area of São Paulo. However, the results of the National Household Surveys in 1972 and 1976 (FIBGE 1972, 1976) provide information on urban areas for the entire state. A comparative analysis of these two sources suggests that the proportion of urban households earning the minimum wage or less declined by 4.3 percentage points between 1972 and 1976. Such a change would contribute to reduced mortality, yet the magnitude of the shift is small and subject to considerable ambiguity.[2] In any event, to attribute the 22 per cent drop in mortality from 1976 to 1979 to a change in the composition of the population by income strata presumes an improvement in income distribution at a pace and to a degree that contradicts, not only the well-known stability of the income distribution profile, but also the very character of the Brazilian style of development.

Water and sewage services

Public officials paid serious attention to the decline in the death rate in the 1970s. This reflects the political importance that the infant mortality trend has assumed in Brazil. During the administration of Governor Paulo Egýdio Martins the state government distributed an elaborate brochure, published in English and Portuguese. The publication gave full credit for the decline in infant mortality to the Governor's effort to extend water and sewage services to the growing urban population (State of São Paulo 1979).

The extension of the city's infrastructure has indeed occurred at a rapid pace. A recent study by the census bureau shows the increase in water and sewage facilities for households with children under three years of age in the metropolitan area of São Paulo. In 1970, 56.1 per cent had running water. In 1976, the proportion rose to 69.4 per cent. Similarly, the proportion of households with sewage services increased from 44 per cent in 1970 to 53.8 per cent in 1976 (FIBGE 1982: 63).

As we noted in chapter 4, running water and the availability of sewage facilities reduce the risk of death in the early years. However, our explanation of the mortality trend shown in Figure 5.1 does not discount the effect of expanded city services. That is, the decline in real wages in the 1960s and early 1970s led to a rise in the infant mortality rate that probably would have risen more sharply if water and sewage facilities had not been extended. By the same token, it is plausible to assume that the decline in the death rate in the late 1970s was caused by an increase in public services *and* a rise in the purchasing power of low-income groups (see Monteiro 1982).

Additional evidence

Additional observations suggest a causal link between the infant death rate and changes in the real minimum wage in São Paulo. The first point to note is that the high infant mortality among the poor is very sensitive to changes in real income. This is because the high death rate among low-income populations is caused by malnutrition and a high incidence of infectious and parasitic diseases. These causes of death are relatively easy to reduce with an improved standard of living. Compared to populations in which these risks have been eliminated, small increases in income result in large reductions in the death rate.

Martine and Peliano (1977) show that 20 per cent of the men and over half of the women (54 per cent) in São Paulo's labor force earn less than the legally established minimum wage. The aggregate infant mortality rate (a weighted average of subgroups' rates) is highly sensitive to changes in infant deaths among the poor because they comprise the lar-

Table 5.2. *Hours of work required to purchase food items for a family of four for one month, São Paulo, 1965 and 1975*

Food item	December 1965	December 1975	Percentage increase
Meat (6 kg)	26 h 24 min	53 h 47 min	103.7
Milk (7.5 l)	4 h 15 min	6 h 45 min	58.8
Beans (4.5 kg)	7 h 8 min	11 h 27 min	60.6
Rice (3.0 kg)	3 h 45 min	7 h 19 min	94.7
Subtotal	41 h 32 min	79 h 18 min	90.9
Other	45 h 48 min	75 h 00 min	63.8
Total	87 h 20 min	154 h 18 min	76.7

Source: Camargo et al. 1978.

gest proportion of the population. Compared to middle and upper income groups, the poor also have a higher weight in the aggregate infant mortality measure by virtue of their higher fertility. This means that the children of low-income women are numerous relative to the total number of children born.

We can therefore expect an inverse, causal link between the aggregate infant mortality rate and changes over time in the real value of the minimum wage because of: (1) the high income elasticity of mortality among the poor; (2) the high proportion of children in low-income families; and (3) the large number of children born to poor women.

Hours worked. Tabulations of the number of hours required to support a family of four in 1965 and 1975 provide a concrete illustration of the magnitude of the decline in purchasing power between the two periods. Table 5.2 shows that a laborer in São Paulo, earning the minimum wage in 1965, had to work 87 hours and 20 minutes to provide the basic food necessities for himself, his wife and two children. In 1975 the same basket of goods required 154 hours and 18 minutes of work, an increase of 76.7 per cent. As indicated in column 4, the relative costs of various items increased at different rates. The sharpest increase was for meat (103.7 per cent), followed by rice, beans and milk.

In response to increased economic stress, households placed additional members into the labor force, especially women and children. Several studies suggest the importance of secondary workers as sources

of supplemental income. Analyses of a sample of 500 legally registered
working minors in São Paulo indicate that 81 per cent turned over all of
their earnings to the family (cited in Schmink 1979). Surveys of
working-class households in 1958 and 1969 show that the employment
of wives and other members softened the decline in purchasing power.
Despite these strategies, however, real family income still dropped in
the 1960s (DIEESE 1974).

Nutrition. In addition to reallocating family labor, households
respond to a decline in real income by changing consumption patterns.
A study of family budgets in 1958 and 1969 in São Paulo found that
workers in low-income households were compelled to spend a substantially greater proportion of their income on food. By Engels's law this
change implies a deterioration in the standard of living during the
1960s. Other findings indicate that the per capita consumption of meat
declined (unsurprising in view of the data in Table 5.2), while the consumption of cheaper and less nutritive foodstuffs increased (cited in
Schmitter 1973).

Inadequate diet is the largest single contributor to child mortality in
developing countries (Berg 1973). Maternal undernourishment leads to
low birth weight among infants, reducing their survival prospects. Malnutrition also makes killers out of otherwise minor childhood ailments
by reducing the resistance to diarrheal diseases and respiratory infections. Poor diet also subjects the child to a repetition of apparently mild
ailments that can have additive or compounded effects (Puffer and Serrano 1973). Because of these interrelationships, referred to as the
"synergism of malnutrition and infection," poorly nourished infants
and children die from a variety of infections (measles, whooping cough,
influenza and pneumonia) and from common gastro-enteritic diseases.
But nutrition is the underlying cause of death.

In selected regions in the state of São Paulo malnutrition was found
to be the primary or associated cause of 51 per cent of deaths among
children under five years of age in 1970 (Puffer and Serrano 1973).
Recent estimates of food consumption from the National Household
Expenditure Survey (ENDEF) provide an indication of the extent of
malnutrition in Brazil. In 1974 a sample of 55,000 families was selected
from the rural and urban areas in each of the major geographic regions
of the country (except Amazônia and the Central West). Quantities of
food consumed were measured for each family over a six or seven day
period. Preliminary findings for the Southeast (which includes the State
of São Paulo) indicate that only 29.6 per cent of the urban population

enjoys a diet considered "adequate" by the standards established by FAO/WHO. Approximately 23 per cent suffer a daily deficit of up to 200 calories. Over 35 per cent experience a deficit of 200–400 calories. The remaining 12.3 per cent of the urban population consume a daily diet that falls short of the minimum basic requirement by over 400 calories (cited in Knight et al. 1979).

Detailed evidence on the relationship between nutrition and child survival by level of household income is not yet available. To date only summary tables for the major regions and selected subregions have been published. But even these aggregate results indicate that the nutritional condition of the Brazilian population is critical. If the average consumption level is so low, the extent of malnutrition among low-income groups must be even more severe.

In summary, four factors suggest a causal interpretation of the inverse relationship between real wage trends and changes in the level of infant mortality in São Paulo from 1963 to 1979: the large proportion of the population earning a salary that is close to or below the officially established minimum wage (and the impact of this on the aggregate mortality rate); the widespread ripple effect that the minimum wage has on prices, and on the salaries of individuals not covered by wage legislation; the high income sensitivity of the mortality of subgroups at the low end of the income range; and the precarious nutritional status of substantial sectors of the urban population.

The declining importance of real wages

Finally, it is important to note that infant mortality is highly sensitive to changes in real wages only within certain ranges. If the overall standard of living reaches a point where infant mortality is very low and caused primarily by bioendogenous factors, a change in the level of income may not have much effect. In the United States, for example, infant mortality may serve as an indicator of socioeconomic status for blacks but not for the white population since the latter experience very few infant deaths (Fordyce 1977). As the mortality rate reaches lower levels we can therefore expect it to become less responsive to changes in income.

Similarly, infant mortality rates respond to wages only in the context of particular political systems. When the provision of health care and basic needs is socialized to the point that access to them does not depend on the individual's purchasing power, there would be little reason to expect mortality to vary with changes in income. Alternatively, if the state provides direct subsidies to the low-income population in the form of water and sewage services or nutrition and health-related programs as it has increasingly done in Brazil, the effect is to attenuate the strength of the income–mortality relationship. Monteiro (1982), for example, argued that the infant death rate in São Paulo was responsive to fluctuations in real wages from 1950 to 1974, but that after 1974 the decline was largely due to greater access to running water. Publicly financed programs which target the poor have similar effect. Such programs include: the Maternal and Child Health Program (Programa de Saúde Materno Infantil – PSMI); the Health and Nutrition Program (Programa de Nutrição e Saúde – PNS), which provides food supplements to poor pregnant women and newborn children of low-income parents; and the Health Assistance Program for Mothers and Children (Programa de Assistência Integral de Saúde da Mulher e da Criança – PAISMC) established in 1984 to immunize children and combat diarrheal disease (Simões and Oliveira 1986). The consequence of initiatives such as these, together with the expansion of water and sewage facilities, is to weaken the association between real wages and the infant mortality rate.

Responses to urban underdevelopment

Contemporary studies of urbanization in developing countries stand at the crossroads of two lines of thought (Portes 1978: 35). One strand, exemplified by the perspective used in the previous sections of this chapter, emphasizes the structural factors that determine the opportunities and the constraints that impinge on the life chances of a city's population. The other line of reasoning takes these structural parameters more or less as given and proceeds to document the way poor people survive under the conditions of underdevelopment to which they are subjected. The former underscores the economic and institutional structures that exist over time, and whose transformations are independent of human will. The latter admits the possibility that institutional arrangements can be changed, even superceded, by the conscious actions of individuals or social classes.

Here we adopt the second view to investigate the various ways underprivileged sectors of the urban population responded to the wage and employment conditions described earlier. We focus on three different categories of behavior: the economic strategies that low-income households pursue in the face of income stress; the mobilization of neighborhood organizations; and the occasional outbursts of collective violence that took place in São Paulo and other cities in Brazil.

Household sustenance strategies and the urban economy

That families experiencing economic stress are compelled to exert greater productive effort is neither a new nor surprising observation. At the same time, students of the Latin American urban economy have found it increasingly useful to focus theoretical and empirical attention on this dynamic aspect of household behavior. The concept of "survival strategies," proposed by Duque and Pastrama (1975) sought to capture the various ways that people respond to the dilemmas of dependent industrial development.

In contrast to earlier conceptual approaches (e.g., modernization theory; the literature on urban marginality) which treat the urban poor as essentially passive folk, the focus on household strategies highlights the multiple initiatives members of the domestic unit undertake to actively negotiate structurally imposed constraints. Specifically, sustenance strategies refer to ways in which the household strives to achieve a "fit" between its consumption necessities, the labor power at its disposal (both determined by the number, age, sex and skills of its members) and the alternatives for generating monetary and non-monetary income (Schmink 1979). In effect, these strategies reflect the way households adapt their internal structure to the forces that lie beyond the unit itself. "The study of household behavior," Schmink (1984: 87) notes, " is pursued primarily as a means of bridging the gap (in social research) between social and individual levels of analysis." From this standpoint, "the domestic unit is conceived as mediating a varied set of behaviors (e.g., labor force participation; consumption patterns and migration) that are themselves conditioned by the particular makeup of this most basic economic unit."

In the advanced economies of the center, where the higher value of labor power has been won through labor militancy, the "family wage" (a single wage sufficient to maintain a working class family), is a dominant characteristic, even among fully proletarianized workers. Such is not the case in peripheral economies where the urban working class lacks the political and economic power to achieve wages sufficient to cover the same expenses (Moser and Young 1981). As a consequence, other members of the family unit, especially wives and children, pick up the slack through productive activities performed mainly within the informal sector of the urban economy.

Table 5.3 *Wife's average income as a proportion of husband's monthly earnings, by income decile, São Paulo, 1970*

Income decile of male heads of household	Wife's average income	Wife's income as a percentage of husband's income
1	23	24.7
2	27	18.8
3	29	11.2
4	35	10.5
5	38	9.3
6	38	8.0
7	44	7.4
8	59	7.0
9	89	6.9
10	173	4.1

Note: In 1970 cruzeiros.
Source: One per cent sample of the 1970 census.

The income earned by wives is of particular importance to low-income households. This is shown by the data presented in Table 5.3. The average income wives earn is higher in the upper socioeconomic groups, as noted in the second column. However, a reverse pattern emerges when we express a spouse's mean monthly earnings as a proportion of her husband's income. In the lowest decile the wife's income is nearly one quarter (24.7 per cent) of the income her husband receives. This figure falls to 4.1 per cent in the highest income decile

The sustenance strategies households undertake have significance, not only as an aggregation of individual means for survival, but also as a structural feature of the process of peripheral accumulation (Portes and Walton 1981: 84). The informal sector encompasses unpaid family labor and, when paid labor is employed, it is well below the official minimum with no social security protection. Informal sector activities therefore result in an output of goods and services at prices below those that could be offered in the formal sector.

The impact on the urban economy is significant in two respects. First, output of cheap goods and services from the informal sector, by reducing labor reproduction costs, maximizes surplus extraction within formal enterprises. Second, the existence of a cheap labor economy means that firms seek to minimize the number of workers protected by labor contracts and legislation (Portes and Walton 1981: 86). In this sense the structure of the urban labor market is, to some degree, a function of the economic strategies followed by individuals and households. "The so-called informal sector," as Klaas Woortman (1984: 28) put it, "mediates between the logic of capital and the logic of the family."

The interdependence that is suggested by these observations (between the productive activities of low-income households and the structural features of São Paulo's urban economy) leads to an ironic conclusion: that the sustenance strategies households pursue in the face of economic stress serve to preserve and perpetuate the very economic conditions to which households are responding in the first place.

Neighborhood organizations

Neighborhood organizations are not a new phenomenon in São Paulo, although the character and the focus of these institutions have changed in recent years. The Friends of the Neighborhood Society (Sociedades Amigos do Bairro, or SABs) founded in the 1950s brought together people on the outskirts of the city to voice local demands to municipal authorities. For the most part the SABs were dominated by liberal professionals and members of the small bourgeoisie closely tied to, and in many instances dependent on, city officials. In the era of political populism of the 1950s and early 1960s, SABs played an important role in the political bargaining for "collectively consumed" goods and services (housing, health, schools, transportation and urban facilities in general). Then it was a matter of mobilizing municipal votes to exchange for public works and city services. In the post-1964 authoritarian period, and with the centralization of political power, the SABs became dominated by ARENA politicians as local demands increasingly came to depend almost entirely on individuals well-placed in the regime's political party (Singer 1982: 289).

As the SABs were co-opted by the dominant political machine and transformed into benign groups, other institutions, notably the Catholic Community Organizations (Comunidades Eclesiais de Base – CEBs), came into prominence. The objectives of the CEBs, unlike the SABs, firmly endorsed the Christian values of equality and solidarity between community members. The CEBs thus tended to express, not only demands for local improvement, but also a more general critique of capitalist society. "Instead of assuming that the needs of the peripheral *bairros* and impoverished population stem from the negligence of the authorities and interested parties, privation is attributed to the very social organization inherent in capitalism" (Singer 1982: 290). The broader philosophy of the Catholic Community Organizations implied a different and more radical stance *vis-à-vis* the political structure. Access to public services came to be viewed as a right to which all of the city's inhabitants are entitled.

No one, not even the National Council of Brazilian Bishops, knows the precise number of CEBs in Brazil. Rough estimates put the number at around 40,000 in 1974 and approximately double that five years later (Pierucci 1982: 48). Whatever the actual total, it is apparent that they have become a major form of community organization, especially in the large metropolitan areas in the center-south, and that their number grew dramatically in the 1970s.

Explanations for the flowering of the CEBs stress the growing incompatibility between the Christian corporatist ethic of traditional doctrine, and the realities of class and class conflict in the modern urban–industrial setting (Camargo 1982). In the face of the brutal social conditions in developing society, organic views of mankind's place in the world have given way, both in theological discourse and in the daily practice of laypersons, to a secularism which endorses the perfectibility of temporal existence. Other observers note that the CEBs arose at a time in Brazil when channels of political expression were closed off by the authoritarian regime. In effect, grass-roots organizations filled the vacuum left by the abolition of the populist electoral process (for a critique, see Ruth Cardoso 1982).

Within the CEBs, such things as education, clean water and sewage services became focal points of community discussion. Often using scientific methods of data collection and analysis, the CEBs represented a dramatic fusion of informed social action and Christian moral ethics (Cardoso 1982). The result was a new form of political expression, quick to identify and denounce injustice and to push for social change, within the confines of the community and *vis-à-vis* public authorities.

The outlook fostered by the CEBs in São Paulo was thoroughly consistent with, and indirectly led to, nationally recognized initiatives, such as the Cost of Living Movement (Movimento de Custo de Vida – MCV). In 1973, the Mothers' Club in several working-class neighborhoods protested the increase in the cost of transportation, health care and food. Two years later community organizers undertook a research project to document the deteriorating economic conditions. Soon other neighborhoods were drawn in. By 1977, 700 delegates met to elect coordinators for what by then had become a grassroots movement of substantial size. The MCV culminated in a petition, signed by over one million people, calling for a freeze on the prices of basic necessities and for an increase in wages. The petition met a cool reception in Brasília when leaders of the MCV tried unsuccessfully in 1978 to present the document personally to the President (Singer 1982).

As Brazil returns to a democratic political system, the Church hierarchy has not been inclined to establish or support a Christian Democratic Party, or any similar such organization. Nor have existing parties made it a point to explicitly embrace ethico-religious themes. Nonetheless, there appears to be a close affinity, at least in places like São Paulo, between the CEBs and the Partido dos Trabalhadores (Camargo 1982: 53).

The future of the CEBs, and their relationship to the various political parties, raises interesting questions for which there are presently no firm answers. Yet the history of community action groups in general suggests that this form of political organization is sure to continue to play an important role in Brazil's urban context. Whatever their successes or failures in the past, entities such as the CEBs and the MCV alerted people to their collective dilemma and, perhaps most importantly, educated them in methods of voicing their discontent and mobilizing grassroots political pressure. Under Brazil's newly established democracy, these lessons may well provide the basis for popular initiatives that will successfully create a more equitable and more humane urban environment.

Collective urban violence

Other forms of protest have not been so peaceful. Under conditions of high urban unemployment and widespread poverty, individual acts of violence are commonplace in the city. In some instances, however, violent outbursts have involved thousands of people. In São Paulo and Rio, collective social actions of this kind have occurred on the commuter trains that connect the workplace to the low-income residential neighborhoods located in the outskirts of the two metropolitan areas. In 1973, three major incidents involved burning train cars and destroying train stations. Six other *quebra-quebras*, as they are popularly known in Portuguese, occurred in 1975. Ten such incidents took place in 1976. Estimates indicate that each one involved somewhere between 3,000 and 5,000 people (Moisés and Martinez-Alier 1978: 26).

A number of interrelated factors account for this kind of urban violence. For one thing, the stock of transportation equipment servicing the urban–industrial center has suffered from poor maintenance. In addition, the number of cars has failed to keep pace with the growing demand for transportation services. The result has been overcrowding, erratic schedules and an increase in the accident rate. At the same time, workers depend on the rail system for their very survival. Being late for work means a loss of pay and, for many, the risk of being fired. In São Paulo, blue-collar workers who live on the urban periphery spend as much as three or four hours a day commuting to and from their job. This often means getting up at three or four in the morning to board the six o'clock train, and then returning home well after dark. An interview with one commuter clearly shows the extent to which workers depend on low-cost transportation:

I leave the house everyday at 5:30 in the morning to catch the train at 6:15, which gets me to work at 8 o'clock. I carry Cr$5.00 in my pocket: Cr$1.20 goes for roundtrip train fare and a few cigarettes. In my lunchbox I carry a handful of rice with some beans and, once a week, some meat. I keep my work card in my wallet at all times; without it I'd be arrested for vagrancy. If I were to use the bus I'd pay Cr$4.70 only on transportation. And if I spend more than Cr$5.00 the kids don't eat (cited in Moisés and Martinez-Alier 1978:28).

Under these circumstances it is easy to see how the daily uncertainty of getting to work and back contributes to a volatile atmosphere in which a train accident, or any delay in the schedule, heightens the level of individual frustration. Moreover, the crowded conditions, and the shared danger of riding the trains, fosters a kind of collective identity among the commuters. As one worker put it, "When things go wrong, it only takes one guy to start yelling *quebra*! for the whole train to explode" (Moisés and Martinez-Alier, 1978).

Underlying these collective outbursts are a number of structural changes in the urban economy. Moisés and Martinez-Alier (1978) summarize the contradictions of industrial development in São Paulo that have increasingly placed the low-income working population at a disadvantage. On the one hand, the locus of heavy industry has beome spatially concentrated in areas that no longer house a sufficient number of people to man the factories. Workers, drawn from outlying communities, rely on public transportation to get to work. Yet the allocation of resources by the Ministry of Transportation has systematically favored roads and other expenses associated with automobile travel. This has benefitted those who are sufficiently well-off to afford a car, not to mention the makers of automobiles who have for many years received favorable tax and other incentives from the government. The daily economic and emotional cost of getting to and from the factory gates is borne by the men and women who work in the plants.

More recently, acts of collective violence have been directed against food stores and supermarkets. Food riots and looting came about with the increase in unemployment and the massive lay-offs that accompanied the economic recession in the early 1980s. Between 1980 and 1983, São Paulo industry shed approximately 477,400 jobs, about a quarter of its labor force. An assessment of the full impact of the recession, according to the Federation of Industrial Employers of São Paulo (FIESP), would also include the number of jobs that in normal circumstances would have been created. On this basis, São Paulo industry lost a staggering 700,000 jobs during the period.

Food riots, Yone and Barreira (1984) contend, cannot be dismissed as irrational acts that take place on a purely spontaneous basis. Rather, the *saques* were another reflection of the deteriorating economic conditions faced by the city's low-income population. Cut off from legitimate channels of political expression, looting was both a short-term solution to hunger as well as a public statement of dissatisfaction.

Although job insecurity is hardly new to the urban working class, the depth of the national crisis after 1981 lent special meaning to being laid off. An unemployed worker in São Paulo explained:

The difference now is that until 1981 you'd lose your job, yet you knew you could find another one. But then, from the beginning of 1982, you knew you'd never get another job if you got laid off. There's not a soul around here who's not scared (cited in Yone and Barreira 1984: 28).

The explanation for the looting Yone and Barreira (1984) offer is consistent with Piven and Cloward's (1971) more general treatment of the relationship between unemployment and civil disorder. When mass unemployment persists for any length of time, Piven and Cloward argue (1971: 6–7), it diminishes the capacity of other institutions to bind and constrain people. Occupational behaviors and outlooks underpin a way of life by which people conform to familiar and communal roles. When large numbers of people are barred from their occupations, the entire structure of social control is weakened. If the dislocation is widespread, the legitimacy of the social order itself may come to be questioned. The result is civil disorder which challenges existing social and economic arrangements.

* * *

Conventional perspectives on the relationship between economic development and demographic behavior do not account for the possibility of a rise in the death rate in developing countries. The demographic transition from high to low mortality levels is attributed to the combined effects of the endogenous development of economic and social organization and to the diffusion of medical and health technology from more to less developed countries. Once a low level of mortality is reached, the death rate in the final stage of the transition is presumed to be irreversible. In an extensive study of life expectancy at birth in Latin America, Asia and Africa, Stolnitz (1965: 131) finds that none of the areas that experienced recent mortality declines gives evidence of recidivism. He concludes on a positive note: "As to the future, I find the evidence far more persuasive that the recent mortality decline will be preserved or enhanced ... Those who fear reversals are conspicuously vague about places, dates or reasons."

The increase in infant mortality in São Paulo from the early 1960s to the mid-1970s, associated with the decline in purchasing power, indicates that such optimism is unwarranted. Once the gain in life expectancy due to the transfer of indirect and relatively cheap death control technology has run its course, additional improvements become increasingly sensitive to the nutritional and general socioeconomic wellbeing of the population. At this stage, there is little reason to assume that mortality will necessarily remain constant. The rise and the subsequent fall in the death rate in São Paulo suggest that the mortality level of the poor is highly responsive to the impact of development planning policies. When government growth strategies entail a deterioration in the absolute standard of living of already disadvantaged subgroups, the infant mortality rate may very well increase.

The conclusion is consistent with other studies of mortality, such as Gwatkin's (1980) summary of recent world trends, that underscore the important role political factors play in the pace and the direction of mortality change. Social class differences in length of life are, after all, only an expression of the more general forms of inequality. Hence, if we ask why a population's mortality profile changes we are, inevitably, searching for an explanation for changes in socioeconomic and political organization. As such, the analysis compels us to examine the structure of production and distribution, as well as the changing nature of class and class conflict, and how the relationships between them result in concrete state policies that enhance the quality of life of one group at the expense of another.

At the same time, an overly structuralist view tells only part of the story. São Paulo's industrial working class, and indeed the city's low-income population in general, are not to be regarded as passive victims of urban conditions, as the macro perspective is wont to do. We can more accurately conceptualize the urban complex as a dynamic interaction between structural phenomena and behavioral responses to them. In some instances, such as the sustenance strategies poor households pursue in the face of income stress, the actions people undertake to survive may preserve and perpetuate the very economic system that forces them into informal sector employment in the first place. On the other hand, organized labor's struggle to defend its interests in the workplace, like the initiatives undertaken by community groups to improve the quality of neighborhood life, represent forms of action consciously undertaken to change the socioeconomic and political system.

6

Racial inequality and child mortality

On his return from a hunting trip to South America in the early 1900s, Theodore Roosevelt noted what he understood to be a fundamental difference between Brazil and the United States. "If I were asked to name one point in which there is a complete difference between the Brazilians and ourselves," Roosevelt proclaimed, "I should say it was in the attitude to the black man ... In Brazil any Negro or mulatto who shows himself fit is without question given the place to which his abilities entitle him" (cited in Silva 1978: 50).

Roosevelt's comment echoed a common and today still popular theme: that, unlike the United States, or other countries such as South Africa, Brazil is a "racial democracy." The racial democracy thesis implies two corollaries essential for understanding the dominant perception of race relations in Brazil. The first corollary concerns the relationship between race, class and prejudice. According to the prevalent notion, if white Brazilians take a dim view of the black and brown population, it is because most nonwhites are lower class. Prejudice, if it exists at all, does not involve racism or racial discrimination, so much as personal prejudice against low status.

The "class over racism" explanation for prejudice was put forth by Donald Pierson (1967), who wrote *Negroes in Brazil: the History of Race Contact in Brazil*, and by the Bahian social scientist Thales de Azevedo (1953). Pierson and Azevedo's work represents what has come to be called the "Bahian school" of thought on race relations in Brazil. Both analysts agree that there are rich and poor people in Brazil, and that the overwhelming majority of rich people are white and that most blacks are poor. They further agree that "whiteness" is regarded as more desirable than "darkness." Yet what determines how an individual is received by the white majority is not exclusively fixed by race or skin tone, but is contingent on the minority person's class position. The conclusion that follows from this argument is that once nonwhites achieve sufficient income or education they will be fully accepted by the white majority. Because inter-group behavior is heavily influenced by the interplay of gradations of blackness and perceptions of social standing, race relations in Brazil are far more subtle and complex compared, say, to the United States where skin color alone is the overriding criterion.

The second corollary of the racial democracy thesis asserts that race is of limited importance as a determinant of opportunities for upward social mobility. The claim raises an important question regarding the indisputable empirical evidence of sharp racial inequalities along numerous dimensions of social stratification: If race is no barrier, why is the average nonwhite person in Brazil poorer and less educated than the average white person? For those who endorse the racial democracy idea, the cause could be traced to a legacy of the slave period. Blacks, who began disadvantaged as a subordinate class in the slave mode of production, have simply not "caught up" with whites since the abolition of slavery in the late nineteenth century. Contemporary inequality, as Degler (1971) contended, is the vestige of an earlier period of subjugation.

In keeping with both classical Marxism and modernization theory, the second corollary of the racial democracy theme suggests that racial inequalities will decline with economic growth. Marx's portrayal of capitalism's "civilizing mission" maintained, among other things, that the expansion of the capitalist mode of production acted as a corrosive force upon traditional group attachments. The proletarianization of the work force under the rule of capital, and the intense inter-capitalist rivalry in a competitive marketplace, would put an end to ethnic and racial (even gender) criteria for recruiting labor into the process of production. Whenever the bourgeoisie got the upper hand, Marx wrote in the *Manifesto of the Communist Party*, the "icy water of egotistical calculation" destroyed all feudal, patriarchal, idyllic relations, leaving no other nexus between people than the "callous cash payment." The tendency is for capitalism to reduce all labor to the commodity of labor power, thereby obliterating qualitative distinctions between different categories of labor.

For modernization theorists, who drew heavily on Weber, discrimination on the basis of racial and ethnic criteria was an aspect of traditional society that would give way to modern values, attitudes and behaviors with the advance of industrial production. Parson and Shils (1951) expressed the value transformation in terms of five "patterned variables," three of which were especially important for contrasting the alternative choices of action in traditional and modern society: diffuseness versus specificity; ascription versus achievement; and particularism versus universalism. In Parsons' scheme, societal roles in traditional societies are ascribed, are functionally diffuse and are oriented toward narrow particularistic preferences and standards. Conversely, social roles in modern societies tend toward specificity, are acquired through competitive striving for achievement, and are oriented toward universal standards and norms. The movement from a traditional value orientation to a modern one thus implied, as it did for Marx, the waning importance of race as criteria for social behavior.

In the absence of racial barriers to social and economic improvement in Brazil, analysts predicted that large numbers of people would rise in social standing as opportunities for advancement increased with economic growth. Writing in the early 1950s, Charles Wagley (1952: 155) concluded his study of caste and class in North Brazil on a note that was both optimistic and fully consistent with the racial democracy assumption. In the course of development, Wagley wrote, "the great contrasts in social and economic conditions between the darker lower strata and the predominantly white upper class should disappear."

If the concept of racial democracy held sway in popular mythology – even among nonwhites in Brazil (Skidmore 1974) – it was through the work of such eminent scholars as Gilberto Freyre (1946) in Brazil and F. Frazier (1944) in the United States that the idea gained wider currency. The assumption that Brazil was a "racial paradise" held special importance to Europeans in the aftermath of the vicious anti-semitism of Nazi Germany, and to North Americans who sought to understand the long history of racial violence in the United States. In comparative terms, Brazil was justifiably famous for its harmonious race relations. Intermarriage, if not the rule, was certainly common; outright segregation was rare; Jim Crow laws were non-existent; and the national consensus against public discrimination on the basis of color was formalized in 1951 by the Afonso Arinos law that made discrimination a criminal offense, punishable by a jail term or a fine. The racial democracy thesis was so firmly entrenched that, in 1950, UNESCO set out to study Brazil's harmonious race relations in order to share Brazil's secret with the world. In fact, this and later research raised serious questions about, and partially discredited, the sanguine racial image of Brazilian society (Skidmore 1985: 13).

Among the first to substantiate the significance of racism and racial discrimination in industrial and capitalist Brazil were scholars from what came to be known as the "São Paulo school." Prominent among them was Florestan Fernandes (1969) who argued that, after the abolition of slavery in 1888, blacks were handicapped for adaptation to the emerging competitive order. The rise of the capitalist mode of production demanded maximum mobility of land, labor and capital. Workers could no longer be immobilized and treated as part of fixed capital stock as they had been under the slave system. The demise of slavery, and the rise of a free labor force in which individuals competed for wages in a fluctuating market for workers, was therefore structurally necessary to the development of capitalism (Graham 1970). Yet former slaves, because they lacked the necessary skills and socialization to adapt to the new economic order, were not integrated into the emerging proletariat. Ill-fitted for wage work, and suffering increased competition from European immigrants, nonwhites in Brazil were bypassed by the development process.

Fernando Henrique Cardoso (1962) and Octavio Ianni (1972) stressed the ideological consequences of the breakdown of the slave mode of production. In colonial Brazil, the legally-sanctioned coercive power of white slave owners was sufficient to insure the subordination of blacks. But the transition from a caste to a class system, and from slave to free labor, required new forms of social and cultural domination. The emancipation of slaves thus gave impetus to theories of natural inferiority. Loosely articulated racial concepts came into the open, giving them the force of formal ideology (Toplin 1981).

Others found the cause of contemporary racial inequality in the dynamics of class conflict in modern capitalism. Whereas classical Marxism as well as modernization theory stressed the tendency of the market to homogenize labor, racial strife could also be functional to the accumulation of capital inasmuch as it served to divide, and thereby weaken, labor's bargaining power in the workplace. Thus, racial prejudice and discrimination did not disappear with abolition, but acquired new meaning within the new social structure. The point was recently made by Hasenbalg (1980: 27) who saw the racial practices of the dominant group in Brazil, not as the vestige of old patterns of prejudice and discrimination, but as behavior that was "functionally related to the material and symbolic benefits obtained by whites through the disqualification of nonwhites as competitors."

The idea that the nonwhite population confronted a systematic disadvantage in terms of jobs and opportunities for advancement called into question the often-cited separation of "prejudice" and "discrimination" in Brazil. Prejudice refers to a state of mind. Discrimination refers to some form of practice. The former, so the argument goes, does not automatically imply the latter. Indeed, the idea that people could be prejudiced against nonwhites without translating their views into discriminatory actions was an assumption central to the racial democracy thesis.

Recent studies of social mobility and wage determination reject the presumed independence of prejudice and discrimination. Hasenbalg (1985) has shown that to be born nonwhite in Brazil usually means to be born into a low-status family. He further concluded that nonwhites are exposed to a cycle of cumulative disadvantages in intergenerational social mobility. Using data from the 1976 national household survey, Hasenbalg demonstrated that, other things being equal, the probability of improving social status from one generation to the next was considerably smaller for nonwhites than for whites. Moreover, interracial differences in the opportunities for upward mobility increased with higher social status of origin. The risk of social demotion among the small group of nonwhites born in families of high social standing was much greater compared to whites of the same background. Hasenbalg (1985: 32) concluded that racial inequalities that began under slavery were perpetuated "through discriminatory practices and cultural stereotyping by whites of the role 'adequate' for blacks and mulattoes."

Nelson do Valle Silva (1985) used the 1976 national household survey to determine if nonwhites were discriminated against in the labor market. His results documented the unequal income returns by race to equal amounts of education. In 1976, average income for whites was twice that of nonwhites. A third of that difference could be attributed to discriminatory labor practices. Silva concluded that the monetary disadvantage suffered by blacks and mulattoes due to discrimination in the labor market was around $60 dollars a month (566 cruzeiros), a finding consistent with the results of his earlier study (Silva 1978) of black–white income differentials in Brazil in 1960.

The studies carried out by Hasenbalg and by Silva represent an important contribution to the literature on racial inequality in Brazil. By using sophisticated statistical techniques on a large data set, they were able to empirically demonstrate what others had concluded on the basis of less reliable sources: that nonwhites suffer systematic disadvantages compared to whites in intergenerational social mobility, and in the labor market. In the analysis that follows, we extend this line of inquiry by exploring racial differences in child mortality. Given racial disparities in income and education, we can predict with certainty a higher probability of death among the children born to nonwhite parents. Yet, at least three important questions remain to be answered: What is the magnitude of the mortality gap between white and nonwhite children? Has this differential narrowed or widened over time? And, do the mortality differences by race persist or disappear after statistically controlling for the relevant social and economic determinants of mortality? Before turning to the results on child mortality, we will review the evolution of the racial composition of the population, and assess the validity of census data on race in Brazil.

White, black and brown in Brazil

Before the Portuguese arrived in the New World, the population of the area of South America which is now Brazil consisted of about 1,500,000 Indians. The native population was divided into linguistic and tribal groups scattered across the land. Since warfare was almost continuous among the tribes, the native population offered no unified resistance to the Portuguese. Expeditions by the early colonists to capture Indian slaves, and the mortality consequences of exposure to European diseases against which the aboriginal groups had no immunity, quickly reduced the native Indian population. By 1750, few Indians remained in the coastal areas the Portuguese had colonized.

The need to look elsewhere for slaves, especially after the introduction of sugar cane in the middle of the sixteenth century, prompted the Portuguese to turn to Africa for needed labor (see chapter 3). The first black slaves arrived in 1538, initiating a 300 year period during which there was a steady flow of Africans to Brazil. The Africans were embarked at the Cape Verde Islands and nearby Portuguese Guinea, on the coast of what is now Ghana, at Cabinda near the mouth of the Congo, and at the ports of Portuguese-dominated Angola and Mozambique. Because the slave system was particularly harsh in Brazil (Degler 1971), a constant supply of slaves from Africa was necessary to compensate for the losses due to high mortality rates. Over the centuries, Brazil received perhaps ten times as many Africans as the North American colonies, but, owing to the high death rate and a low rate of reproduction, the Brazilian slave population of 1860 was only about half as large as that in North America. Conservative estimates put the total number of slaves that entered Brazil at approximately 3,300,000 in the seventeenth and eighteenth centuries alone, although the number was probably greater (Wagley 1952: 142).

The "whitening" of the population

From the first days of the colonial period the relative absence of white women and the inferior place of women in the family gave white men unhampered access to Indian and later African female slaves. The matings between persons of various degrees of mixed blood rapidly diffused white blood throughout the veins of most of the population. Miscegenation was furthered by the numerous illegitimate progeny of upper class men, and later by the immigration of large numbers of Europeans in the late nineteenth and early twentieth centuries.

The whitening, or *branqueamento*, of the country's population, was both a demographic fact and, at one time at least, a political doctrine. In the first half of the twentieth century, white–black miscegenation was proposed as a natural solution to the race problem. Drowning black blood in imported European white blood would make the population whiter, and therefore "better." Skidmore's (1974) explanation of the "whitening ideal" is that it was a solution, largely devised by Brazilian intellectuals, to reconcile the contradiction posed, on the one hand, by the racist doctrines that dominated the scientific community at the end of the nineteenth century, and, on the other, by the reality of the racial situation in Brazilian society.

The first general census, taken in 1872, showed that the population consisted of 3,787,289 whites (38.1 per cent), 1,954,543 blacks (19.7 per cent) and 4,188,737 of mixed blood (42.2 per cent). Although the reliability of the census classification is open to question (discussed below), the figures nonetheless provide a general idea of the relative importance of the three major racial groups. Subsequent censuses show how the racial composition of the population has changed over the years. By 1940, when the total number of Brazilians reached 41 million, 64 per cent were classified as white, 21 per cent as brown and 15 per cent as black. The results of census enumerations over the last four decades, shown in Table 6.1, reveal a clear pattern: the proportion of whites and blacks has declined, while the proportion of people in the intermediate classification has increased. At the time of the last enumeration in 1980, whites, browns and blacks respectively accounted for 54, 39 and 6 per cent of the total population.

Census categories and subjective classifications

How valid are census data on the racial composition of the Brazilian population? The question is pertinent in light of anthropological re-

Table 6.1. *The racial composition of the population, 1940–80*
(in thousands)

Race	1940		1950		1960		1980	
	N	%	N	%	N	%	N	%
White	26,172	(63.5)	32,028	(61.7)	42,838	(61.0)	64,540	(54.2)
Brown	8,744	(21.2)	13,786	(26.5)	20,706	(29.5)	46,233	(38.8)
Black	6,036	(14.6)	5,692	(11.0)	6,117	(8.7)	7,047	(5.9)
Yellow	242	(0.6)	329	(0.6)	483	(0.7)	673	(0.7)
Missing	42	(0.1)	108	(0.2)	47	(0.1)	517	(0.4)
Total	41,236	(100.0)	51,943	(100.0)	70,191	(100.0)	119,010	(100.0)

Source: Demographic Censuses 1940, 1950, 1960 and 1970.

search on race relations in Brazil that amply documents the fine distinctions Brazilians make when asked to identify a person's race. Harris (1964), for example, used a set of nine portrait drawings to explore the range of terms that might be applied to a given individual. Variable in hair shade, hair texture, nasal and lip width and in skin tone, the pictures elicited forty different racial types. The wide range of terms people use to identify color variations between the two extremes of black and white would appear to invalidate the simple fourfold classification system used in the census.

In 1940, census enumerators asked people if they were black, white or yellow. Individuals who declared themselves to be somewhere in between (e.g., *mulato, caboclo, moreno, indio,* etc.) were classified as brown (*pardo*). The same system was used in 1950. The method was modified in 1960 when, in addition to the three standard possibilities (white, black and yellow), two pre-coded intermediate categories were introduced for the first time (*pardo* and *indio*). Although the 1960 census was never fully completed, the published tables that do exist for certain states collapsed the two intermediate categories into a single grouping – *pardos*. The race item was not included at all in the 1970 census. It was reintroduced in the 1980 enumeration, which used the self-identification method and a four-category scheme: white, black, brown and yellow.

Compared to the many terms that people in Brazil commonly use to identify shades of "darkness," the four-category scheme used in the censuses obviously simplifies the classification of people by race. The crucial question is the extent to which the census scheme departs from people's self-classification if they are allowed other options. Fortunately, the 1976 National Household Survey addressed this very issue. The survey included two items on race. The first was an open-ended item which permitted respondents to use whatever term they wished. The second was the standard fourfold classification. Analyses of the open-ended item showed that, despite the wide range of terms, the four categories (white, black, brown and yellow) accounted for about 57.1 per cent of the responses. Three additional classifications proved to be important: *clara* (2.5 per cent); *morena clara* (2.8 per cent); and *morena* (34.4 per cent). Further analyses found that nearly all of the people who declared themselves *morena* in the open-ended question classified themselves as brown (*pardos*) when confronted with the pre-coded options. The four-category scheme thus accounted for approximately 95 per cent of all responses (Oliveira, Porcaro & Costa 1981). Analysts in the Census Bureau concluded that the forced-choice method, although not perfect, was sufficiently reliable to be used in the 1980 round of data collection.[1]

Racial differences in child mortality

The 1950 census was carried out long before Brass (1968) developed the technique to estimate child survival probabilities from data on the proportion of surviving children classified by mother's age (see the Appendix). Yet, it is fortunate that the necessary data were nonetheless collected in 1950, and that the published information was disaggregated by the mother's race. On the basis of these tabulations we are able to derive estimates of probabilities of child survival to exact ages 2, 3 and 5 (the $2q_0$, $3q_0$ and $5q_0$ life table functions) for the white and nonwhite populations. The same items, repeated in the 1980 census, allow us to determine whether the mortality differential by race has changed over the span of three decades.

Using the same methods followed in chapter 4, and described in the Appendix, the three survival probabilities can be converted into a single mortality measure: the average number of years of life expected at birth. Because the measure is generated from retrospective information provided by women 20 to 34 years of age, the estimate refers to the average level of mortality during the decade prior to the census. Hence, the results derived from the 1950 census refer to the 1940/50 period; those from the 1980 census refer to the 1970/80 decade. The rates generated in this manner are interpreted as the life expectancy that corresponds to the mortality experience (i.e., the xq_0 values) of children born to women who were 20 to 34 years of age at the time of the interview (1950 and 1980), and who identified themselves as being white or nonwhite. The nonwhite category refers to women who declared themselves to be either "black" or "brown."[2]

Social change and the persistence of the white-nonwhite mortality gap

The results of applying the Brass method to 1950 and 1980 census data, shown in Table 6.2, indicate the magnitude and the persistence of racial inequalities in length of life in Brazil. In 1940/50, the mortality experience of children born to white mothers was equivalent to an average expectation of life at birth of 47.5 years. The comparable figure for nonwhite children was 40.0 years, a value that is 7.5 years below the white life expectancy rate. In the thirty years since the 1950 census, both groups experienced substantial improvements in length of life. By 1970/80, whites reached an average expectation of life of 66.1 years. The rate for nonwhites rose to 59.4 years. Yet despite the gains achieved by both groups, the gap between the two remained high. In 1970/80 white life expectancy rates exceeded that of nonwhites by 6.7 years.

The figures in Table 6.2 are especially significant in light of the profound changes that took place in Brazil between 1950 and 1980. As the analysis in chapter 4 showed, the country experienced significant gains in per capita income and educational achievement in recent decades. Non-agricultural employment rose substantially, and the population became predominantly urban. Marked improvements were also achieved in the distribution of public services, such as water and sewage facilities, and the life expectancy rate for the population as a whole increased about 37 per cent over the period (see Table 4.1). Yet these transformations in social, economic and demographic structure apparently did little to reduce the relative inequality between whites and nonwhites in Brazil. If we interpret child mortality rates as an indicator of quality of life, the data show that the gap between the two racial groups was about the same in 1970/80 as it was three decades earlier.

Further disaggregation of the 1980 census data enables us to explore some of the reasons for racial differences in child mortality. If the white–nonwhite mortality gap were due solely to differences in income or education, then we would expect mortality differentials observed in the aggregate to disappear when we estimate life expectancy rates within strata of household income or within categories of educational achievement. Yet the results of such an analysis, presented in Table 6.3,

Table 6.2. *Life expectancy at birth by race, 1950 and 1980*

Race	1950	1980	80–50
White	47.5	66.1	18.6
Nonwhite	40.0	59.4	19.4
White–nonwhite	7.5	6.7	

Table 6.3. *Life expectancy at birth by household income, education and race, 1980*

			Race		White–nonwhite (3)
			White (1)	Nonwhite (2)	
A	Household income[a]	1	59.5	55.8	3.7
		2	64.4	59.8	4.6
		3	66.2	61.2	4.8
		4	70.4	63.7	6.7
B	Education[b]	None	59.4	54.9	4.5
		1–4 years	66.2	62.2	4.0
		over 4 years	72.3	66.6	5.7

Notes: [a]Total monthly household income. Categories are the same as the four strata used in other chapters (1 = 1–150; 2 = 151–300; 3 = 301–500; 4 = 501+, in 1970 cruzeiros).
[b] Education refers to the mother's years of schooling.

indicate that racial differences in the average number of years of life expected persist even after introducing such controls. Within the poorest stratum of the population, whites outlive nonwhites by an average of 3.7 years. Moreover, the mortality gap appears to become larger in the middle and upper income groups.

The results disaggregated by years of schooling approximate the same pattern found when we controlled for income. That is, the children of uneducated white women (those with no schooling) outlive the children of uneducated nonwhite women by an average of 4.5 years. And, as in the case of household income, the difference in life expectancy was greatest among the children born to women in the highest of the three categories of educational achievement (5.7 years for children of women who completed primary school).[3]

The persistence of racial differences in length of life, even after introducing controls, could be due to other factors that distinguish the two racial groups, but which are not captured by the income and education variables. Perhaps the most important of these is the geographic distribution of the population. Since most nonwhites are concentrated in the NORTHEAST, where mortality is higher than in the rest of the country, nonwhites may be subject to higher risks of death even within the same stratum of household income. Similar arguments can be advanced for the rural–urban distribution of population, and for the distribution of other variables that affect child survival, such as access to running water.

Table 6.4 demonstrates the importance of spatial differences when it comes to social indicators such as mother's educational attainment and access to piped water in the household, two variables known to have a strong depressing effect on mortality rates among children in the early years of life (see chapter 4). Panel A shows the percentage of women of 20 and 34 years of age who have completed primary school. In light of the sharp regional inequalities in economic development in Brazil, it is hardly surprising to find that, on average, women are more educated in urban compared to rural places, and that educational achievement is higher in areas outside of the relatively backward NORTHEAST. Yet the percentages shown in Table 6.4 also reveal an unexpected pattern: the white–nonwhite differences in educational attainment are pronounced even after controlling for region, place of residence and monthly household income. To take one example, 37 per cent of the poorest white women in the urban NORTHEAST completed primary school. This figure is substantially higher than the proportion of educated nonwhite women (29 per cent) who share the same spatial and socioeconomic characteristics. The ratios of the two proportions, given in column 6 of Table 6.4, indicate that – even within the same stratum of household income – nonwhite women are at a relative disadvantage compared to whites in both rural and urban areas, as well as in the NORTHEAST and in other regions of the country. The same pattern holds when we examine racial differences in the proportion of households with running water, as shown in panel B.

Race as an independent predictor of child mortality

The findings presented in Tables 6.3 and 6.4 raise an important issue: If we simultaneously control for all of the most significant predictors of

Table 6.4. *Selected indicators by region, place of residence, household income and race, 1980*

Indicator	Region (1)	Place of residence (2)	Income (3)	Race White (4)	Race Nonwhite (5)	White/ nonwhite (6)
A Education	NORTH-	urban	1	37	29	1.28
(% with	EAST		2	57	46	1.24
more than			3	76	64	1.19
four years)			4	89	75	1.19
		rural	1	15	10	1.50
			2	22	14	1.57
			3	39	26	1.50
			4	56	45	1.24
	Other	urban	1	46	37	1.24
			2	57	52	1.10
			3	70	59	1.19
			4	89	76	1.17
		rural	1	31	18	1.72
			2	43	20	2.15
			3	57	31	1.84
			4	72	43	1.67
B Water (% of	NORTH-	urban	1	32	18	1.72
households	EAST		2	47	36	1.31
with piped			3	61	50	1.22
water)			4	90	77	1.17
		rural	1	2	2	1.00
			2	6	5	1.20
			3	15	14	1.14
			4	36	31	1.16
	Other	urban	1	46	36	1.28
			2	61	45	1.36
			3	77	59	1.31
			4	94	83	1.13
		rural	1	20	8	2.50
			2	32	15	2.13
			3	40	17	2.35
			4	60	31	1.94

mortality in the young ages, do the children of nonwhite women continue to experience higher death rates compared to children born to white women? An answer to this question is of great substantive interest to analyses of racial inequality in Brazil. If race ceases to explain variance after removing the effects of social and economic determinants of mortality, then we can assume that the mortality gap is due to socioeconomic factors. On the other hand, if race continues to be important, it suggests that nonwhites are subject to disadvantages other than those associated with lower socioeconomic standing, access to piped water and with place of residence.

In principle it is possible to use the Brass technique for such an investigation. Yet, the analysis would be cumbersome and subject to error. The Brass method generates estimates of child mortality rates for groups of women of different ages (20–24; 25–29, etc.). In order to introduce the necessary controls, we would have to cross-classify the number of children ever born and the number surviving at the time of the census by age of mother, region of the country and place of residence. Within each of these groups, we would have to further disaggregate the child survival ratios by four strata of household income, three categories of education and, finally, by the presence or absence of running water in the household. The problem with such an approach is that (even with the Public Use Sample of the 1980 census, which contains information on nearly 50,000 women aged 20 to 34) we would soon run low on the number of cases in each cell, causing the mortality estimates to become unstable.

Trussell and Preston (1982) have suggested a method for analyzing mortality differentials that, instead of translating survival ratios into rates for groups of women, adjusts the ratio of dead children to the number ever born for each individual woman. The goal of the Trussell–Preston procedure is to construct an index of child mortality which can then be compared to the index value for women in different socioeconomic circumstances. Adjustments are required for two reasons: to account for mother's age and to normalize the mortality ratio. Adjustment for the effect of mother's age is necessary because differences in survival ratios reflect not only the particular mortality regime to which their children are subject, but also differences in these children's exposure to the risk of dying. Children of older women are exposed to the risk of mortality for a longer period of time. Hence, other things being equal, age alone accounts for a higher proportion of children who have died. Additional adjustment is required because the ratio of dead children to the number ever born is a binomially rather than normally

Table 6.5. *Means and standard deviations of dependent and independent variables used in analysis of mortality index of mothers aged 20–29, 1980*

Variable	Description	Urban		Rural	
		Mean	SD	Mean	SD
Mortality index	Standardized index	.803	2.285	.921	2.266
Household income	Total monthly income	21,519	36,012	7,857	20,852
Race	Dummy variable (nonwhites = 1)	.390		.520	
Education	Years of school of mother	3.8	1.94	1.9	1.90
Region	Dummy variable (NORTHEAST = 1)	.20		.41	
Water	Dummy variable (Household with piped water = 1)	.69		.21	

distributed variable, making ordinary least squares an inappropriate estimating technique.

In the Trussell and Preston method, the mortality index for each woman is equal to the number of her dead children divided by the expected number of dead children. The latter is derived by multiplying her number of births by the expected proportion of children dead. This expected proportion is based upon general mortality conditions in the population, as well as upon the distribution of exposure times of children to the risk of dying, as measured by the mother's age and the timing of births. The expected mortality value is taken from a family of model life tables that reflect as accurately as possible the age pattern of mortality for the country in question. In this case, the mortality standard chosen was the Coale-Demeny South model (level 19, with a life expectancy at birth of 65 years).

The mortality index (MI) calculated in this manner refers to the ratio of observed to expected deaths. The advantage of MI as a dependent variable is that we can apply ordinary regression techniques to simultaneously control for numerous other independent variables.[4] Table 6.5 shows the units in which the variables used in the regressions are measured, and provides sample means and standard deviations. For Brazil in 1980, the mean value of MI for urban women 20 to 29 years of

Table 6.6. *Mortality index for mothers aged 20–29 regressed on selected indicators in urban and rural areas, 1980 (standardized beta coefficients)*

Independent variable	Urban			Rural		
	(1)	(2)	(3)	(4)	(5)	(6)
Race	.086*		−.035*	.062*		.008
Log of household income		−.031*	−.027*		−.047*	−.008
Education		−.117*	−.096*		−.108*	−.057*
Region			.069*			.097
Piped water			−.030*			−.009
R^2	.007	.017	.030	.004	.009	.019
Standard error	2.276	2.264	2.019	2.256	2.250	2.240
Constant	.645	1.865	1.628	.772	1.292	.916

* = significant at .001 or less

age was .803, with a standard deviation of 2.285. The average MI for rural women in the same age range was .921, with a standard deviation of 2.266.

Three separate regression models were run within urban and rural areas (Table 6.6). The first model (columns 1 and 4) includes only the dummy variable for race. Since nonwhites are coded as 1, the positive sign of the coefficient indicates that the ratio of observed to expected deaths (MI) is significantly higher among the children of nonwhite women, as anticipated.

The second model (columns 2 and 5) regresses MI on household income and education. We take the log of household income because of the non-linear relationship between income and mortality due to the diminishing returns to income as income rises (see chapter 8). The results of the second model indicate that both variables are statistically significant in rural and in urban settings. The negative sign shows that the effect of increases in income and education is to reduce the ratio of observed to expected deaths.

The third, and most important model, introduces all of the independent variables, including dummy variables for region (NORTHEAST = 1) and whether or not the household has running water (yes = 1). The coefficients given in column 3 indicate that, in urban places, race remains a statistically significant variable even after the model controls for household income, mother's education, region of the country and access to piped water. Examining the size of the beta coefficients, we conclude that the most important predictor of MI is the mother's education, followed by the effect of region. Race appears to be the third most important variable, having approximately the same impact on child mortality as running water. In rural areas (column 6), only education and region are statistically significant.

Why does race have an effect on child mortality in urban areas net of statistical controls for indicators of socioeconomic standing and region of residence? One answer points to discrimination. It is possible that nonwhite women are discriminated against in terms of access to health care or other services associated with the proximate determinants of child mortality (maternal nutritional status; diet and feeding variables during pregnancy and following birth; and child care, especially in response to illness). Other explanations turn to more structural considerations. It is possible, for example, that nonwhite children live in more hazardous areas within cities. Or that nonwhite mothers receive a poorer quality of education as a consequence of residential patterns and the distribution of funds for public schools, and therefore experience lower health returns to education. Whatever the actual cause, the findings nonetheless suggest that, beyond the negative effects of lower socioeconomic status and region of residence, there are additional costs associated with being nonwhite in urban Brazil.

* * *

Estimates of racial inequality in Brazil do not support the convergence hypothesis put forth by most theories of development and social change. Despite the considerable economic growth that has taken place since the abolition of slavery a century ago, sharp inequalities remain between the country's white and nonwhite populations. Differences in social and economic standing are reflected in racial differences in the survival probabilities of children born to white and nonwhite parents. The mortality gap, which was around 7.5 years of average life expectancy in 1940/50, remained about the same thirty years later (6.7 years in 1970/80). Other findings presented in this chapter indicate that the mother's race continues to be associated with child mortality after removing the effects of social and economic determinants such as income, education and access to clean water.

The character of racial inequality in contemporary Brazil is the legacy of historical events. Under the slave mode of production, which dominated the country's colonial history, race and social class were one and the same. With the exception of a minority who had been freed, all blacks were members of the subordinate and highly stigmatized class of slaves. By the middle of the nineteenth century, the economic and social changes began to erode the power of the slave-owning class. Once a sleepy, rural-based society, Brazil started to lose its provincial character with the onset of the coffee boom. Commerce surged, and the capital accumulated from the international sale of coffee was invested in railroads and steamship lines. Small industries sprouted, especially in textiles. A polytechnic school opened to train engineers, and military academies gave emphasis to technical training and to ideas that linked modernization to nationalism. Urban centers were filled with an expanding number of merchants, bureaucrats and entrepreneurs who shared a belief in a society characterized by social mobility and economy dominated by the profit motive. Industrialists, along with numerous other social groups, increasingly came to believe that the substitution of a free work force for the slave one was the solution to Brazil's labor shortage. The demand for labor to meet the needs of an expanding coffee economy, and the rise of urban groups dissatisfied with slavery as a system, were the two most important factors that made abolition a necessity (Graham 1970).

The end of slavery in the late nineteenth century, and the growing importance of a free labor market, altered the social and economic bases of racial inequality. Theories of racial inferiority, although present during the slave period, assumed particular vehemence in the transition to abolition as defenders of the status quo eagerly reached for racial concepts to defend their endangered institution. Ideas about the natural inferiority of blacks gained prominence and acceptability, leaving an impact on the relations between blacks and whites in the period after emancipation. Lack of property, inadequate job skills and shortcomings in education represented major impediments for freedmen and their descendants (Toplin 1981). If blacks ceased to be slaves after abolition, the quality of "blackness" remained a stigma.

In terms of the framework developed in chapter 2 (Figure 2.2), we can say that, in the course of Brazilian development, the locus of the cleavage between white and black shifted from infrastructure (where class and race were coincident within the slave mode of production) to more complex and subtle forms of inequality within the stratification system. Social definitions of skin color, although finely graded and often contingent on other attributes, continue to affect the character of interpersonal relations. Racial discrimination is also associated with systematic differences in intergenerational mobility, labor market discrimination and, as we have shown here, in differential rates of childhood mortality.

7

The "baby bust"

Available data indicate that fertility rates in Brazil remained fairly constant through the first half of this century. In the late 1960s, the birth rate then began a sudden and rapid decline. The pace of the transition from high to lower fertility was arguably the most significant demographic event in the country's recent history. The change was all the more remarkable because of the pattern of the fertility change by socioeconomic strata. The common expectation is for the onset of lower fertility to begin among the urban middle class, gradually spreading downward through the social ranks and outward to the countryside. Recent estimates for Brazil, in contrast, show a sharp and simultaneous drop in the birth rate among all social groups, both urban and rural.

In keeping with the perspective adopted in previous chapters, we reject the assumption that social change had equal consequences for all socioeconomic groups. Instead, our objective is to examine the manner in which recent transformations in Brazilian social and economic structure unequally affected different subclasses of the population, stimulating a reduced demand for children. If fertility fell in all socioeconomic strata, the point we wish to make is that this common outcome was caused by factors that were more or less specific to different sectors of the population. Comparing rural and urban areas, and middle and lower income groups, we find different macrostructural processes working to alter reproductive behavior in favor of a smaller family size.

The explanation for the drop in the fertility rate is cast at two different levels of analytical abstraction. The first deals with the "proximate determinants" of fertility, a perspective that identifies an increase in contraceptive use among married couples as the primary factor in the fertility decline. The second moves beyond the proximate determinants to ask: What caused the increasing use of contraceptives? The answer can be found in the reproductive consequences of social and economic changes that increased the costs and reduced the benefits parents derive from children.

The fertility decline

The registration of vital events in Brazil is far from perfect. Although the quality of vital registration has been greatly improved, there is still no complete record of the number of births in the country. This means that we cannot study fertility with conventional demographic methods that rely on vital registration statistics. Instead, we derive fertility estimates using the indirect technique developed by William Brass (1968). The Appendix describes the method, and discusses its assumptions and limitations.

The Brass technique permits estimates of age-specific fertility rates from census or survey data. It uses two kinds of information, classified by age of woman: (1) the number of live births during the 12 months preceding the census, and (2) the total number of live births. These age-specific fertility rates are added up to yield an estimate of total fertility. The total fertility rate is the number of children that an average woman would have during her childbearing experience (were she subjected to the estimated age-specific fertility rates during her reproductive period).

Table 7.1 presents estimates of total fertility for Brazil and the ten regions of the country. As shown in the last row, the average number of children per woman was 6.5 in 1940. This value remained fairly constant in the next decade (6.3 in 1950), dropping to 5.8 children in 1970. In the thirty years between 1940 and 1970, the level of fertility in Brazil declined about 11 per cent. Unfortunately the 1960 census was never published in its entirety and reliable estimates for that year are lacking.

Regional estimates for the 1940–70 period, however, indicate widely divergent patterns in the different geographic areas of the country. The more developed regions experienced a fertility decline. The total fertility rate in São Paulo fell from 5.6 in 1940 to 4.2 in 1970, a 25 per cent change. A similar reduction is found in the South (a 17.7 per cent drop) and, to a lesser degree, in Minas. Fertility rose in other regions, such as Amazônia, the Central Northeast and Paraná. The fertility decline in the more developed central and southern regions partially offset the increase in the less developed areas of the country so that the result was a national fertility rate that showed only modest change between 1940 and 1970.

Table 7.1. *Total fertility rates by region, 1940–80*

	1940	1950	1970	1980	% change 1940–70	% change 1970–80
Amazônia	6.9	7.3	8.1	6.2	17.4	−23.5
N. Northeast	7.0	7.0	7.3	6.6	4.3	−9.6
C. Northeast	7.9	7.7	7.8	5.5	−1.3	−29.5
S. Northeast	6.9	7.3	7.6	5.8	10.1	−23.7
Minas	7.2	6.8	6.5	4.1	−9.7	−36.9
Rio	4.2	4.0	4.0	2.7	−4.8	−32.5
São Paulo	5.6	5.1	4.2	3.1	−25.0	−26.2
Paraná	5.9	5.9	6.5	3.9	10.2	−40.0
South	6.2	6.2	5.1	3.2	−17.7	−37.3
Central West	6.2	6.4	6.6	4.5	6.5	−31.8
BRAZIL	6.5	6.3	5.8	4.2	−10.8	−27.6
Rural			7.7	6.0		−22.1
Urban			4.8	3.5		−27.0

In the following decade Brazil entered a new phase in its demographic history. In the short span of about ten years the fertility level declined a full 27.6 per cent.[1] In 1970 the average number of children born was 5.8 and yet the total fertility rate reached a low 4.2 in the late 1970s. All regions experienced considerable reductions with the exception of the Northern Northeast, where the drop was a modest 9.6 per cent. Between 1970 and 1980 the per cent decline in fertility exceeded 30 per cent in Minas, Rio, Paraná, South and Central West. The birth rate also dropped in both rural and urban Brazil (22.1 and 27.0 per cent, respectively).

The most recent estimates of fertility rates in Brazil come from the 1986 demographic and health survey, jointly carried out by the BEMFAM (Sociedade Civil Bem-Estar Familiar no Brasil) and DHS (Demographic and Health Surveys of Westinghouse Corporation). The findings, based on interviews with 3,414 women of 15–44 years of age, is representative at the national level (except sparsely settled places, such as Rondônia, Acre, Roraima and Amapá and the rural areas of the North and Central West regions). The results show that the decline in the birth rate that took place during the 1970s continued on into the 1980s. Survey findings for 1986 indicate a total fertility rate of 3.1 for the country as a whole (a decline of 26.9 per cent since 1980). Similar reductions occurred in rural and urban places, where the total fertility

Table 7.2. *Total fertility rates by household income and place of residence, 1970 and 1980*

Place of residence	Income	1970	1980	% change
Total	1–150	7.5	6.1	−18.7
	151–300	6.7	5.6	−16.4
	301–500	5.4	4.2	−22.2
	500+	3.3	2.9	−12.1
Urban	1–150	7.0	5.2	−25.7
	151–300	6.0	4.0	−33.3
	301–500	4.8	4.0	−16.7
	500+	3.1	2.8	−9.7
Rural	1–150	7.8	6.6	−15.4
	151–300	8.0	6.2	−22.5
	301–500	7.7	5.2	−32.5
	500+	5.9	4.0	−32.2

Note: Income in 1970 cruzeiros.
Source: 1970 estimates from Carvalho and Paiva 1976; 1980 estimates derived from the 0.8 per cent sample of the census.

rate fell to 4.4 and 2.7 children, respectively (BEMFAM/DHS 1986: Table 2).

The sharp fertility decline observed across regions of the country indicate that the change in reproductive behavior occurred in both developed and less developed areas. The findings presented in Table 7.2 further show that the decline in the birth rate was not restricted to a particular socioeconomic stratum of the population, but took place among women at all levels of household income. When the estimates of fertility change are broken down by rural and urban areas, an interesting pattern emerges. In urban places the percentage decline in the birth rate was higher among the two lower income groups. In rural areas, the reverse was true. Larger rates of change occurred among the two higher strata of monthly household income. It was the joint effect of these two patterns of change that accounted for the relatively uniform fertility decline found across income categories for the country as a whole.

The proximate determinants of fertility

The level of fertility in a population is the product of the interaction between biology, social organization and individual behavior. In 1956,

Davis and Blake (1956) set forth a conceptual framework that identified the variables directly connected with the stages of human reproduction: (1) intercourse, (2) conception and (3) gestation and parturition. Eleven factors were associated with the three steps: age of entry into sexual unions, celibacy, time between unions, voluntary and involuntary abstinence from intercourse, involuntary fecundity or infecundity, contraceptive use, voluntary fecundity or infecundity and foetal mortality (from voluntary and involuntary causes).

These "intermediate variables" specify the avenues through which, and only through which, cultural and material conditions can affect fertility. Any factor that affects the level of reproduction must do so in some way classifiable under one or more of the eleven elements of the scheme. Each of the intermediate variables can have a positive or negative effect on fertility. The actual birth rate is a function of the net balance of the various values. Thus, societies with different types of social organization may have the same level of fertility, yet reached this common outcome through quite different institutional mechanisms.

The value of the Davis–Blake framework is that it pinpointed the specific channels through which socioeconomic factors influence the birth rate. The distinctive features of an intermediate variable is its direct influence on fertility. If an intermediate variable changes (such as the age of marriage), then fertility also changes if other factors remain constant. This is not necessarily the case for the indirect determinants of fertility, such as income and education. Consequently, differences in the birth rate among populations, and fertility trends over time within the same population, can be traced to variation in one or more of the intermediate fertility variables.

Although demographers have long recognized these relationships, it has been difficult to quantify the link between a set of intermediate variables and fertility. An important exception is John Bongaarts's (1978, 1980) work. Drawing on the work by Davis and Blake, he identified a limited number of conceptually distinct and quantitatively important variables, called the "proximate determinants" of fertility. A set of equations measure the influence of the proximate determinants and parcel out the separate influence of each. These include the index of the proportion married (C_m, equals one if all women of reproductive age are married; zero if none are); the index of contraception (C_c, which equals one in the absence of contraception and zero if all fecund women use 100 per cent effective contraception); the index of abortion (C_a, equals one in the absence of induced abortion and zero if all pregnancies are aborted); and the index of postpartum abstinence infecundability

Table 7.3. *Estimate of proximate determinants of total fertility rate 1970–81*

Measure	1970	1976	1981
Total fecundity rate	15.3	15.3	15.3
Postpartum infecundity (Ci)	0.89	0.91	0.93
Total natural fertility	13.6	13.9	14.2
Abortion (Ca)	0.96	0.94	0.82
Contraception (Cc)	0.72	0.54	0.55
Total marital fertility	9.34	7.04	6.42
Non-marriage (Cm)	0.63	0.63	0.64
Total fertility rate	5.89	4.43	4.11

Source: Merrick and Berquó 1983: Table 15.

(Ci, equals one in the absence of lactation and postpartum abstinence and zero if the duration of infecundability is infinite). The method starts with the total fecundity rate, defined as the number of births a woman would have in her reproductive lifetime if none of the inhibiting factors were operative. This value, multiplied by each of the indices in succession, provides an estimate of the relative magnitude of the factors that reduce fertility from the theoretical maximum to its observed level.

By quantifying the relative importance of key intermediate variables, the Bongaarts framework is an important advance over the original Davis–Blake model. The drawback to the technique is that the data required to calculate the four indices are generally available only in national level fertility surveys that include questions on breastfeeding, abortion and current contraceptive use. Census data do permit the calculation of the marriage index, but national information on the three remaining variables is unavailable in Brazil. Despite this limitation, Merrick and Berquó (1983) were able to piece together census data and information from numerous subnational surveys. Using this information, they estimated the value of the four indices that Bongaarts proposed.

Table 7.3 presents their findings for 1970, 1976 and 1981. The primary factor accounting for the decline in the total fertility rate, from 5.89 in 1970 to 4.43 in 1976, is the decline in the value of Cc. The index of contraception varies inversely with prevalence and use effectiveness of contraception practiced by couples in the reproductive age. The drop in Cc therefore reflects the combination of increased contraceptive use, and the spread of more effective means of fertility control. In Brazil, the availability of modern contraceptives is related to broader issues associated with national population policy, family planning institutions and the role of the Catholic Church.

Population policy and family planning

The increased use of contraception has occurred even though Brazil has never established an official family planning program. Until recently the government's policy regarding population was decidedly pronatalist. National security and the desire to colonize frontier regions were among the factors that explained official reluctance to endorse any policy that seemed to threaten the growth of population. The pronatalist position was compatible with the doctrines of the Catholic Church, whose teachings found their way into public pronouncements. In 1967, President Costa e Silva commented on Pope Paul VII's encyclical, 'Humanae Vitae' in a statement that shows a telling merger of religion and politics: "As governor of a country that is trying to occupy more than half of its territory and is still exposed to the risk of demographic density incompatible with the global needs of its development and security, I do not depend on our unshakable faith in the Christian commandments to applaud this notable document" (cited in Mello, Silva and McLaughlin 1978: 15).

The Church has been important in national policy-making, but less so among the population at large insofar as contraception is concerned. Although officially opposed to "artificial" methods of birth control, the Church's position has become less rigid in recent years, especially at the level of individual counseling by the clergy (Carvalho et al. 1981: 23). A 1986 survey of contraceptive use in Brazil showed that only 1.5 per cent of currently married women aged 15–44 gave religious reasons for their decision (BEMFAM/DHS 1986: Table 12). The figures are somewhat higher in northern Brazil, yet they are still low compared to popular impressions of the significance of the role of the Church in Latin America. In the SOUTH region, none of the respondents cited religion as the reason for not adopting contraception.

Political and economic events have played a role in the evolution of population policy in Brazil. In 1967 and 1968 a controversy involving the IUD made front-page headlines. Newspapers charged that foreign missionaries were committing genocide by sterilizing women in the Amazon region in order to depopulate the area and take possession of the land. A parliamentary commission was appointed to investigate the charges. This inquiry coincided with the onset of Brazil's economic boom, when the rate of growth in the national product substantially exceeded the rate of population increase. Delfim Neto, then Minister of Finance, and outspoken opponent of population control, held that the economic and political costs of any attempt to lower fertility would far outweigh its benefits. In keeping with this view, Brazil took a strong stand against the control of population growth at the Stockholm Conference on Environment in 1972, and later, in 1973, at the meeting held in Geneva in preparation for the World Population Conference planned for the following year in Bucharest (Sanders 1973b).

In the early 1970s it appeared that the government would refuse to support family planning for many years to come. But, despite the monolithic appearance of the official stance, there was considerable variance of opinion among the technocrats directing the economy (Merrick 1976: 183). Influential figures, such as Rubens Vaz da Costa, once head of the Bank of the Northeast and of the National Housing Bank, and Mário Henrique Simonsen, former President of the national literacy program (MOBRAL) and Minister of Finance, offered counter-arguments to the pronatalist view (cited in Merrick 1976).

The dissenting voices were apparently heard. At the 1974 World Population Conference, where Argentina and Algeria led a coalition of countries that attacked fertility control policies, the statement presented by the Brazilian representative departed from the hard-line pronatalist view. The main text denounced population control as a solution to Third World problems, yet the last paragraph contained a surprisingly positive statement regarding the obligations to provide birth control information. "Being able to resort to birth control measures," the representative claimed, "should not be a privilege reserved for families that are well-off, and therefore it is the responsibility of the state to provide information on the means that may be required by families of limited income" (cited in Mello et al. 1978: 16).

Public support for family planning by a Brazilian president came in January 1978 when President Geisel told the press during a visit to Mexico that he was concerned with his country's population growth and that family planning would be a means of improving the standard of living. A year later, his successor, President Figueiredo, told the cabinet:

In present conditions in Brazil the success of social development programs depends in large measure on family planning, but with respect for the freedom of decision of each couple. While the principles and methods of responsible parenthood are well known to those of higher income, they are unknown to precisely those who are economically less fortunate. It behooves the state to make this knowledge available to all families.

The first concrete steps towards "democratizing" access to birth control began in 1978, when family planning services were offered through federal health agencies as part of a new "Program for the Prevention of High Risk Pregnancies." This policy, implemented by the Maternal and Infant Health Program, later formed part of Prev-Saúde, announced in 1980. In December 1982 Brazil signed the declaration of the Western Hemisphere Conference of Parliamentarians on Population and Development, which called on governments to "ensure that all individuals can exercise their basic right to decide freely and reasonably the number and spacing of their children by providing family planning information and services."

Even before the public statements in 1974, and the later decision to offer limited family planning services through public agencies, the government tolerated the presence of private organizations. The Brazilian Association for the Welfare of the Family (BEMFAM), with financial backing from the International Planned Parenthood Federation and other foreign sources, has actively promoted family planning in Brazil since its founding in 1965. In addition to lobbying and publicity efforts, the organization signed contracts with state governments to make contraceptives available through a community-based distribution system. BEMFAM operates primarily in the northeast (Pernambuco, Rio Grande do Norte, Paraíba, Alagoas and Piauí).

The BEMFAM/DHS survey in 1986 offers the most recent estimates of contraceptive use in Brazil and selected regions (Table 7.4). In São Paulo, 72.8 per cent of married women aged 15–44 were using contraception at the time of the survey. This compares to 53.0 per cent in the Northeast. The distribution by type of birth control indicates the predominance of oral methods and sterilization. The latter is most common in the North-Central West where the proportion of female sterilization reached 42.0 per cent.

Table 7.5 presents information on the sources of contraceptive devices. In Brazil, pharmacies supplied 38.5 per cent of birth control devices. In the North-Central West, the majority of users obtained contraception from private hospitals and state health agencies. Private sources are more important in the southern, more developed regions of the country where pharmacies provided 54.5 per cent of contraceptive devices (BEMFAM/DHS 1986).

Today, discussions of birth control in Brazil have taken on new dimensions. This has occurred partly because of the diminished relevance of the old terms of the debate, and partly due to the presence of new actors on the scene and new perspectives and concerns voiced in the arena of political discourse. A key factor, as Ruth Cardoso (1983) argued, has been the emergence of the women's movement in Brazil. While women's groups always felt uneasy about a completely *laissez-faire* attitude about contraception (endorsed by the reactionary right as well as the revolutionary left), the issue of sexuality, abortion and individual rights were themes that inevitably made their way into attempts to mobilize women, such as the neighborhood organizations discussed in chapter 5. Protests of social injustice, planned and coordinated by women, cultivated the idea that women had an active role to play *vis-à-vis* the society of which they were a part and with regard to their own personal lives. When housewives in low-income neighborhoods escaped the "domestic ghetto" and took to the streets to denounce the high cost of living and the deterioration of the community, it was only a short step for them to endorse the equality of men and women in all walks of life (Cardoso 1983: 4). Birth control has thus become an issue inextricably bound up with the social and economic questions raised by community action groups, by feminists' demands for sexual equality and the "right to choose," as well as Catholic couples' concern for "responsible parenthood."

Perspectives on the fertility transition

Knowledge of the proximate determinants of fertility, and information regarding the prevalence of contraceptive use in Brazil, facilitate rather than preempt a socioeconomic explanation for the reduction in the birth rate. The quasi-definitional accounting identities that constitute the intermediate variable scheme tell us little about the broader structural changes that lead to lower fertility. Identifying changes in the values of the proximate determinants is clearly an important first step, yet the central question remains unanswered. If the fertility decline in Brazil can be traced to reduction in marital fertility as a result of an increase in contraception, what caused this change in behavior? In effect, what determines the proximate determinants of fertility?

In order to answer this question we first summarize the most important socioeconomic explanations for a decline in the birth rate. These frameworks fall into three groups: the theory of the demographic transition, economic analyses of the costs and benefits of children and studies of household sustenance strategies. The distinction between

Table 7.4. *Percentage distribution of currently in union women 15–44 according to current contraceptive method, by region, Brazil, 1986*

Current use and method	Brazil	Rio de Janeiro	São Paulo	South	Central east	North-east	North-central west
Using	65.3	70.7	72.8	72.6	61.6	52.9	63.3
Female sterilization	27.2	33.6	31.5	18.3	25.1	25.3	42.0
Pill	25.0	25.2	24.7	39.6	23.1	17.4	13.5
Withdrawal	5.0	3.1	6.6	7.5	2.9	4.2	1.9
Periodical abstinence*	4.3	5.3	3.4	3.7	5.5	4.5	3.5
Condom	1.6	1.8	3.2	1.4	2.0	0.4	0.7
IUD	0.9	1.1	0.7	1.4	1.8	0.4	0.5
Male sterilization	0.8	0.2	2.0	0.5	0.6	0.2	1.2
Vaginal methods	0.5	0.4	0.7	0.2	0.6	0.5	0.0
Not using	34.7	29.3	27.2	27.4	38.4	47.1	36.7
Total	100.0	100.0	100.0	100.0	100.0	100.0	100.0
(Number of cases unweighted)	(3,414)	(453)	(441)	(573)	(545)	(971)	(431)

* Includes Calendar, Rhythm and Billings methods.
Source: BEMFAM/DHS 1986.

Table 7.5. *Percentage distribution of currently in union women 15–44 currently using contraception according to source of contraception, by region, Brazil, 1986.*

Source	Brazil	Rio de Janeiro	São Paulo	South	Central-east	North-east	North-central west
Pharmacy	38.5	36.7	36.8	54.5	39.1	28.2	23.1
Private hospital/doctor	21.2	28.1	21.5	16.0	26.0	15.8	36.5
Social Security hospital/doctor	18.6	17.9	24.8	9.5	19.0	19.5	24.2
State/municipal health facility	5.8	3.7	0.6	1.4	2.3	20.2	5.8
BEMFAM	0.6	0.9	0.0	1.4	0.3	0.4	0.0
CPAIMC[a]	0.4	3.1	0.0	0.0	0.0	0.0	0.0
Friends/relatives	4.7	2.8	3.1	4.3	7.0	7.1	3.6
Church	0.1	0.0	0.3	0.0	0.3	0.0	0.4
Other	3.5	2.8	4.3	4.6	2.6	2.5	4.0
Not applicable[b]	6.5	4.0	8.6	8.3	3.5	6.3	2.4
Total	99.9	100.0	100.0	100.0	100.1	100.0	100.0
(Number of cases unweighted)	(2,214)	(324)	(326)	(420)	(343)	(524)	(277)

[a]Centro de Pesquisa de Assistência Integrada à Mulher e à Criança.
[b]Current method is withdrawal.
Source: BEMFAM/DHS (1986)

these categories is somewhat arbitrary because there is considerable overlap between them. Nonetheless, the division facilitates our summary of the vast literature on the relationship between socioeconomic change and fertility patterns. We will use key elements of the following discussion in our subsequent analyses of Brazilian data.

The demographic transition

In a well-known re-assessment of the theory of the demographic transition, Ansley Coale (1973) noted three general conditions that must be met before a fall in marital fertility can occur. First, reproduction must be something couples consider to be within the realm of choice. This condition would exclude the Hutterites, the Amish or any other group that rejects the idea that human intervention can determine family size. Second, social and economic circumstances must be such that reduced fertility is seen as advantageous to the individual couple. Finally, effective techniques of fertility control must be available and used. It is only when all three prerequisites are met that fertility falls.

Coale's second precondition is central to an explanation of the fertility decline in Brazil. What are the macrostructural forces that stimulated the desire for fewer children? In one of the initial formulations of the theory of the demographic transition, Notestein (1953) listed the factors associated with the shift from high fertility in premodern society to lower fertility in the urban–industrial context. Although it contains a mixture of empirical generalizations and *ad hoc* explanations, the passage is worth citing. If nothing else, it captures the complexity of the relationships commonly understood to account for the drop in the birth rate.

It is impossible to be precise about the various causal factors (that led to the new ideal of the small family), but apparently many were important. Urban life stripped the family of many functions in production, consumption, recreation and education. In factory employment the individual stood on his own accomplishments. The new mobility of young people and the anonymity of city life reduced the pressures toward traditional behavior exerted by the family and community. In a period of rapidly developing technology new skills were needed, and new opportunities for individual advancement arose. Education and a rational point of view became increasingly important. As a consequence, the cost of children grew and the possibility for economic contributions by children declined. Falling death rates at once increased the size of the family to be supported and lowered the inducements to have many births. Women, moreover, found new independence from household obligations and new economic roles less compatible with childbearing...Under these multiple pressure old ideas and beliefs began to weaken, and a new ideal of the small number of children gained strength (Notestein 1953, cited in Coale 1973: 54).

Notestein's reference to the increasing importance of a "rational point of view" reveals a persistent strain in the literature on the demographic transition. The debate centers on whether the birth rate responds to changes in material conditions or in response to "new" norms and values that accompany the "modern" lifestyle. Caldwell (1976) claims that many theorists (especially Notestein) incorrectly assume traditional societies are irrational, brutish and bound to custom. The corollary is that rationality, and hence lower fertility, is the exclusive domain of urban, industrial society. In Caldwell's view, this is what accounts for the repeated reference in the sociological literature to attitudes, beliefs and traditions that presumably impede the adoption of the small family norm. Adopting a long-term perspective, anthropologists argue the contrary. Throughout human history, people have used one means or another to adjust their family size in response to changes in the materially determined advantages and disadvantages of children (Harris and Ross 1987).

Rationality and the costs and benefits of children

In contrast to the sociological emphasis on norms and values, economic perspectives on reproduction assume that rationality is universal. Leibenstein (1954) explained the drop in the birth rate in terms of the way the utilities and costs of children shift in the course of economic development. Rising per capita income is associated with a decline in the utility of children, both as a productive resource and as a source of security in old age. Their reduced utility is accompanied by a rise in their direct and indirect costs. Direct costs refer to the usual expenses of maintaining a child (food, clothing) at the prevailing social standard. The indirect costs are the opportunities foregone, especially as they apply to the earnings lost by the mother's inability to work. Inasmuch as parents are cognizant of the change in the costs and benefits of children, the model of individual rationality predicts a decline in the demand for children with a rise in per capita income.

Caldwell (1976) is more explicit about the family's role in the changing costs of children. The direction and the magnitude of intergenerational flows of wealth is fundamental to his framework. The transition from high to low fertility depends on the net balance of two flows, one from parents to children and the other from children to parents. The structural changes that occur in the course of development, including changes in family organization, alter the pattern of the intergenerational transmission of resources. In primitive societies children are, on balance, an asset. "Then there is a great divide, a point where the compass hesitatingly swings around 180 degress, separating the earlier situation in which the net flow of wealth is toward parents, and in which high fertility is rational, and the later situation in which the flow is toward children and in which no fertility is rational" (Caldwell 1976: 345).

Caldwell's notion of intergenerational wealth flows stresses historical changes in social and economic organization. This differs from the neoclassical approach that focuses exclusively on the rational calculus of parents within a given institutional context. In this view, the satisfactions or utilities to be derived from an additional birth are assessed against the costs, both monetary and psychological, of having another child. In this framework the demand for children depends on the balancing of subjective preferences for goods and children relative to externally determined constraints of price and income. While there are many variants of this approach (see Easterlin 1980) the model posits that variations in preferences, price and income can be expected to cause changes in the demand for children and, hence, in the motivation for fertility control. For the individual household an increase in contraceptive use, and a reduction in fertility, occurs when the supply exceeds the demand for children (Coale's second precondition), and when methods of reproductive control are available (Coale's third precondition) at a cost (both monetary and otherwise) that is not prohibitive (see Easterlin 1975: 59.61).

The economic model of household behavior has had a marked influence on demographic studies of fertility. In contrast to the analyses of the proximate determinants, which merely identify the variables that have a direct influence on the birth rate, the microeconomic perspective offers an explanation for the individual motives for reduced family size. Key elements of the scheme – changes in prices, preferences and costs – nonetheless remain exogenous to the framework.

Household sustenance strategies

If neoclassical economic explanations center on the rational calculus of parents at the expense of an explicit concern for macrostructural change, the opposite tends to be true for the historical–structural perspective. The latter, formulated primarily by social scientists in Latin America and Africa, draws heavily from Marxist materialism. The historical–structural approach, applied to the study of demographic behavior, pays special attention to the role of the household as it responds and adapts to changes in the political economy of development. The household is conceptualized as a decision-making unit that allocates the time and resources available to it through a series of "survival" or sustenance strategies (Schmink 1979). The latter refer to the ways in which the household actively strives to achieve a fit between its consumption necessities, the labor power at its disposal (both of which are determined by the number, age, sex and skills of its members) and the alternatives for generating monetary and nonmonetary income. These strategies must necessarily be dynamic, even in a stable socioeconomic and political environment, if only because household composition changes with different stages of the life cycle. Under conditions of social change, the households must devise especially flexible and innovative strategies compatible with shifting productive opportunities. Changes in biological reproduction (fertility, mortality), as well as shifts in the patterns of material production (e.g., labor force participation, intra-household division of labor, labor migration) are thus explained in terms of household responses to the shifting constraints and opportunities that affect the sustenance capacity of the household unit (Lerner 1980; Torrado 1980; Wood 1981).

Socioeconomic determinants of the fertility decline

Despite conceptual advances in the field of fertility research, a striking aspect of the present state of knowledge is the absence of an accepted theory of fertility (Miró and Potter 1980: 94) that links structural change in the society and economy to individual fertility decisions. Indeed, it has been argued that contemporary perspectives have not gone much beyond Notestein's writings on the demographic transition (Caldwell 1976: 325–6). In the absence of a theoretical framework that specifies the connection between macrostructural process and individual or family behavior, the link between the two levels of analysis remains casual. At the same time, the perspectives summarized above, whatever their respective emphases, repeatedly resort to one variant or another of the same theme. Societal level change affects fertility by changing the relative costs and benefits of children. In the following section we report on a number of social indicators that reflect the changes underway in Brazil that have a bearing on reproductive decisions.

Table 7.6. *School enrollment and educational attainment, 1960 and 1970*

Sex	Age	1960	1970	(1970–1960)
Male	15–19	19.3	38.7	+19.4
	20–24	5.5	17.7	+12.2
Female	15–19	15.7	35.4	+19.7
	20–24	3.0	13.7	+10.7

Source: Demographic Censuses 1960 and 1970.

The increase in educational attainment

Among the most important changes in the recent period has been the increase in educational attainment. Table 7.6 shows the proportion of the young population enrolled in school in 1960 and 1970. For both males and females the proportion of 15 to 19 year olds attending school more than doubled during the decade. Enrollment rose even more among those 20 to 24 years of age. Between 1960 and 1970 the proportion of males in school increased 22.8 per cent, while the proportion of females more than tripled. These are the age cohorts that are particularly relevant to fertility behavior in the 1970s.

The increase in educational attainment was not restricted to daughters of middle and upper income families. The figures presented in Table 7.7 show the percentage of women aged 20 to 34 years who completed more than four years of school. Between 1970 and 1980 the proportion rose 6.5 percentage points among women in the lowest income households. Greater educational attainment among poor women was especially high in urban areas, where the proportion completing primary school grew by 11.5 percentage points over the decade. More modest increases took place in rural areas among women in all but one income stratum. The marked improvement in educational achievement had especially significant fertility consequences because it took place among women in the prime reproductive years.

While the overwhelming weight of the evidence shows that increases in female (and to a lesser extent, male) education, leads to lower fertility (Cochrane 1979), it is important to note that greater educational achievement also has the opposite effect. Improved health conditions through the diffusion of knowledge about personal hygiene, food care and environmental dangers tends to enhance the potential supply of

Table 7.7. Percentage of women aged 20 to 34 with more than four years of school, by household income and place of residence, 1970 and 1980

Income	Total			Urban			Rural		
	1970	1980	1980–1970	1970	1980	1980–1970	1970	1980	1980–1970
1–150	9.3	15.8	+ 6.5	19.9	31.4	+11.5	3.5	7.8	+4.3
151–300	29.3	36.7	+ 7.4	38.9	49.7	+10.8	15.8	17.8	+2.0
301–500	51.6	58.7	+ 7.1	58.1	67.1	+ 9.0	28.8	27.8	+1.0
500+	74.6	86.7	+12.1	77.2	90.2	+13.0	45.0	49.4	+4.4

Source: Public Use Samples of 1970 and 1980 censuses.

children by raising natural fertility. It also reduces infant and child mortality, leading to a higher number of surviving children. More education is further associated with shorter lactation time, thereby reducing the latent depressing impact of lactation on fecundity.

The second (and much stronger) effect is for increases in educational attainment to depress fertility, a consequence that operates through a wide range of factors. Arguing from a broad historical perspective, Caldwell (1976) maintains that the timing of the onset of the fertility decline is determined by the effects of mass education on the family economy. Mass education reduces the child's potential for work inside and outside the home. It also increases the costs of children, and speeds the process of cultural change. Universal schooling is also associated with the dissemination of western middle-class values and ideologies, and is related to protective legislation that reduces the economic productivity of children.

By leading to older ages at first marriage, greater educational attainment affects the proximate determinants of fertility by reducing the years of exposure to pregnancy. Other intermediate variables are also involved. Sociologists typically interpret educational level as a proxy measure of the knowledge and use of contraceptives, a line of reasoning that extends to social psychological factors related to birth planning. Compared to women with lower educational attainment, educated women have a positive attitude toward contraceptive use, enjoy greater communication with their husbands and have a greater sense of personal efficacy.

The economic perspective stresses the decline in the demand for children associated with the rise in educational attainment of parents, especially mothers. In the microeconomic model of reproductive behavior, a higher level of education implies an increase in the opportunity cost of childbearing. Other things being equal, the rise in the wife's potential market earnings is associated with higher indirect costs of children and, hence, to a desire to limit family size. Education may also lead to higher standards of childcare, creating greater emphasis on quality rather than quantity of children. The effect is to increase the subjective attractiveness of expenditures that compete with children, thus tending to lower demand.

The rise of an urban–industrial economy

Throughout most of its history Brazil was an essentially rural society. The proportion of the population found in urban areas was 31 per cent in 1940 and 36 per cent in 1950. By 1960 the proportion urban rose to 45 per cent, increasing to 56 per cent in 1970. By 1980, seven out of every ten Brazilians resided in an urban place. The increase in the proportion of the total population living in cities caused in large part by heavy rural out-migration in the 1960s and 1970s (see chapter 9), was accompanied by a change in the size distribution of urban places. Between 1950 and 1960 the growth rate was highest in cities with more than 500,000 inhabitants (6.3 per cent per year). In the following decade the most rapid growth (8.7 per cent) occurred in places between 50,000 and 500,000, indicating a larger proportion of the population in middle-sized cities across the country (Carvalho, Paiva and Sawyer 1981: 29).

The urbanization of Brazil was associated with sectoral changes in the economy. In 1960, 54 per cent of the labor force was engaged in agricultural activities. By 1970 the proportion of the work force in agriculture fell to 44.3 per cent, and dropped to 29.9 per cent in 1980. Agriculture's share of domestic income followed the same tendency, falling from 26.7 per cent in 1960 to 17.7 per cent in 1969. As agriculture declined in importance, the secondary sector's share of the labor force grew from 12.9 per cent in 1960 to 24.4 per cent in 1980. Service sector employment also grew, absorbing nearly half (45.7 per cent) of the labor force by 1980. The growing importance of the urban–industrial economy was accompanied by a rise in income. From 1965 to 1974, Brazilian per capita income (in 1970 dollars) grew from US$392 to US$698 (Carvalho et al. 1981: 29).

The various indicators point to fundamental changes in Brazilian society: the redistribution of population from rural to urban areas; the decline of agriculture; the growing importance of the industrial and service sectors; and a rise in per capita income. Together these transformations in social, economic and demographic structure define new cognitive perspectives and new material conditions conducive to lower fertility via the numerous mechanisms Notestein summarized in his statement of the demographic transition. Easterlin (1983: 571) provides a similar inventory of the various reasons that urbanization leads to a lower birth rate. On the demand side, urban as opposed to rural living raises the relative cost of children because the price of food is higher, and because urban children take more time away from the mother's paid work and contribute less toward family income than do children in rural areas. On the supply side, access to fertility control knowledge is likely to be greater and market costs lower in high-density population centers. The subjective costs of contraceptive use are also likely to be lower than in rural settings because of the tendency of city life to weaken traditional attitudes. By reducing the demand for children, and reducing the monetary and psychic costs of contraception, urbanization contributes to a fall in fertility.

The increase in women's participation in the labor force

Data on wage and price changes in the 1960s and 1970s showed an increase in economic stress, especially among the population in the lower income strata. As noted in chapter 5, the real value of the minimum salary in São Paulo fell sharply between 1964 and 1974. For the country as a whole, information on wages paid to unskilled labor indicated a decline in the purchasing power of the wages received by urban workers (Bacha 1979).

The rise in the number of hours required to purchase food for a family of four reflected the erosion of the purchasing power among low-income groups. In São Paulo, a worker earning the minimum wage in 1965 had to labor 87 hours to sustain himself, his wife and two children. In 1975, the hours required to do so rose 76.7 per cent, to 154 hours and 18 minutes (chapter 5). The trend was especially significant for the urban poor because a rise in the cost of food has a much larger effect on low-income families due to fact that the proportion of total expenditures on food items is substantially greater compared to more affluent households. Hence, the welfare cost of food inflation is disproportionately borne by the poor.

Putting more members to work is one of the strategies households use to respond and adapt to deteriorating economic conditions (Schmink 1979). Data for 1970 and 1980, presented in Table 7.8, show a marked rise in female labor force participation rates across all age groups, including the very young (10 to 14 years of age). Participation rates rose 34.1 per cent for women 20 to 24 years old. Even larger increases took place among those aged 25 to 29 (+59.2 per cent) and 30 to 34 (+65.6 per cent) years old – precisely the age groups where most fertility takes place. Additional information provided by Castro (1987) indicates that wives constituted the bulk of the new female entrants to the labor force during the 1970s, and that significant changes took place in the distribution of women workers by industry. Comparing the three sectors, the largest increase in female employees occurred in the transformative sector, especially as wage earners within capital-intensive industrial firms.

Table 7.8. *Age-specific labor force participation rates for women aged 10–49, 1970 and 1980*

Age	1970	1980	% increase
10–14	6.4	8.4	31.3
15–19	25.5	31.4	23.1
20–24	28.7	38.5	34.1
25–29	22.8	36.3	59.2
30–34	21.2	35.1	65.6
35–39	20.4	34.2	67.6
40–44	20.3	31.7	56.2
45–49	18.7	28.5	52.4

Source: Demographic Censuses 1970 and 1980.

Researchers have advanced numerous arguments to explain the inverse relationship between a rise in female labor force participation and a decline in the birth rate (Standing 1983). Some of the mechanisms are indirect, such as the tendency for the work experience to raise both the age of marriage and the age of the onset of fertility. Women's work, and their monetary contribution to household sustenance, is also thought to foster more egalitarian gender relations, making women less subordinate to men in decision-making, particularly with regard to fertility and childrearing. Other analysts have shown that the type of jobs women engage in is relevant to the work–fertility relationship. It is generally accepted that the opportunity costs of children is low for women doing agricultural work, especially on family farms where work schedules are presumably flexible. On the other hand, in urban areas, wage employment away from the home is particularly incompatible with the demands of childrearing, at least among less affluent households. If middle and upper income families can afford to purchase childcare (because of the relatively high opportunity income compared to the cost of domestics), the same is not true among the urban poor. Hence, the observed increases in female labor force participation rates, as well as other evidence on type of employment involved, suggest that the rise in the number of working women between 1970 and 1980 was an important factor contributing to the decline during the period in the birth rate among lower income women in urban Brazil.

Relative deprivation and the urban middle class

The relationship between wage and price changes and reproduction can be conceptualized in terms of the interplay between aspirations and resources, or what Easterlin termed the "relative affluence" of the married couple. When the material resources available to the couple are abundant relative to consumption aspirations, they will feel free to have children. On the other hand, if the resources are scarce relative to aspirations, they will be hesitant to do so. We can conceptualize the recent fertility decline in Brazil in terms of the conflict between resources and aspirations in order to account for the changes in the birth rate for the low and middle-income strata (Carvalho et al. 1981).

The data reviewed above suggest a deterioration in the material well-being of low-income groups, a trend households sought to counter by placing wives and children into the labor market. In contrast to the poor, the middle and upper income population gained in real income during the recent period of economic growth, as shown in the analyses of income distribution in chapter 3. However, as Carvalho, Paiva and Sawyer (1981) argue, middle-class aspirations may have exceeded their resources once additional goods and services became increasingly available to them. The National Housing Bank, for example, placed the purchase of houses and luxury apartments well within the reach of middle-income groups. Yet, because of the indexing of long-term mortgages and other loans, a sizeable part of the family income became committed for long periods of time. Similarly, the ideology of social mobility led families to extend the number of years of schooling desired for their children. The increase in the proportion of sons and daughters attending universities and private colleges placed greater constraints on the family budget. Moreover, the rapid growth in the production of consumer durables, such as automobiles and electrical appliances, together with the ready availability of consumer credit, stimulated a growing diversification of consumption patterns. Although these observations are mainly suggestive, they point to a shift in the tastes and preferences among middle-income sectors of the population, especially compared to earlier generations. Such changes in aspirations and consumption patterns almost certainly induced members of the middle class to have fewer births, or to postpone childbearing (Carvalho et al. 1981).

A framework similar to the aspirations/resources model stresses the relationship between the individual and his or her "reference group." An accepted principle in sociology is that a person's attitudes and conduct are shaped by the group to which he or she belongs. In the 1940s this was extended to the idea of relative deprivation, a concept that invoked the idea that deprivation was not dependent on any absolute scale but was related to the perception of the person's position *vis-à-vis* a reference group. In a study of fertility in the United States, Freedman (1963) developed a measure of relative income status. Regression analysis was used to estimate the earnings expected on the basis of background characteristics, such as age and education. The value predicted from the individual's human capital endowments was then compared to actual earnings. If actual income exceeded the predicted value, relative income was positive; if the actual amount fell short of predicted earnings, relative income would be negative. Using the relative income measure as a proxy for the relationship to one's reference group, Freedman found that an income level above (below) the average for one's status was associated with more (fewer) children.

Merrick and Berquó (1983) applied the relative income concept to the study of fertility in Brazil. In this case the measure is intended to capture the effects at the individual level of structural changes in the economy, especially inflation. Interpreted in this way, the gap between the observed and the predicted income indicates the degree to which a household is vulnerable to inflationary pressures. In an analysis of 1970 census data, and of the 1976 PNAD survey, Merrick and Berquó found a positive association between relative income and the number of children ever born. Although the contribution of the relative income variable to the total variance explained was small, the results for the two periods were the same: the more the husband's actual earnings fell below the income predicted from his background, the lower the average number of children. These empirical findings are consistent with the idea that relative deprivation reduces the demand for children, and that it leads to a decline in fertility.

Agrarian structure and rural fertility

The proletarianization of rural labor

Lower birth rates in the countryside are undoubtedly associated with the massive transformations that have taken place, and that are currently underway, in the social relations of production in the agricultural sector. Landowners in Brazil have increasingly found that wage labor is less costly relative to payments in kind and/or usufruct of land. Tenant and sharecropping arrangements are rapidly being replaced by temporary workers, hired through intermediaries during peak periods of labor demand. Between 1970 and 1975 alone, the number of tenant and sharecropping establishments dropped by 10.5 and 21.3 per cent, respectively. Similarly, the area cultivated under these forms of land tenure declined by about 30 per cent. The number of temporary or seasonal wage laborers, on the other hand, grew from 3.9 million in 1967 to 6.8 million in 1972 (Kohl 1981: 211). Many of these part-time agricultural workers have migrated to the periphery of cities and small towns where they also engage in urban-based occupations (see chapter 9).

Changes in the social relations of production alter the function and the character of the family unit. When the household is the locus of production and consumption, the greater the number of laborers in proportion to consumers, the greater is its productive capacity. Under the *colono* system, that evolved in the coffee growing areas in southern Brazil, income depended, not only on the number of trees under the care of a family, but also on the task rate set by the planter. The basis of the task rate was a family with three adult workers. This form of remuneration placed a premium on large family size as those with few children were at a disadvantage throughout the family life cycle (Stoelke 1984). Moreover, the principal subsistence items, such as food, were produced by the domestic unit. Thus, larger families, through economies of scale and the possibility of dividing labor, had a comparative advantage in terms of monetary wages. Moreover, additional children did not represent a proportional increase in the costs borne by the family unit. In this way the *colono* system, and sharecropping and tenant arrangements generally, constituted specific conditions where large family size enhanced productive capacity and contributed to lowering the cost of the maintenance and reproduction of the household (Carvalho et al. 1981: 36–43).

With the breakdown of these forms of land tenure through the proletarianization of the work force, the household becomes a partial or total wage-earning unit. The separation of the home and the workplace has profound repercussions on the family economy. The advantages of scale and division of labor derived from large families is eliminated, and the cost of subsistence rises relative to the subsistence capacity of the unit. Food and housing are purchased in the marketplace, while the sale of labor, contracted individually rather than on a family basis, increases economic uncertainty. The burden of rent, and the imposition of other monetary expenditures, place the rural household in a tenuous economic position, especially during periods, such as the first half of the 1970s, when the purchasing power of wages declined (Stolcke 1984). When the wage is insufficient to meet household needs, parents consider children a burden as they make it difficult for the wife to work.

Stolcke's (1984) interviews with former *colonos*, now working as seasonal wage laborers, clearly reveal the fertility consequences of these changes in agrarian structure. "For those who had many children," one informant explains, "it was better before; those who had 12, 13 children could raise them easily...now, those who have only small children, for the father to work alone, it is very hard." Under the circumstances, a drop in the desired number of children is hardly surprising. In the words of one woman, "Nowadays nobody wants to have children any more...the thing is to close the factory gates; to close it and lose the key."

If the proletarianization of sharecroppers and tenant farmers leads to lower fertility, as suggested here, what about smallholders who still retain ownership or access to land? Although the literature on Brazil is sparse, the question has been the object of study in a wide range of other countries. Two research foci dominate the literature on this topic (for a review, see Schutjer and Stokes 1984). One examines the relationship between the size of holding and fertility. The theoretical rationale for such a connection usually invokes the value and the demand for children as laborers. Where family labor and land are the major inputs to the production process, larger holdings are expected to be associated with larger family size (see Schutjer and Stokes 1984).

Another approach concerns the availability of land. An increase in the number of available plots influences fertility by lowering the age at marriage and increasing the number who eventually marry, and, secondarily, through a rise in marital fertility. Conversely, land scarcity is related to lower fertility. In a study of the United States in the nineteenth century, Easterlin (1976) proposed a bequest theory in which inheritance was an important link between land availability and fertility. Farmers in newly settled and sparsely populated areas found it relatively easy to preserve and increase their holdings, and transmit their wealth to the next generation. This was more difficult to accomplish in older, more densely populated places. Easterlin concluded that this was the cause of the decline in rural fertility with the closing of the frontier in the United States in the 1860s.

Anthropological studies of rural Brazil suggest the relevance of land scarcity in the study of fertility. In the long-settled areas of São Paulo, Shirley (1971, cited in Merrick and Graham, 1979: 272) documented the struggle for land due to fragmentation of farms caused by the Brazilian tradition of multigeniture inheritance. Similarly, Margolis (1973) has shown that the rise in population density in northern Paraná, and the decline in available land that occurred as a result of intense immigration, had a negative impact on household formation. Building on the earlier work by Easterlin, Merrick (1978) analyzed rural fertility differentials between frontier regions and the older, more settled areas of the country. The data showed a negative correlation between fertility levels and the degree of land utilization, a finding consistent with the bequest model.

*   *   *

Estimates of the level of fertility between the 1940s and the 1960s indicate that the aggregate birth rate remained fairly constant for most of the period. Small increases in the total fertility rate occurred in some regions, while modest declines took place in others. The picture of stability at the national level gave way in the 1960s and 1970s to a rapid reduction in the average number of children born. Places which had high and increasing fertility in the 1940–60 period, such as Amazônia and the Northeast, reversed this trend in the subsequent decade. In the more developed regions of southern Brazil the decline in fertility, which was already underway at a slow pace, accelerated in the 1970s. Analyses of the proximate determinants of fertility show that the drop in the birth rate was associated with the increased prevalence of contraceptive use, and the reliance on more effective means of birth control among married couples.

Explanations for these changes are more or less consistent with the model of the demographic transition. The various indicators of socioeconomic development show that Brazil has become an increasingly urban society with an expanding industrial base and a more highly educated population subject to lower death rates. By implication, the population adapted its reproductive behavior in response to the growth of the economy and to the structural transformations that accompany the process of development. However, the surprising pace and the extent of the drop in the birth rate suggest that this interpretation, by itself, is incomplete. Only a relatively small proportion of Brazilians benefitted from the economic growth that took place from the late 1960s to the mid–1970s. In addition, there is evidence of a considerable fertility decline, even in those classes that participated in the benefits of development only marginally, if at all. Evidence of lower fertility among all socioeconomic subgroups of the population, including women in the poorest stratum of household income, is a pattern of fertility change that does not conform precisely to the common expectation of a gradual diffusion of the small family size norm, beginning among middle and upper income urban couples and only later spreading downward through the social ranks and outward into rural areas. The Brazilian case does not reject the general assumptions of the demographic transition so much as call attention to the need to examine reproductive change from the standpoint of the manner in which the rapid restructuring of Brazilian society provoked a broad spectrum of social, economic and cognitive changes – some of which are more or less specific to different population subgroups – that altered the incentive structure of childbearing in favor of a reduced number of offspring.

The acceleration of the fertility decline in the 1970s coincided with a period in which urban middle-income households raised their consumption expectations in favor of material possessions, and in terms of 'higher quality' children though increased investments in education. High rates of inflation, and the indexing of credit obligations may have resulted in a gap between a couple's material aspirations and their resources, a condition that depressed the demand for children.

Lower-income urban households were particularly hard hit by the joint impact of an erosion in real wages from the mid-1960s through the mid-1970s, and an increase in the cost of food, housing and public services, especially in urban areas. The data on labor force participation rates indicate substantial increases in the number of working women between 1970 and 1980. The rise in the proportion of women in the labor force had a significant depressing effect on fertility for at least two reasons. First, the increase in participation rates took place primarily among wives, and in the prime reproductive years. Second, the pattern of the rise in female employment was not restricted to the traditional female-dominated occupations. Although the personal service sector in 1980 continued to absorb the bulk of women workers, the rise in female employment between 1970 and 1980 took place primarily in modern industry (transformative sector) and related activities (producer services). Jobs of this type, which are outside the home and characterized by rigid scheduling, are especially incompatible with the demands of childrearing in an urban environment.

The changes that took place in the eco-demographic infrastructure, such as those noted above, also brought about new cognitive orientations that weakened traditional gender relations, especially among urban women. Economic factors were undoubtedly important, such as the increase in female labor force participation rates, and the growing economic importance of women within the household. Other factors were political, associated with the mobilization of urban women in neighborhood organizations and behind such causes as the Cost of

Living Movement, discussed in chapter 5. Protests of social injustice, planned and coordinated by women, cultivated an attitude that brought to the forefront of daily life the issue of gender inequality and the right of women to control reproduction.

In rural settings, the story was a different one. Here the most significant structural modifications were associated with fundamental changes in the organization of agricultural production, and in the manner in which labor was recruited and remunerated in the countryside. Traditional tenancy and sharecropping gave way, at least in many parts of the country, to the wage relationship in which workers were hired individually, often on a seasonal basis. Some of these changes, notably in southern Brazil, took place as a consequence of the country's new position with the international market system, specifically the growing importance of non-traditional agricultural exports, such as soy beans (chapter 3). The separation of families from access to land, and the breakdown of the *colono* system on the coffee plantations where large family size was clearly an economic asset, restructured the household decision environment, thereby changing the dominant mode of reproduction (see chapter 2) in the countryside. The demographic outcome of the proletarianization of the rural labor force included a decline in the birth rate, as well as the massive rural-to-urban migration flow, discussed in chapter 9.

The analysis of fertility change would be incomplete if we did not also emphasize the role of political superstructure. There is little doubt that many of the most significant social and economic changes were caused, at least in part, by the economic growth strategies endorsed by Brazil's military regime. The emphasis on urban–industrial growth and the wage-squeeze policies adopted in the late 1960s and early 1970s are among the more salient examples of the manner in which public policy influenced the pace and the direction of changes in Brazil's eco-demographic base. Also important was the decision to mobilize financial resources, much of it borrowed abroad, to expand water and sewage services, and to increase investment in public education. Finally, the shift in official policy away from the traditional pronatalist stance to the public endorsement of the inherent right, regardless of social class, to access to methods of family planning was a move that represented an important turning point in public policy.

Pulling back from a particular concern for the actions of the state, and from the manner in which macrostructural changes differentially affected middle and lower income households in urban and rural Brazil, the causes of the decline in the aggregate birth rate can be summarized in terms of a change in a few basic relationships. The restructuring of Brazilian society in recent years created an array of pressures that directly or tangentially altered the incentives and disincentives of child-bearing. The rise in the direct and indirect costs of children, and the decline in the market and the subjective costs of the means of reproductive control, reduced the demand for children and permitted couples to adjust their fertility accordingly. Because the preference for fewer children was manifest across social groups (albeit for different reasons), the overall result was an unprecedented 28 per cent decline in the average number of children born to women in Brazil.

8

Income distribution and population growth

Contrary to theories of development popular in the post-World War II period, data for developing countries (Chenery et al. 1974; Adelman and Morris 1973; Weiskoff and Figueroa 1976) showed that the process of economic growth did not necessarily lead to a more equitable distribution of income. In some cases, such as in Brazil in the late 1960s and early 1970s, high rates of increase in Gross Domestic Product were associated with a rise rather than a decline in the degree of income concentration.

In light of the socioeconomic and political significance of changes in the distribution of income, researchers devoted considerable effort to measuring and explaining the degree of income concentration (see chapter 3). Among the causal variables singled out, few have been subjected to less systematic analysis than population growth. Most analyses in the field of development studies seldom go beyond the general assertion that a low rate of population increase contributes to a more equitable distribution of income (Ghai 1975: 506). At times the observation amounted to little more than an article of faith. A World Bank Staff Report, for example, concluded that "there appears to be no explicit dissent from the view that lower fertility contributes to greater income equality" (King et al. 1974: 35). In Cassen's (1976: 812) view, the state of the literature is a "sad reflection" on the separation of demographic and economic studies and the prolonged debate on "growth versus distribution" has largely overlooked the feedback of demographic change.

This chapter explores the relationship between population growth and the distribution of household income in Brazil. The analysis addresses three questions: (1) In light of the fertility and mortality differentials noted in chapters 4 and 7, to what extent does the rate of population growth among the poor exceed that of the middle and upper income groups? (2) What is the impact of these differential rates of natural increase on the distribution of income? And, conversely, (3) how does a change in the level of real income affect subgroup rates of population growth?

Fertility and the distribution of income

Both macro and microeconomic reasoning suggest that a high fertility rate in a population contributes to an increase in income inequality. At the micro level, high fertility adversely affects the per capita accumulation of assets and human capital. Large family size reduces savings, leads to a fragmentation of landholdings and shifts resources to consumption at the expense of productive investment. The macroeconomical model predicts the same outcome through different channels. Since the wage share of total income declines with a rise in the supply of labor, a high rate of population growth has negative effects on the distribution of income (Rodgers 1978).

Other perspectives link the birth rate and income inequality but reverse the causal direction. In this view, the high concentration of income is the cause (not the effect) of sustained high fertility. Proponents of this view base their argument on the relationship between income and a couple's demand for children and their capacity to control reproduction (Kocher 1973; Rich 1973). Because the desire for and capacity to achieve small families is closely tied to standard of living, the poorest members of society are unlikely to reduce their number of offspring. When income is concentrated in the hands of a small elite (with low fertility) and when the largest proportion of the population is poor (with high fertility), the birth rate for the population as a whole will necessarily be high. Studies that use countries as the unit of analysis therefore find a positive association between the degree of income concentration and the aggregate fertility rate (Repetto 1974, 1977, 1978).

Most studies of the relationship between population growth and income distribution rely on aggregate estimates of the birth rate for countries as a whole. This method has two important limitations. First, it overlooks the mortality component of the natural increase equation. This is significant because the higher fertility of the poor does not necessarily mean that their numbers are increasing. If mortality is also very high among the poor, then the high birth rate will be completely offset by the high death rate, and the rate of growth will be zero. It is more likely, however, that mortality only partially offsets fertility, leading to an increase in the number of children born to the poor. Hence, the rate of natural increase that corresponds to different socioeconomic groups is determined by the group's age structure and by the magnitude of the difference between birth and death rates.

The second limitation associated with the use of aggregate measures is that such a perspective fails to account for the fact that vital rates do not tend to fall at the same time and at the same pace in all population subgroups. The trend toward a lower aggregate birth rate is usually initiated by a fertility decline among the relatively wealthy and better educated women while lower status women continue to have large families. The result is an increase in differential fertility by social strata. Now, if child mortality stays the same, this pattern of demographic change implies a lower rate of population growth among women in the middle and upper income groups and a sustained high rate of natural increase among the poor. Since assets and human capital are unequally distributed to begin with, the widening gap in the rate of population growth contributes to greater not lesser income concentration. Hence, the initial decline in the aggregate birth rate can cause a rise in inequality, an outcome that is exactly the opposite of the conventional expectation.

Child mortality rates are not likely to remain constant, however. If an increase in income causes the birth rate to fall, such a change will also lead to fewer deaths. Demographic outcomes of a rise in income are further complicated by the fact that increments to income may have a larger effect on mortality than it does on fertility, at least among the poor. The effect of an increase in income on the rate of population growth will therefore depend on the income elasticities of fertility and mortality, which vary by social stratum. We can begin to unravel these complex relationships using population projections to measure the extent to which the various combinations of births and deaths lead to differential rates of population growth within the various income strata.

Population growth and the distribution of income

Table 8.1 presents fertility and mortality rates for 1960/70 by four categories of household income in Brazil. The total fertility rates shown in column 1 indicate the marked differences in the average number of births for women in different income strata. On average, poor women have a total of 7.6 children during their reproductive period, more than double the number born to women in the highest income group (3.3).

The estimates of average life expectancy presented in column 2 illustrate the substantial mortality differences between the rich and poor strata of the population. As we noted in chapter 4, people in high

Table 8.1. *Measures of fertility and mortality and rates of growth of the Brazilian population by four categories of household income in 1970 with projections to the year 2000*

Household income (in Cr$)	Total fertility rate (1)	Life expectancy ($e°$) (2)	Population total (3)	1970 % (4)	Population total (5)	2000 % (6)	Annual rate of increase (7)	Doubling time (in years) (8)
1–150*	7.6	49.9	29,113	34.2	82,025	41.2	3.2	21.7
151–300	6.7	54.5	24,057	28.3	63,346	31.8	3.0	23.1
301–500	5.4	57.6	13,098	15.4	28,078	14.1	2.4	28.9
500+	3.3	62.0	18,773	22.1	25,855	13.0	1.1	63.0
Total	6.0	53.4	85,041	100.0	199,304	100.1	2.7	25.7

Note: $US1.00 = Cr$4.6 in 1970

income households enjoy an average length of life of 62 years, twelve years longer than the expectation of life among the poorest sector of the population (49.9 years).

Projections to 2000

The total fertility rate (column 1) and the level of life expectancy (column 2) provide the basis for a forward projection of the population in each income class (column 5).[1] If fertility and mortality remain constant, and there is zero mobility from one income level to another, then the total population of Brazil would grow at an average rate of 2.7 per cent per year (column 7). This implies a doubling time of 25.7 years, as noted in column 8.[2]

Because the assumptions of the first projection are highly unrealistic, the results given in Table 8.1 are primarily of hypothetical interest. We know that fertility and mortality have declined in the past and will probably continue to do so in the future, and that upward and downward social mobility are an important aspect of the process of change in Brazil. Later in this chapter we will incorporate these factors into the analysis. But the findings based on fixed demographic parameters and zero mobility nonetheless provide important information. The rates of increase given in column 7 reflect the pace of population growth associated with the 1960/70 levels of fertility and mortality for each category of household income. Other things being equal, the exercise shows that the particular combination of births and deaths among the poor leads to a rate of population growth that is three times as fast as that for the rich. The rate of increase is 3.2 per cent per year for those earning Cr$1–150, a value that implies a doubling time of 21.7 years. In the highest income strata, the comparable rates are 1.1 per cent and 63.0 years, respectively.

The proportional distribution of the population by income is modified by different rates of demographic increase among population subgroups. We can see this shift by comparing the percentage of people in each category of household income in 1970 and 2000. In 1970, 34.2 per cent of the population was found in households with total monthly earnings of Cr$1–150 and 22.1 per cent in the highest income group (column 4). Projections to the end of the century indicate that the proportion in the lowest interval rises to 41.2 per cent while the percentage in the high income category drops to 13.0 per cent of the total population, a decline of 9.1 percentage points. Other things being equal, the effect of a high rate of natural increase among the low income groups is to change the socioeconomic composition of the Brazilian population by increasing the relative proportion of the poor.

Changes in the Gini coefficient between 1970 and 2000 given in the last row of Table 8.1 show the effect of differential rates of population growth on the concentration of income. The decline in the index from .4986 to .4885 indicates a more equal distribution by the end of the century. At first glance this appears paradoxical in light of the increase in the proportion of the population in the lower income categories. However, the Gini coefficient is a measure of relative inequality. As such, the index falls in 2000 because the population has become more homogeneous at a lower income level.

In order to obtain a more disaggregated picture of socioeconomic differentials, we apply the same procedures to smaller intervals of household income. Table 8.2 shows the results based on twelve categories of monthly household income. As expected, there is a much wider range in the levels of fertility and mortality. The total fertility rate (column 1) exceeds seven children in the lower four income categories and falls to two children in the highest income group. Similarly, average life expectancy at birth (column 2) is 46.7 years in the poorest stratum and reaches 63.9 years among the richest population.

A significant finding in Table 8.2 is the small increase in fertility that occurs when moving from the lowest income strata (7.4 children in Cr$1–50) to the next higher one (7.6 children in Cr$51–100). It is possible that malnutrition is the cause of slightly lower fertility among the most destitute stratum of women. Frisch (1975) has proposed that malnourishment affects the female reproductive system, hence the supply of children, by inducing later menarche and earlier menopause, and by lengthening postpartum amenorrhea and increasing the frequency of anovulatory cycles. Others have argued that nutritionally caused changes in age of menarche and portpartum amenorrhea only have a marginal impact on fertility (Bongaarts and Menken 1983). On balance, the data suggests that nutrition significantly affects fertility only under conditions of extreme famine. It is therefore likely that the observed increase in the total fertility rate at the low end of the income scale in Brazil may be due to other factors, such as the effects of unstable unions on the birth rate and the wide range of health problems and economic disruptions that afflict the poor.

Differences in birth and death rates are reflected in the substantial variation in the annual rates of population increase. The estimates shown in column 7 indicate that the poorest population would grow at 3.0 per cent per year doubling every 23.1 years. The rate increases

Table 8.2. *Measures of fertility and mortality and rates of growth of the Brazilian population by twelve categories of household income in 1970 with projections to the year 2000*

Household income (in Cr$)	Total fertility rate (1)	Life expectancy (e°) (2)	Population total (3)	1970 % (4)	Population total (5)	2000 % (6)	Annual rate of increase (7)	Doubling time (in years) (8)
1–50	7.4	46.7	4,316	5.1	11,248	5.7	3.0	23.1
51–100	7.6	49.6	13,541	15.9	38,079	19.2	3.2	21.7
101–150	7.5	51.6	11,256	13.2	32,155	16.2	3.2	21.7
151–200	7.3	54.0	12,207	14.4	34,168	17.2	3.1	22.4
201–250	6.1	54.4	5,369	6.3	13,047	6.6	2.8	24.8
251–300	5.9	56.1	6,481	7.6	15,690	7.9	2.8	24.8
301–400	5.7	56.8	7,478	8.8	16,516	8.3	2.5	27.7
401–500	4.9	58.8	5,621	6.6	11,339	5.7	2.2	31.5
501–1,000	4.0	60.9	11,311	13.3	17,318	8.7	1.4	49.5
1,001–1,500	2.7	64.0	3,323	3.9	4,157	2.1	0.7	99.0
1,501–2,000	2.5	65.5	1,653	1.9	2,020	1.0	0.7	99.0
2,000+	2.0	63.9	2,486	2.9	2,736	1.4	0.3	231.0
BRAZIL	6.0	53.4	85,042	99.9	198,473	100.0	2.7	25.7

slightly to 3.2 per cent in the next higher group reflecting the increase in fertility from 7.4 to 7.6 children. The rate of population growth then steadily declines as income rises. The growth rate for the highest income group is a low 0.3 per cent a year.[3] With a growth rate close to zero, the doubling time of the population in the Cr$2000+ range is 231 years, ten times the number of years required to double the size of the rapidly growing poor population.

Social mobility and changes in vital rates

Table 8.3 simulates the effect of changes in vital rates and upward inter-generational social mobility. Panel A presents the size and distribution of the population by income in 1970. This panel serves as a reference point in assessing the results of subsequent projections. Panel B, for example, shows the effect of projecting the population to 2,000 assuming constant fertility and mortality and no mobility between income levels. The results, noted earlier, show a greater proportion of the population in the poorest stratum and a decline in the relative number of people in the highest income category (rows 2 and 5).

Panel C simulates upward social mobility. The projection assumes that 20 per cent of the children born to parents in a given income category (i) move up to the next income level (i+1) as they enter the labor force (ages 15–24).[4] The model incorporates mobility at three points during the projection period: 1970, 1980 and 1990. Compared to panel B (constant vital rates and no mobility), upward mobility reduces the proportion of the population in the lowest income group by nearly seven percentage points (rows 5 and 9). The proportion in the inter-mediate income levels (columns 2 and 3) remain about the same since these strata both send and receive mobile individuals. The percentage in the highest income group rises by two percentage points by the year 2000. The expected positive effect of upward mobility on the distri-bution profile is indicated by a drop in the Gini coefficient from 0.4885 (panel B) to 0.4830 (panel C). For the population as a whole, per capita income increases by 10 per cent, from Cr$62.36 to Cr$68.80.

Panel D simulates the effects of a decline in fertility and mortality in the absence of mobility. The projection assumes that the fertility and mortality rates of income stratum (i) decline linearly to levels corre-sponding to i+1 by 1980 and to i+2 by 1990. In the case of the highest income group in 1970, panel D posits a total fertility rate of 2.2 (re-placement level) and a life expectancy of 65.5 years (the highest re-corded in Table 8.2) by 1985, remaining constant thereafter. The results

Table 8.3. *Population projections to the year 2000 with social mobility and changes in vital rates*

	Income Strata				
	1–150	151–300	301–500	500+	
	Per capita household income				
	18.55 (1)	41.97 (2)	74.99 (3)	237.61 (4)	Total
A. Population 1970*					
Total (1)	29,113	24,057	13,098	18,773	85,041
Percentage (2)	34.2	28.3	15.4	22.1	100.0
Gini coefficient (3)					0.4986
B. Population 2000: Constant fertility and mortality, no mobility*					
Total (4)	82,025	63,346	28,078	25,855	199,304
Percentage (5)	41.2	31.8	14.1	13.0	100.1
Rate of increase (6)	3.2	3.0	2.4	1.1	2.7
Gini coefficient (7)					0.4885
C. Population 2000: Constant fertility and mortality, upward mobility					
Total (8)	67,268	65,867	32,631	29,297	195,063
Percentage (9)	34.5	33.8	16.7	15.0	100.0
Rate of increase (10)	2.8	3.1	2.8	1.4	2.6
Gini coefficient (11)					0.4830
D. Population 2000: Declining fertility and mortality, no mobility					
Total (12)	76,524	52,572	21,323	22,494	172,913
Percentage (13)	44.3	30.4	12.3	13.0	100.0
Rate of increase (14)	3.0	2.5	1.6	0.6	2.3
Gini coefficient (15)					0.4984
E. Population 2000: Declining fertility and mortality, upward mobility					
Total (16)	64,220	53,513	24,950	27,228	169,911
Percentage (17)	37.8	31.5	14.7	16.0	100.0
Rate of increase (18)	2.6	2.5	1.9	1.1	2.2
Gini coefficient (19)					0.4966

Source: Table 8.1

of this exercise indicate that the simulated decline in fertility and mortality does not lead to greater income equality. The Gini coefficient in 2000 (0.4984) is nearly identical to the original distribution in 1970 (0.4986).

The index of income concentration, however, is a relative measure of inequality and does not reflect changes in the absolute number of poor people. Panel D, for example, indicates that a decline in fertility and mortality leads to a substantially smaller total population in 2000 (compared to panel B with constant vital rates) and to a smaller absolute number of people in the lowest income bracket. Compared to the impact of constant vital rates, the decline in fertility and mortality significantly reduces the incidence of poverty.

Panel E illustrates the joint effect of a change in vital rates and upward social mobility. Numerous comparisons are possible in Table 8.3. The most pertinent observation pertains to the original distribution of the population by income in 1970 (panel A). A comparison of the results in panel A to those in E shows a rise in the number of poor from 29,113,000 in 1970 to 64,220,000 in 2000 and an increase in the proportion of the population in the lowest income stratum (from 34.2 to 37.8 per cent). According to panel E, despite the simulated levels of upward intragenerational mobility and the assumed declines in fertility and mortality, the relatively high rates of natural increase among the poorer subgroups of the Brazilian population leads to an increase in the relative and absolute number of poor people by the year 2000.

Income distribution and population growth

On the basis of hypothetical assumptions regarding fertility, mortality and social mobility, the previous section used projection models to explore the impact of differential rates of population growth on the distribution of income and on the absolute size of the poor population. The analysis that follows reverses the direction of causal reasoning. Here we investigate the impact of the rise in real income between 1970 and 1980 on the actual differences in fertility and mortality and on the associated rates of natural increase corresponding to different income strata of the population. The issue is important given the recent changes in real income in Brazil reported in chapter 3 of this volume, and in light of the relationship between population growth and income distribution discussed above.

Average real income rose 48 per cent in Brazil between 1970 and 1980, with substantial gains recorded in all deciles of the economically active population (see Table 3.6). Since fertility and mortality rates respond to a change in the level of wellbeing, we can assume that both rates were affected by the increase in real income over the period. Indeed, the findings presented in chapters 4 and 7 document the decline in fertility and the increase in life expectancy in all strata of monthly household income. The question is, has the decline in births and deaths across population subgroups significantly changed the rates of population growth associated with each category of household income?

Determining the impact of the rise in income on subgroup rates of population growth is not straightforward. This is because a rise in income has two effects that pull in opposite directions. On the one hand, a decline in fertility – under conditions of constant mortality – implies a *decrease* in the rate of growth. On the other hand, reduced mortality – under conditions of constant fertility – leads to an *increase* in the rate of population growth. Since both fertility and mortality change at once, the income effect on demographic increase is ambiguous. For a given income group, the net outcome of a change in birth and death rates is contingent on the relative magnitude of the two opposing effects.

Anticipating the impact of real income change is further complicated by non-linear effects. The demographic response to a rise in income varies by social strata. The income–fertility relationship in 1970, for example, is inverse over much of the income range, except in the poorest group where a rise in standard of living may cause an increase in fertility. Subsequent increases in income are associated with reduced fertility, although there are diminishing returns to the income effect in the upper ranges. Thus, the relationship between income and fertility varies in magnitude (and in some cases may vary in direction) across income classes.

The association between income and mortality is also non-linear. Within the poorest stratum of the population small increases in real income permit significant gains in reducing the death rate. This is because the poor are subjected to a high risk of death from infectious and parasitic diseases that are relatively easy to eliminate. However, less tractable afflictions assume proportionately greater significance at higher income levels where mortality is much lower. Differences in the causes of death imply that the mortality of the poor is highly responsive to changes in income. The death rate of more affluent groups, on the other hand, is less sensitive to a comparable change in earnings. Hence, the income–life expectancy relationship defines a logistic curve that is steep in the lower income range and flattens out as income increases

Table 8.4. *Total fertility and life expectancy rates and intrinsic rate of natural increase per year by household income in 1970 and 1980*

Household income	1970			1980		
	Total fertility (1)	Life expect- ancy (2)	Intrinsic rate of increase (3)	Total fertility (4)	Life expect- ancy (5)	Intrinsic rate of increase (6)
1–50	7.4	46.7	3.10	7.0	53.8	3.52
51–100	7.6	48.6	3.40	6.1	51.0	2.91
101–150	7.5	51.6	3.47	6.0	56.0	3.13
151–200	7.3	54.0	3.39	5.8	58.2	3.01
201–250	6.1	54.4	2.82	5.7	58.2	2.95
251–300	5.9	56.1	2.76	5.2	58.8	2.71
301–400	5.7	56.8	2.60	4.5	61.6	2.23
401–500	4.9	58.8	2.18	3.8	62.0	1.65
501–1,000	4.0	60.9	1.62	3.3	64.5	1.23
1,001–1,500	2.7	64.0	0.43	2.9	68.5	0.93
1,501–2,000	2.5	65.5	0.97	2.5	66.3	0.31
2,000+	2.0	63.9	−0.55	2.4	70.1	0.26

(and as life expectancy reaches biological limits).

Total fertility rates and the number of years of life expected at birth for twelve categories of household income in 1970 and 1980 are presented in Table 8.4. These values are plotted in Figures 8.1 and 8.2. The graphs illustrate the non-linear relationship between income and fertility, and between income and life expectancy. Comparing the curves for 1970 and 1980 further suggests that, in addition to the expected change in the height of the fertility and life expectancy curves, the nature of the relationship between vital rates and household income may have changed somewhat over the decade. In the case of fertility (Figure 8.1), the increase observed at the low end of the income scale in 1970 disappeared in 1980. The slope of the income–fertility relationship also seems to have become somewhat flatter in the middle-income range in 1980 compared to the estimates a decade earlier. The same flattening tendency appears to be true for the income–life expectancy relationship. In 1970 the curve was somewhat steeper than in 1980, at least among lower income groups. Despite these rather subtle changes, the findings for both 1970 and 1980 confirm the general pattern of diminishing income effects on fertility and mortality in the upper income range.

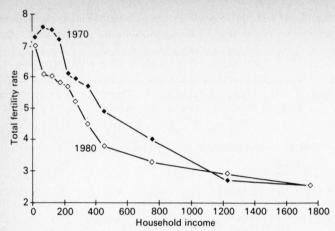

Figure 8.1 Total fertility rates by household income, 1970 and 1980

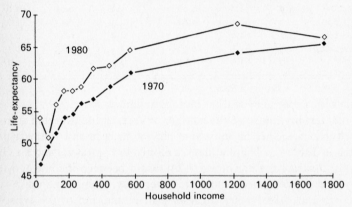

Figure 8.2 Life expectancy at birth by household income, 1970 and 1980

How have the changes in differential fertility and mortality between 1970 and 1980 affected the rates of population growth that correspond to each income group? A conclusive answer to this question is elusive. The major difficulty is that a population's actual growth rate is determined, not only by its level of fertility and mortality, but also by other factors, namely the age distribution of fertility, and the age distribution of the population to which the vital rates are applied. While the latter is not hard to obtain if the unit of analysis is a region or a country, the age distribution of a population is more problematic when the population of interest is defined according to a socioeconomic characteristic, such as household income. The problem is compounded when we adopt a disaggregated approach, focusing attention on twelve categories of household income as opposed to the four strata used earlier, and when both fertility and mortality rates are changing, as was the case during the 1970s.

An alternative to estimating the actual rate of population growth within each income stratum is to generate estimates of the "intrinsic rate of natural increase" and to compare the 1970 and the 1980 results. In 1907, Alfred J. Lotka demonstrated that, if a population is subject to a fixed schedule of age-specific fertility rates and a fixed schedule of age-specific mortality rates for an indefinite period of time, and if meanwhile there is no migration, ultimately the age composition of the population would assume a fixed distribution (stable age distribution). In 1925, Lotka further proved that a closed population with constant age-specific fertility and mortality schedules (stable population) would have a constant rate of growth. The intrinsic rate of natural increase (IRNI) thus refers to the rate of population growth "intrinsic" to a particular combination of fertility and mortality rates (by age).

The IRNI assumes that age-specific birth and death rates remain constant for an indefinite period – hardly a realistic assumption in Brazil. Yet, the IRNI value is nonetheless of interest here because we can use it to measure the rate of growth that is implied by the fertility and mortality levels specific to each category of household income, and to assess how the change in birth and death rates during the 1970s may have affected the income-specific rates of natural increase.

Table 8.4 (columns 3 and 6) presents intrinsic rates by strata of household income in 1970 and 1980. The values are plotted in Figure 8.3. The vital rates that correspond to households with earnings be-

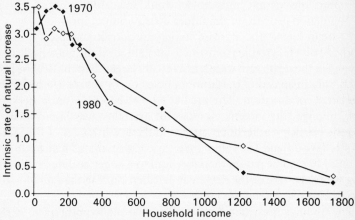

Figure 8.3 Intrinsic rates of natural increase by household income, 1970 and 1980

tween Cr$151–200 provide a useful example of the relevant relationships. Fertility estimates derived from the 1970 census indicate that women in households in this income range had an average of 7.3 children. Mortality estimates for the same group showed a life expectancy at birth of 54.0 years. Estimates derived from the 1980 census show a drop in the total fertility to 5.8 children, and an increase in life expectancy to 58.2 years.

Given that a decline in fertility tends to reduce the rate of growth, while lower mortality tends to increase it, what was the net effect of the observed changes in vital rates? The IRNI value indicates that, if the 1970 birth and death rates were to remain unchanged for an indefinite period of time, the result would be a population of a given age distribution, and with rate of natural increase of 3.39 per cent per year. If the 1980 fertility and mortality rates were to remain constant, the result would be a population with an annual rate of natural increase of 3.01 per cent. Comparing the IRNI estimates for 1970 (3.39 per cent) with those for 1980 (3.0), we conclude that the net effect of lower fertility and mortality for this particular category of household income (Cr$151–200) was to reduce the intrinsic rate of natural increase.

The pattern of change in vital rates across income strata during the decade has important implications for the relationship between population growth and the distribution of income, discussed in the first part of this chapter. It is possible, for example, that a change in the profile of income-specific fertility and mortality rates could lead to a rise in the rate of natural increase among the poor. Other things being equal, such a pattern of demographic shift, by increasing the number of children born into low-income households, would intensify the negative effects of population growth on the future distribution of income.

A rise in the natural increase among the poor is possible if mortality were to fall while fertility remained constant, or if the magnitude of the decline in the death rate were substantially larger than the decline in the birth rate. In an earlier publication, based on 1970 data, we anticipated the latter combination. The prediction was based on the observation that, in 1970, the income elasticity of mortality was higher than the income elasticity of fertility, at least in the lower ranges of the income profile (Wood and Carvalho 1982: 63). Other things being equal, an increase in income would therefore lead to a larger decline in mortality relative to the size of the decline in fertility, causing the rate of natural increase to rise among the poor.

The findings presented here confirm that the hypothesized increase in the rate of population growth occurred, at least in the poorest category of household income. Although fertility among women in the poorest households declined from 7.3 to 7.0 between 1970 and 1980, the drop in mortality was proportionately much larger. Hence, the tendency for the lower birth rate to reduce the rate of natural increase was more than offset by the decline in mortality, which tends to increase the rate of growth. The net effect of the two opposing tendencies was therefore a rise in the rate of demographic increase in the poorest households. This particular combination of demographic events did not characterize the entire lower income population, however. With only one exception (income range Cr$201–250), the fertility decline that took place over the decade (which was unexpectedly large) led to lower rates of natural increase among households earning less than Cr$1,000 per month.

The upper end of the income range showed a different pattern of change. Among rich households (Cr$1,501–2,000 and Cr$2,000+), the IRNI rose somewhat between 1970 and 1980 because of slight increases in the total fertility rate. However, the higher rate of increase among wealthy households is not likely to have much effect on the aggregate relationship between population growth and income distribution owing to the small proportion of the population in these income strata.

* * *

Studies of the relationship between population growth and income distribution typically relate aggregate rates of demographic increase to measures of income concentration across countries. Such an approach does not account for differences in the rate of natural increase among socioeconomic strata of the population. Although it is hardly surprising that the poor have higher birth rates than do the rich, this pattern does not necessarily imply a greater rate of growth given that the poor are also subject to higher mortality rates. It therefore becomes important to account for both the fertility and mortality rates that correspond to women in households with different levels of income in order to determine income-specific rates of population growth. The empirical results presented here empirically verify the commonly held assumption that the poor population in Brazil (despite its relatively higher mortality) grows at a substantially faster rate than does the population in the middle and the upper income range. The findings indicate that the doubling time that corresponds to the fertility and mortality rates of affluent households is about ten times greater than the doubling time of the most destitute population.

Population projections that simulate upward social mobility and a decline in vital rates do not appreciably alter the conclusion that the poor population grows at a more rapid pace than the rate of increase of the rich. The projections further indicate that the simulated decline in fertility and mortality, together with the assumed rates of social mobility, do not lead to greater income equality. The Gini coefficient in 2,000 (0.4984) is nearly identical to the original distribution in 1970 (0.4986). The findings emphasize the importance of turning attention from aggregate measures of population growth in favor of a disaggregated approach that accounts for the fertility and mortality patterns among different socioeconomic subgroups of the population.

Conclusions about the relationship between demographic increase and the distribution of income should not be confused with the impact of population growth on the degree of absolute poverty. Income distribution, measured by the Gini coefficient, is an index of relative inequality. Indices of absolute poverty, on the other hand, refer to the number of people below some defined income level. The structure of population growth by income strata in Brazil has different implications for measures of relative inequality compared to measures of absolute poverty. If the simulations that project the population to 2000 indicate that the Gini coefficient remains stable (leaving relative inequality more or less unchanged), the projections also show a substantial rise in the number of people in the lowest income stratum (indicating an increase in the magnitude of absolute poverty).

The analysis in the last section of this chapter addressed a different issue: How did the increase in real income between 1970 and 1980 affect subgroup rates of population growth? To answer the question we examined the income elasticities of fertility and mortality in 1970 and 1980. The findings for both years clearly show that birth and death rates are highly sensitive to changes in income in the lower income range, but that there were diminishing income effects on fertility and mortality in the upper income range. In order to identify the net effect of changes in births and deaths within each income group, we estimated intrinsic rates of natural increase that corresponded to the various combinations of total fertility and life expectancy rates. The results showed that the net effect of the fertility and mortality decline that took place in Brazil during the 1970s reduced the rate of natural increase in all but the lowest and the highest income strata.

9

Agrarian structure and the rural exodus

Only a few years ago, when the modernization perspective dominated the development literature, rural-to-urban migration was viewed as a positive aspect of structural change. W. Arthur Lewis's influential two-sector model was premised on the idea that the marginal productivity of labor in the countryside was zero. Economic growth meant the with-drawal of labor from agriculture and its incorporation into the urban industrial sector. For economists who stressed the benefits of labor transfer, the concern was how to *increase* the urbanward flow. Indeed, as Richard Jolly (cited in Todaro 1981: 231), director of the Institute of Development Studies at the University of Sussex noted, "one of the reasons given for trying to increase productivity in the agricultural sector was to release sufficient labor for urban industrialization. How irrelevant most of this concern looks today!"

In contrast to the earlier view, contemporary perspectives see rural out-migration in a very different light. Today, urbanward migration is no longer seen as a beneficent process necessary to solve the problems of growing urban labor demand but, instead, as a major factor con-tributing to urban surplus labor. The effect of internal migration, in Todaro's (1981: 231) view, is to exacerbate rural–urban structural im-balances in two ways. On the supply side, the rural exodus dispro-portionately increases the growth rate of urban job seekers relative to urban population growth. On the demand side, most urban job cre-ation is more difficult and more costly to achieve compared to rural employment creation as a consequence of the need for complementary resource inputs. "Together this rapid supply increase and lagging demand growth tend to convert a short-run problem of manpower im-balances into a long-run situation of chronic and rising urban surplus labor" (Todaro 1981: 231).

If there is redundant labor in the cities, what accounts for the massive and increasing volume of rural–urban migration in Brazil in recent decades? A narrow microeconomic perspective calls attention to the individual calculus involved in the decision to move, and concludes that people travel to metropolitan areas because the benefits of doing so outweigh the costs. Yet explanations of this kind, which prevail in the literature on population and development, leave much to be desired. A perspective that limits its analytical focus to individual rationality is at pains to account for the structural context that motivates the decision in the first place. Lest we remain at the level of micro observations, analyses of rural out-migration must necessarily delve into structural phenomena that determine the "push" factors in the countryside.

The explanation of rural-to-urban population movement put forth in this chapter stresses the importance of five aspects of Brazil's agrarian structure: the concentration of land ownership, the commercialization of agriculture, the mechanization of production and the impact of credit policies and land price inflation. A summary of two competing theoretical traditions introduces the discussion of the relationship between population growth, agrarian structure and rural out-migration.

Perspectives on urbanward migration

Explanations for rural–urban migration largely depend on the researcher's conceptualization of the migration process, and on the preferred unit of analysis for data collection and interpretation. In recent years the literature on this subject has become increasingly polarized around two competing schools of thought (Wood 1982).

The equilibrium model of migration

In the neoclassical economic framework, population movement is conceptualized as the geographic mobility of workers who are responding to imbalances in the spatial distribution of land, labor, capital and natural resources. The skewed geographic location of the factors of production determines the unequal returns to each factor. This influences the direction and the magnitude of migratory streams. Labor moves from places where capital is scarce and where labor is plentiful (hence remuneration to the workers is low) to areas where capital is abundant and where labor is scarce (hence remuneration is high). By conquering the "tyranny of space," and by redistributing human capital from places of low productivity to places of high productivity, migration is considered a "development fostering" process that corrects rural–

urban, interurban and interregional imbalances in factor returns (Spengler and Myers 1977: 11).

To achieve equilibrium in the distribution of the factors of production, and hence a more efficient allocation of a country's resources, workers must seek out those employment opportunities that give them the greatest return. In a formal sense the aggregate process of labor mobility can, therefore, be interpreted as a special case of the microeconomic theory of consumer choice (Shaw 1975: 54). In the broadest form, migration flows are assumed to be the cumulative result of individual decisions based on the rational evaluation of the benefits to be gained and the costs entailed in moving. The model can be extended to include variables such as the character and the extent of the information available, the utility significance of the costs and benefits to the individual (Rothenberg 1977: 186) and "lifetime income," defined as the present value of expected future income due to migration (Sjaastad 1962). The model has been modified to account for the highly segmented labor markets in urban areas of developing countries by including the probability of obtaining desirable employment in the modern sector of the economy (Harris and Todaro 1970).

By providing a formal theory of individual behavior, the microeconomic model highlights a common set of variables (e.g., costs, benefits, distance, wage differentials), and generates empirically testable hypotheses. Because of these advantages, the microeconomic framework has tended to dominate the migration literature. Still, the internal consistency of the approach is at the expense of a broader understanding of the structural factors that propel population movements.

The main problems with the neoclassical economic perspective are its ahistorical character, and a reductionist bias that precludes attention to the underlying structural causes of migration. The cost–benefit analysis conducted at the level of the individual migrant presupposes (and hence fails to explain) the unequal distribution of land, labor and capital. As a consequence, the microeconomic framework offers little insight into the macro-level conditions that compel the decision to move in the first place. To the extent that the etiology of migration is sought exclusively among individuals, the conclusions derived are necessarily restricted to the realm of secondary causes.

Under conditions of extreme deprivation, and in cases where extra-economic coercion is involved, the microeconomic model also lends an unwarranted veneer of free choice to the analysis of migration (Amin 1974). When a population strives to merely maintain subsistence requirements, a deterioration in rural conditions or the violent expulsion of peasants from their land (see chapter 10) leaves the individual with no real alternative but to migrate.

The assumed universal applicability of the neoclassical approach (e.g., Rothenberg 1977) also overlooks the fact that the existence of free labor is contingent on the historically specific relationship between migration and economic organization. Under a slave mode of production labor is immobile. The same is true of traditional forms of labor use that are based on permanent residence on the plantation, and that are solidified by patron–client relationships between the landowner and the worker and his family. It is only when arrangements such as these break down that there emerges a mobile labor pool that "spontaneously" transports itself to areas where labor is needed.

A structural model of push factors

In contrast to the microeconomic model of migration, the structural perspective assumes that explanations for population movement must first account for the factors that modify the organization of production. The approach seeks to make explicit the mechanisms by which social, economic and political forces directly and indirectly affect the demand for labor and the associated forms of labor recruitment and remuneration (Balan 1973; Portes 1978). Accordingly, migration is conceptualized as a class phenomenon where the unit of analysis is the stream as opposed to the atomistic approach that treats migration as the sum of individual decisions.

In his study of rural out-migration, Paul Singer (1973) draws a distinction between "factors of stagnation" and "factors of change." Stagnation produces excess population when demographic increase occurs under conditions where the availability of additional land is limited by the structure of land tenure, or when land is physically insufficient either in size or fertility to support a greater number of people. Factors of change account for surplus population where the introduction of capitalist social relations destroy sharecropping and tenant arrangements, where the work process is mechanized, or where changes in agricultural production, such as the switch from one crop to another, reduce the demand for labor. In short, stagnation refers to population increase against fixed resources. Factors of change refer to modifications in the structure of agricultural production that reduce the rural sector's capacity to sustain population.

Both stagnation and change result in out-migration. However, the underlying causes of population movement, and the economic implications of the two types of push factors, are quite different. Factors of change are an integral part of the industrialization of agriculture. This process is associated with the technification of production, an increase in productivity of labor and a rise in the demand for more highly skilled workers. Areas that experience this transformation lose population, yet the rise in productivity permits, at least in principal, an increase in wages and standard of living for the remaining labor force. In places where the factors of stagnation predominate, out-migration is more closely associated with the rate of demographic increase. The material conditions of those who remain in the rural area continue at the same level, or may actually deteriorate.

The relative importance of factors of stagnation and change is difficult to quantify, especially in areas where both phenomena occur simultaneously. Yet the merit of Singer's model is to call attention to regional differences in the way that population growth interacts with agrarian structure. The general characteristics of the major regions of Brazil suggest that net rural out-migration in the Northeast is associated with stagnation, while the push factors in the more developed Center-south are largely related to changes in the structure of agricultural production.

Agrarian structure and the rural out-migration

The concentration of land ownership

Despite substantial changes in the structure of agricultural production since the colonial period, a high concentration of land ownership remains one of the most significant aspects of Brazilian agrarian structure (see chapter 3). Table 9.1 gives an indication of the degree of land concentration in the country. In 1975, 52.1 per cent of all rural establishments were less than ten hectares in size. However, small farms occupied only 2.7 per cent of total land under cultivation. At the other end of the distribution, only 0.8 per cent of farms exceeded 1,000 in size, yet large agricultural establishments controlled nearly half of the land in rural areas.

A comparison of data for 1960 and 1975 shows that the proportion of small farms rose by 7.4 percentage points. For the most part, however, there are only minor changes over the fifteen year period. Gini coefficients for concentration in land distribution for the census years 1950, 1960 and 1970 hover around 0.84. Coefficients for different regions indicate that concentration is greater in the NORTH, NORTHEAST and

Table 9.1. *Distribution of rural properties by number of establishments and total area, 1960 and 1975 (percentage distribution)*

Size of properties (in hectares)	Number of establishments			Area		
	1960	1975	(1975)–(1960)	1960	1975	(1975)–(1960)
Less than 10	44.7	52.1	+7.4	2.4	2.7	−0.3
10–100	44.6	38.0	−6.6	19.0	18.6	−0.4
101–1,000	9.4	9.0	−0.4	34.4	35.8	+1.4
1,001–10,000	0.9	0.8	−0.1	28.6	27.8	−0.8
10,001–100,000	0.4	0.0	−0.4	15.6	15.1	−0.5
Total	100.0	99.9		100.0	100.0	

Source: FIBGE, Anuário Estatístico, 1976; FIBGE, Agriculture Census, 1975.

CENTRAL WEST and smallest in the SOUTH. This reflects the wide diversity in economic activities ranging from the small family farms of descendants of European immigrants in southern Brazil, to the giant ranches of Mato Grosso, to the traditional sugar estates in northeastern Brazil (Baer 1979: 215–16).

The distribution of landholdings by size of farm does not fully capture the degree of land concentration. Comparisons between regions that are characterized by different climates, soils, markets and level of technology can be misleading. When such variability is present plot size is not a comparable unit of measure since the sustenance capacity of a farm in one place may not be equal to that of a farm of the same size in another. With the objective of providing a standard unit of analysis, the Land Statute of 1964 established the concept of a "rural module" as the basis for official data collection and evaluation. A module is defined as the size of plot unique to a particular region that is required to absorb the year-round labor of the farmer family, and that is sufficiently large that it can, with the help of hired hands, permit the "social and economic progress of the domestic unit."

The module, which varies in size by region and type of production, is the basis for defining four types of landholdings. A plot smaller than one module is classified as a *minifúndio*. A holding 300 modules or larger is called a *latifúndio*. Farms in the intermediate range, from 1 to 300 modules, can be of two types according to their productivity: the "rural enterprise" (*empresa rural*) is a farm that is "rationally and economically exploited." Landholdings of 1 to 300 modules that remain uncultivated, or are poorly exploited, or are held for speculative purposes, are called *latifúndios por exploração*.

Because the concept of farm size is based on the area of land needed to provide remunerative employment to a typical farm family, the distribution of rural establishments according to this typology provides a more useful description of the structure of land tenure in Brazil. According to the INCRA cadastre of 1972, nearly three quarters of all farms (72 per cent) were classified as *minifúndios*. Whereas *minifúndios* occupied only 12.5 per cent of the total area, 72 per cent of the remaining land was uncultivated or held for speculation by large landholders (*latifúndios por exploração*). Rural enterprises, or large farms that are productively operated, constitute only 4.8 per cent of the total farm establishments and occupy less than 10 per cent of the occupied land (Graziano da Silva 1978).

Where the means of production are monopolized by a minority of *latifundistas* and the vast majority of rural inhabitants are relegated to plots of land smaller than the minimum necessary for subsistence, a high rate of demographic growth creates an imbalance between the availability of productive resources and the sustenance requirements of rural households. The economic stress caused by this deficit is a major factor contributing to the out-migration of surplus population. In the context of rapid demographic increase, the concentration of land ownership is thus a primary cause of the rural exodus.

The commercialization of agriculture

Although the commercialization of agriculture is hardly a new phenomenon in Brazil, commodity production has accelerated as mechanized technologies, urban-based communications systems and the market economy increasingly penetrate rural areas. The emphasis on export crops, first stimulated by the colonial regime, continues to be encouraged by the government as a source of tax revenues and urgently needed foreign exchange. Commercialized agriculture tends to use capital intensive methods of production whenever possible. In some areas of Brazil such as Paraná, coffee, which requires large inputs of labor, is being replaced by soybeans, a crop that uses far less labor per unit of land or value of product. The result is a decline in the demand for the services of agricultural workers and tenants.

For Brazil as a whole, the production of soybeans rose at an average annual rate of 29.8 per cent between 1967 and 1978. In contrast, the growth rate for rice (3.21 per cent per year) only slightly exceeded the increase in population. The averages for black beans and manioc were negative (−1.60 and −1.63 per cent, respectively) (Kohl 1981: 231). The decline in the production of such crops as black beans and manioc is an indication of the increasingly precarious economic viability of small farms. Analysts attribute the stagnant or declining production of traditional foodcrops to credit and subsidy policies that discriminated against small farmers in favor of large establishments that produce for export. This has had important repercussions in urban areas. The low supply of basic commodities was a major contributor to the rise in the cost of living in the 1970s (Kohl 1981: 237), a factor associated with the rise in infant mortality in São Paulo (chapter 5).

With the weakening of small-scale agriculture, large agro-industrial firms have assumed a dominant role in Brazil's rural sector (Sorj 1980). Linked to urban and international finance, processing and market networks, these enterprises enjoy a strong competitive advantage in the marketplace. The use of vertically integrated production and transport methods displaces small farmers as well as numerous petty suppliers and traders.

The commercialization of Brazilian agriculture, and the growing importance of new, highly mechanized export commodities, have had a regressive effect on income distribution. Between 1970 and 1980 measures of rural income concentration soared (Denslow and Tyler 1984). The Gini coefficient rose from 0.44 to 0.54; the Theil index, another commonly used indicator, nearly doubled, from 0.43 to 0.80. The income share of the bottom 40 per cent of the population fell from 15.6 per cent to 12.4 per cent, while the share of the top decile rose from 36 to 49 per cent. Denslow and Tyler (1984) partly attribute this increase in income inequality to the surge in the production of export crops such as cocoa and soybeans. The latter exercised an especially severe impact on the distribution of earnings in places where soybeans replaced the more labor-intensive crops, such as coffee in Paraná.

The social and political consequences of the increasing commercialization of agriculture are also significant. The wealth, status, and power hierarchies that differentiate the rural population are closely tied to the ownership and control of land. Within these strata there are informal solidarity networks based on kinship or neighborhood relationships that provide mutual assistance, sharing and protection. Crosscutting these horizontal networks are vertical relationships based on patron–client arrangements. Even though highly unequal, these relationships incorporate mutual obligations that protect clients and provide for their basic subsistence (Esman 1978: 4).

In Brazil and in many other parts of Latin America, rural social structure evolved to meet the needs of traditional agricultural production. In the colonial period, for example, labor requirements were more or less uniform throughout the agricultural cycle and labor was in short supply. Resident farm labor and personalized patron–client relationships between landowner and tenant became the norm. However, when the rhythm of work accelerates such that peaks in labor use get very steep and deep troughs appear in other seasons, there is no good reason to support workers full-time on the farm. Under these circumstances, wage-laborers are substituted for resident employees. There is little doubt that workers under the traditional system were exploited, but as they become proletarianized they are denied the benefits of the old system and must fend for themselves. Changes in the social relations of production, and the emergence of a highly variable market for rural labor erode both the horizontal and vertical solidarity structures, leaving the rural poor more vulnerable than before.

The mechanization of production

The mechanization of production has gone hand in hand with the increasing commercialization of agriculture. In terms of population movement, the most significant aspect of this trend is a reduced demand for labor and the tendency for mechanized farms to replace permanent employees and tenant farmers with temporary wage laborers. The data presented in Table 9.2 show the increasing technification of agricultural production in Brazil. The use of fertilizer rose nearly 300 per cent be-

Table 9.2. *Indicators of agricultural inputs*

	1960	1970	1975
A *Use of fertilizer* (kilograms per hectare)			
Brazil	11.5	27.8	44.6
NORTHEAST	—	5.6	—
SOUTHEAST	—	34.4	—
SOUTH	—	46.6	—
SÃO PAULO	—	72.8	—
B *Hectares cultivated per tractor*			
Brazil	430	218	137

Source: Baer 1979: 214.

Table 9.3. *Changes in agricultural production, São Paulo 1940–70,*
selected indicators

| | Year | | | | % Change |
	1940	1950	1960	1970	1940–70
A *Machinery*[a]					
1. Tractors	1.4	3.8	21.2	67.2	+4700
2. Plows	168.1	224.9	272.5	401.6	+ 139
B *Forms of labor*					
3. % permanent	54.6	34.3	24.4	19.3	
					− 56.8
4. % sharecroppers	(b)	15.5	7.5	4.3	
5. % temporary	7.4	10.1	23.1	19.9	+ 168.9
6. % family	37.9	40.1	44.9	56.5	+ 49.1
7. Total %	99.9	100.0	99.9	100.0	—
8. Total N[a]	1,995	1,514	1,869	1,547	− 22.5

Source: Lopes 1977.
[a] In thousands
[b] In 1940 sharecroppers were classified as permanent laborers.

tween 1960 and 1975, with the largest gains taking place in São Paulo
and the SOUTH region. The use of tractors also increased, as shown in
panel B.

In his study of Latin American agriculture, Ambercombie (1972)
noted that the impact of mechanization on labor absorption is conditioned by the size of farm. Using data from Colombia he found that
an average of around nineteen workers were displaced per tractor on
farms in the 50 to 200 hectare range. The substitution ratio steadily
declined with the increase in the number of hectares cultivated. Crop
type also influenced the relationship between mechanization and labor
displacement. For potatoes, the introduction of machinery reduced
labor requirements by only 6 to 19 per cent, compared to a 50 to 90 per
cent reduction for wheat.

Data for São Paulo reflect the impact of mechanization on the
demand for labor and on changes in the social relations of production in
the countryside. As shown in Table 9.3, there were only 1,400 tractors
in use in 1940. Thirty years later the number rose to 67,200, and the
number of plows more than doubled. These changes brought about significant modifications in the size and composition of the labor force.

The proportion of permanent employees and sharecroppers declined 56.8 per cent while the proportion of temporary workers rose 168.9 per cent. The overall number of people employed in the rural sector fell 22.5 per cent between 1940 and 1970 (Lopes 1977).

Aggregate indicators of agricultural production conceal significant variation among different types of farms. The emergence of large-scale agriculture was accompanied by an increase in the number of small farms and by a rise in the total area cultivated by establishments less than fifty hectares in size (Lopes 1977). This trend accounts for the 49.1 per cent increase in family labor in São Paulo's rural labor force (row 6, Table 9.3). However, the expansion of small, family-based farms did not offset the overall reduction in the demand for labor in the state's rural sector as a whole.

The transformation of Paulista agriculture was partly stimulated by government wage policy. The Statute of the Rural Worker in 1962, for example, extended minimum wage, paid vacations and holiday benefits to the rural sector. Despite such good intentions, the Statute provided farmers the incentive to replace permanent employees and tenant farmers with temporary workers (Gonzales and Bastos 1975). By raising the cost of labor relative to capital, the legislation also stimulated the use of machinery. However, as the data in Table 9.3 indicate, the reorganization of production was well underway much earlier. The proportion of permanent workers already suffered a decline from 34.3 per cent in 1950 to 24.4 per cent in 1960. Although this observation does not entirely discount the effect of the Statute, it does suggest that the impact of minimum wage legislation should not be overemphasized in explanations for the mechanization of production and the changes in rural social structure (Lopes 1977).

The proletarianization of the labor force has led to the emergence of a large contingent of landless laborers, known as *bóias-frias*, who live in urban areas, but who travel to work in the fields every day during the harvest. When employment declines in the off-season, workers re-enter the informal sector in the city (D'Incão e Mello 1976 5; Martinez-Alier 1975). The *bóias-frias* thus represent a new type of worker who is highly mobile between urban and rural labor markets. Although data on the number of *bóias-frias* are fragmentary, there is a general consensus that in southern Brazil this type of temporary employment is increasing at the expense of resident workers and various forms of tenant farming (Goodman and Redclift 1977).

Inflation and land values

Land is an especially attractive investment in a high-inflation economy. Using time-series on the sale prices of pastureland, Mahar (1979: 124) showed that the real value of rural property in Brazil increased at an annual rate of approximately 9 per cent between 1966 and 1975. This rate increased to around 25 per cent during the 1970–5 period. Land values in frontier areas, such as northern Mato Grosso, increased at a nominal rate averaging 65 to 70 per cent per year in the first half of the 1970s, or about 38 per cent annually in real terms.

Because rural land is an excellent hedge against inflation, corporate enterprises as well as individuals put their resources into land. Their willingness to buy at high prices further inflates the value of rural property, encouraging local money lenders to foreclose and indebted small holders to sell out. This produces greater concentration of land ownership, less efficient use of scarce land resources and converts small farmers to tenant and wage laborers (Esman 1978: 19).

Credit policy

Modern productive estates (as well as a substantial proportion of land speculators) often benefit from government support in the form of favorable tax breaks and credit terms. From 1960 to 1975 the real value of new agricultural loans increased more than sixfold. Most agricultural credit originated with the Banco do Brasil, although various measures have been used to induce private banks to extend credit to farmers. In the mid-1970s, when inflation exceeded 35 per cent, loans for agricultural inputs carried interest rates of only 7 per cent. The difference between the two rates implies a substantial transfer of income to the agricultural sector (Baer 1979: 218).

The policy of providing support to agriculture represents a significant departure from earlier development strategies. Throughout the 1950s the agricultural sector was subordinate to industrialization. The principal objective of public policy at that time was to exploit Brazil's exportable surpluses of coffee, cotton and cocoa to finance industrial development. This was accomplished through an elaborate system of exchange rates that discriminated against traditional exports while favoring the import of machinery and producer goods.

In the 1960s and 1970s credit became a major policy instrument to stimulate agriculture, although the amount of money available fluctuated, especially in recent years. As part of the government's recessionary policy, credit was curtailed in 1977. However, the negative impact of the cutback on the commercial trade balance, as well as the decline in the demand for modern inputs and machinery, forced a renewed expansion of credit in 1979. This decision was again reversed in 1980 when agricultural credit was blamed for the inflationary expansion of the money supply (Kohl 1981: 14). These fluctuations in available credit, and indeed the evolution of rural development policy in general, reflect the interdependence of the agricultural and industrial sectors in Brazil.

Agricultural credit support did not benefit everyone equally. The distribution of subsidies through negative interest credit has been quite lopsided because larger firms have usually been the greatest beneficiaries. Although national data are not available, the figures for São Paulo are indicative of the pattern that most likely prevails elsewhere. In 1974–7, 15.7 per cent of farms larger than 50 hectares captured 72.3 per cent of total production and investment credit. Small farmers (less than 20 hectares) received only 9.4 per cent even though they comprise 42.4 per cent of all farming establishments (Kohl 1981: 153).

Summary

Figure 9.1 portrays the principal mechanisms through which the commercialization and mechanization of agricultural production lead to rural out-migration. While the figure does not exhaust the causes of the rural exodus, it nonetheless provides a convenient summary of many of the key relationships referred to above. It is important to note, however, that "factors of change" do not invariably lead to the dissolution of the peasantry and to out-migration. On the contrary, increased use of seasonal wage labor by large commercial farms in many cases provides jobs to semi-proletarianized smallholders. Supplemental income derived from part-time wage work often contributes to the survival of peasant producers who might otherwise be forced to abandon their farms. That the industrialization of agricultural production has two contradictory tendencies – one to dissolve and the other to maintain the peasantry – has been the subject of considerable debate.

The fate of the peasantry

Economists in the neoclassical tradition, along with social scientists in the modernization school, endorse the assumption that the industrialization of agriculture leads to the destruction of "backward" forms of production. It is perhaps ironic that this conclusion bears a striking re-

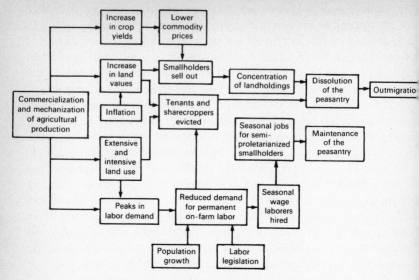

Figure 9.1 Mechanisms through which commercialization and mechanization of agricultural production lead to rural out-migration

semblance to the position of classical Marxists, although the latter hold different ideas as to the road one travels to reach that outcome, not to mention the social and political implications of the result. Although Marx's analysis of the peasantry was never fully explicit (Heynig 1982), the weight of his argument remains clear. In the world historical process, Marx considered peasants a residual category, based on obsolete forces of production and doomed to be replaced by scientific ones. Reviewing these issues, Goodman and Redclift (1982: 5) conclude that " ... both Marx and Engels believed that the fate of the peasant economy was sealed, as a consequence of increased indebtedness and technological change, and that pauperization was only the prelude to proletarianization." Earnest Feder (1978: 193), in an extreme expression of this idea, equates the peasants' fate to that of mammals with the coming of the ice age: "The latest species threatened with extinction," he argues, "(is the) peasant of the nonsocialist underdeveloped regions ... Further generations will know of their existence only through the vast peasant literature..."

Yet Marx's thinking, as many have noted (Goodman and Redclift 1982; Heynig 1982; Bartra 1975), was hardly as mechanical and dogmatic as Feder's prognosis would suggest. In his writings on the relationship between capitalism and the peasantry in England, France and Russia, Marx alludes to the importance of concrete situations in the respective countries, a view that prevents a simplistic application of his observations to peasants in other historical, social and geographical contexts. Lenin, for his part, put a fine point on the issue when he wrote that "the most varied combinations of the elements of one type or another of capitalist evolution are possible, and only incorrigible pedants would claim to be able to resolve the peculiar complicated questions which arise in these cases solely by citing one opinion or another of Marx referring to a different historical era" (cited in Heynig 1982: 123).

Students of rural Latin America have found it useful to examine the functional interrelationships between capitalist and non-capitalist modes as a way to explain the persistence, and in some cases the expansion, of peasant production To explore this interaction, reasearchers have amended the classic Marxist view of the *Communist Manifesto*. Rejecting the idea that noncapitalist economic formations are destroyed everywhere that capitalism expands, Laclau (1971) argued that various modes of production exist simultaneously within a given social formation, and that these modes are "articulated" with one another. The precise meaning of this term is much debated, and its usage has changed over time. The term, as Foster-Carter (1978: 214), put it, is not "simply a long-winded synonym for (say) 'link,' and thus a typically sociological instance of never using words of one syllable when five will do." Rather, it refers to capitalism's paradoxical relationship to other modes of production: on the one hand capitalism undermines noncapitalist formations; on the other, it serves to preserve, and in some instances even extend, the noncapitalist economy.

To say that modes of production are articulated implies, specifically, that a transfer of value takes place from one mode to another. One form of articulation is through seasonal labor migration. According to this argument, the preservation of semi-autonomous households, that are compelled to send some members into the market in search of part-time wage employment, facilitates the expansion of the capitalist enterprise by serving as a source of "cheap" labor during periods of peak labor demand. Labor power produced in the non-capitalist economy is cheap inasmuch as workers need only be remunerated at a level that covers the immediate sustenance of the worker while on the job. Easily laid off at the end of the season, the worker returns to the subsistence plot that is managed by other household members during the period of absence. In effect, the maintenance and the reproduction costs of labor power are shifted back to the subsistence economy until the next season, when the cycle is repeated (Long 1977: 101; Portes 1978a; Wolpe 1980).

The availability of low-cost labor to employers of wage workers thus stems from the patterns of seasonal labor migration that constitute the sustenance strategies formulated by households in the subsistence sector (Wood 1981). Since wages are low (relative to a thoroughly capitalized system), the articulation via migration increases the rate of profit and bolsters the economic viability of capitalist enterprises. Alternatively, the wages earned by seasonal workers serve to preserve semi-proletarianized households in rural areas. In this way, there exists a "functional dualism" between the capitalist and peasant forms of production in the countryside (de Janvry 1981).

Numerous aspects of social change in rural Brazil undoubtedly work against small farmers. At the same time, this does not preclude the fact that other processes, some of which form part of the very same structural transformations, may work to sustain and sometimes contribute to the expansion of the peasantry. Hence, the opposition between capitalist and small farmer agriculture is only one aspect of the interaction between the two forms of production. In addition to the direct and unequal competition between them, functional relationships also exist that link the capitalist and non-capitalist sectors. The two forms of production are neither separate nor autonomous, as the dualist model would have it, but are, instead, integral parts of the same system.

The magnitude of the rural exodus: 1960–70 and 1970–80

In the absence of direct information on individual mobility histories, the "residual" method is the most common indirect technique for estimating the volume of net migration. In a closed population, where there is no in- or out-migration, growth is solely due to the rate of natural increase – the excess of births over deaths. However, in an open population, demographic change is due to the joint effect of natural increase and net migration. The residual procedure uses a population projection to separate the two components of demographic change. Our application of the technique involves estimating net rural out-migration in Brazil and its ten geographic regions.

Using the age distribution of the population (at time 1), and an estimate of fertility (age specific rates) and mortality levels (a life table), we first project the population forward to the next census date. The projected size (at time 2) is an estimate of the number of rural inhabitants we would expect to find as a result of natural increase alone. The actual number of persons enumerated by the census at the end of the period (time 2), minus the projected value, provides a measure of net mi-

Table 9.4. *Estimates of net rural to urban migration, Brazil, 1960–70 and 1970–80 (in thousands)*

A 1960–70	
1. Rural population in 1960	38,767
2. Projected rural population in 1970	54,844
3. Actual population in 1970	41,054
4. Net migrants (3–2)	−13,790
5. Net migration rate	−35.6[a]
B 1970–80	
6. Rural population in 1970	41,054
7. Projected population in 1980	55,944
8. Actual population in 1980	38,616
9. Net migrants (8–7)	−17,328
10. Net migration rate	−42.2[b]

[a] Rate = (net migrants 1960–70/rural population 1960) × 100
[b] Rate = (net migrants 1970–80/rural population 1970) × 100
Source: Fundação IBGE, Demographic Census for 1960 and 1970: Advanced Tabulations for 1980.

gration. We infer the magnitude of population movement from the residual between the total change in population size during the intercensal period, and the change due to natural increase. A negative sign indicates a net loss of people; a positive sign a net gain.[1]

Table 9.4 illustrates the steps taken to estimate the volume of net rural to urban migration in Brazil. As shown in the first row of panel A, the total rural population in 1960 was 38,767,000. Using estimates of rural fertility and mortality for the decade, we projected the population forward ten years. Given the age structure of the population and the particular combination of rural birth and death rates, the expected number of rural inhabitants, assuming zero geographic movement, was 54,844,000 in 1970 (row 2). This value is considerably above the number of persons actually enumerated in the countryside by the 1970 census (41,054,000). The 1970 projected population, minus the actual number, is an estimate of net rural to urban movement. The figures in row 4 show that, between 1960 and 1970, rural areas of Brazil experienced a net loss of about 13,790,000 people.[2] This implies an annual departure of 1.3 million persons, if we assume that the rate was constant over the period. Row 5 indicates that the net migration rate in the 1960s was −35.6 per thousand rural inhabitants.

The results of the 1980 census show that the number of people in rural Brazil declined in absolute terms from 1970. The rural population was 41,054,000 in 1970. Ten years later it fell to 38,616,000, an average annual change of −0.6 per cent. This figure alone means that the magnitude of the rural exodus was so large in the 1970s that it drained off all of the demographic growth due to the natural increase of the population, *plus* additional people. This phenomenon is unprecedented in Brazil and reflects the enormity of the urbanward flow during the last decade.

Panel B shows the estimate of net rural-to-urban migration between 1970 and 1980. In rows 7 and 8 the projected population far exceeds the actual number of people enumerated in 1980, and there is an estimated net loss of 17,328,000 persons over the decade (row 9). Compared to the 1960s, the absolute number of net migrants grew by 3.5 million. This increase is reflected by the rate of net migration, which rose from −35.6 per thousand in 1960–70 to −42.2 per thousand in 1970–80.

The aggregate net rural to urban migration rate masks the considerable diversity among the ten regions of Brazil. To analyze these differences, we generated disaggregated estimates of net urbanward movement by applying the residual technique to each geographic area.[3] The findings presented in Table 9.5 show the importance of the Northeast as a major sending region. Between 1960 and 1970, rural areas of the Northern, Central and Southern Northeast experienced a net loss of −50.2, −32.5 and −31.0 per thousand population. Together the three contributed 32.9 per cent of the total net rural to urban movement in the 1960s. This is a finding consistent with common perceptions of population movement. The plight of subsistence farmers in this drought-ridden area, and their dramatic treks to urban centers in search of a livelihood, are popular themes in Brazilian literature and folklore.

Out-migration was also high in central and southern Brazil. Minas alone, with a net rate of −41.7, accounted for 20 per cent of all net rural out-migration during the decade. In rural São Paulo, the net rate reached −63.4 per thousand, the highest estimate for any region of the country. Column 2 shows that well over a third (37.5 per cent) of the total net urbanward movement originated in São Paulo and the South. Paraná is the only exception to this pattern. The net increase of the rural population there was associated with the movement of the agricultural frontier into the state, a process that began in the 1940s and continued well into the 1960s.

The estimates for 1970–80 shown in columns 3 and 4 reveal important changes in the last decade. Unlike the 1960s, when the net rate of population movement was negative, rural areas in Amazônia and the

Table 9.5. *Rates of net rural out-migration by region, 1960–70 and 1970–80*

REGION	1960–70		1970–80	
	Rate of net out-migration (1)	% of total net out-migration (2)	Rate of net out-migration (3)	% of total net out-migration (4)
Amazônia	−26.4	3.1	*	*
N. Northeast	−50.2	5.8	*	*
C. Northeast	−32.5	17.3	−33.2	15.9
S. Northeast	−31.0	9.8	−34.1	9.9
Minas	−41.7	20.1	−53.0	19.8
Rio	−55.6	5.3	−51.2	3.3
São Paulo	−63.4	22.0	−43.0	8.9
Paraná	*	*	−67.2	17.6
South	−48.4	15.5	−48.5	13.6
Central West	−8.0	1.1	−70.7	11.0
BRAZIL	−35.6	100.0	−42.2	100.0
No. of net migrants		13,790,000		17,328,000

* designates regions that experienced net in-migration

Northern Northeast experienced net gains. The reverse was true in Paraná: net migration was positive in the 1960s, but the estimate for the following decade showed a heavy population outflow from the rural area (−67.2 per thousand). Between 1970 and 1980 Paraná contributed a full 17.6 per cent of the total rural exodus. This dramatic turnaround reflects the closing of the agricultural frontier in Paraná, and the expulsion of population due to changes in agricultural production, especially the expansion of labor-saving soybean cultivation.

The Central West followed a similar pattern. In the 1960s rural out-migration was low: −8.0 per thousand. In the next ten year period the net rate was the highest in the country (−70.7 per thousand population). As in the case of Paraná, the sudden rise in urbanward migration marked the end of frontier expansion in the area. The growth of Brasília, along with other regional centers, such as Goiánia and Campo Grande, further contributed to the urbanization of the Central West (Merrick and Graham 1979: 131–2).

A full account of the causes of the rural exodus would specify the relative impact of push and pull factors, and would trace the various ways that modifications in agrarian structure influence the material conditions of the rural population, including those tendencies that permit people to stay in the countryside. This would necessarily be done at the microregion level given Brazil's geographic diversity and the regionally specific character of many of the changes underway. In the absence of a definitive study of this kind, we can only single out the major forces at work, and draw conclusions as to their net effect on migration. Within these limitations, the empirical results presented here show that Brazil's rural areas experienced a massive outflow of population in the 1960s, and that the magnitude of rural to urban migration grew larger between 1970 and 1980.

10

Colonization and frontier expansion in Amazônia

In the 1970s, population movement became a major policy concern in Brazil. Rural to urban migration and the heavy interregional flow of people from the Northeast into cities in the Center-south increasingly strained the capacity of metropolitan areas to absorb population. The city of São Paulo, which already held over 10 million residents in 1970, continued to grow at an alarming rate, as did Rio de Janeiro and Belo Horizonte. To counter the increasing size and density of the urban population in industrialized regions, the government launched a plan to redirect the flow of migrants away from the south and into the sparsely populated Amazon. The Transamazon Highway and a public colonization project were cornerstones of the ambitious development scheme that began with the National Integration Plan in 1970.

In view of the vast expanse of relatively uninhabited territory in the tropical lowlands of northern Brazil, the move to occupy Amazônia presented a seemingly plausible solution to the maldistribution of population. For the military regime, the plan was also politically compelling. The colonization of new lands addressed the conditions of the rural poor yet sidestepped the issue of land redistribution in the old established regions of the country. Moreover, by portraying colonization as a geopolitical necessity that would protect Brazil's vulnerable interior from foreign encroachment, the regime identified itself with a longstanding nationalist theme.

Aside from what may be politically expedient, is the opening of Amazônia a realistic solution to population pressure and rural poverty? To answer this question we first review the unique history of population and development in the Amazon region. We then describe the colonization project and outline the reasons why the settlement scheme was declared a failure by the mid-1970s. The subsequent analysis of the shift in development priorities away from small farmer colonization and in favor of large-scale capitalist ventures helps explain the growing incidence of violent social conflict in the area. In the final section of this chapter we estimate the volume of net migration to the region between 1970 and 1980. The results, along with our sociopolitical analysis, raise serious doubts as to the Amazon's capacity to absorb Brazil's surplus rural population.

Population and development policy in the Amazon

The Amazon has been the object of proposed colonization since colonial times. Under the Papal demarcation of Spanish and Portuguese possessions in the New World in 1494, Portugal would have had almost none of the Amazon region. But following Cabral's discovery of Brazil in 1500, explorers, traders, settlers and missionaries steadily moved westward to occupy the heartland of South America. The stipulations of the Treaty of Tordesillas notwithstanding, Brazil achieved *de facto* control of strategic spots through a fragile yet effective occupation of the land. Following the principle that "possession is nine-tenths of the law," Brazil took the lion's share of the southern continent.

The Portuguese westward expansion took place despite the fact that Spaniards were the first to explore the length of the Amazon. In 1510, Vicente Yañez Pinzón, who mistakenly thought he had reached the Ganges, sailed fifty miles up the Amazon River to a place he called Mar Dulce, which he claimed for Spain. The most daring adventure was the downstream trip by Franciso de Orellana who joined Pizarro in his expedition from Quito in search of the fabled Land of Cinnamon, reputedly located east of the Andes. After seven months of travel, Pizarro's band arrived at the Coca River, sending Orellana, his second in command, downstream for food. Orellana never returned. Instead, he and his crew continued downriver and reached the mouth of the Amazon in 1541. The chronicles of this expedition were recorded by Chaplain Gaspar de Carvajal. He wrote of Indian tribes where women fought alongside men and this became the source of the legend of the Amazons and the origin of the great river's name.

The rubber boom

Control over the sparsely populated Amazon region has been a long-standing government concern. In the nineteenth century, the rubber boom provoked a dispute with Bolivia over its rubber-rich territory of Acre, a prized possession covering an area of 73,000 square miles in the westernmost Amazon. The demand for natural latex circa 1890 attracted people to the far reaches of the Amazon. The population that numbered 300,000 in 1892 increased threefold by 1906, as migrants from the drought-stricken Northeast flowed into the region in search of "white gold." By the turn of the century, nearly 100,000 Brazilian rubber tappers had swarmed into Acre, and Bolivia threatened war. Armed conflict was averted by the Treaty of Petropolis in 1903. The agreement ceded Acre to Brazil in exchange for the construction of the Madeira–Mamore railway that would provide landlocked Bolivia with a transportation outlet to the world market.

The dispersed nature of natural rubber trees and the lack of a stable labor force in the Amazon proved to be fatal disadvantages in the increasingly competitive struggle for the world rubber market. Using rubber seeds pirated from Brazil by the British botanist, Sir Henry Wickham, growers in the Orient established highly efficient rubber plantations spelling an end to Brazil's commanding market position. During the peak years of the boom (1910–12) Brazilian exports accounted for around 88 per cent of the world's supply. By 1919, Brazil's share dropped to less than 10 per cent. Workers who had ventured into the region either left for other parts of Brazil or reverted to subsistence agriculture and fishing to survive.

After the rubber boom, the Amazonian economy entered a period of stagnation interrupted only by an occasional rise in the price of rubber. At one point the Ford Motor Company tried to establish plantations on the Oriental model. But South American leaf blight repeatedly attacked trees that were artificially planted in close proximity, and the plantation was abandoned. The United States' entry into World War II temporarily resuscitated the rubber trade through the "Washington Accords," of 1942, whereby Brazil agreed to cooperate with the Allied forces by supplying strategic raw materials, including latex. However, at the end of the war, Asian rubber re-entered the world market and the Amazon's economy once again slipped into decline.

The rise and fall of the rubber trade reflects Amazônia's traditional economic dependence on the extraction of forest products as a source of income and employment. This factor accounts for the geographic dispersion of the riverine communities in the region and for the ebb and flow of population over the years.

Contemporary initiatives

In recent decades the federal government has adopted a succession of policies to stimulate the Amazonian economy. In 1946 the Brazilian Constitutional Convention approved article 199. It earmarked 3 per cent of all federal revenues for the development of the region. Administered by the Superintendency for the Economic Valorization of Amazônia (SPVEA), these resources were largely spent on improvements in infrastructure. These included energy, port facilities and water supply systems in sixteen "growth poles" selected as priority areas (see Cardoso and Müller 1977: 109–11).

In 1966 SPVEA was replaced by the Superintendency for the Development of the Amazon (SUDAM). Although national funds allocated to SUDAM were cut from 3 to 2 per cent of the federal budget, the newly created institution adopted far-reaching fiscal and tax incentive programs. The purpose of the new policies was to mobilize entrepreneurs in other parts of Brazil to reinvest taxable incomes in the Amazon. Companies established in the region before December 1974, and considered to be of regional economic interest to SUDAM, would be exempt from taxes for a period of ten years. Funds were also made available through the Bank of the Amazon for loans or as equity for approved projects. Originally, the investor had to put up one dollar for every two received through the fiscal incentive system, but the equity requirement eventually dropped to 25 per cent of the total cost of the investment (Katzman 1976; Mahar 1979). In addition, a Free Trade Zone was established in Manaus in 1967 in order to provide cheaper commodites to residents of the area and to stimulate commercial growth.

The Brazilian government took a more aggressive and more direct approach in 1970. This decision was to alter the character of state involvement in the planning and execution of development projects in the region. The catalyst for this new attitude was a devastating drought that struck the Northeast in the spring of that year. The new President, General Médici, visited the stricken area and was reported to have been deeply moved by the sight of thousands of famished refugees seeking work and food along the roadside. Ten days later Médici announced the Program for National Integration (PIN) that called for the construction of the Transamazon and Cuiabá–Santarém Highways, and declared a commitment to finance and administer the colonization of new lands made accessible by the roads. The Transamazon, Médici told the Brazilian press, was intended to connect "men without land in the northeast, to a land without men in the Amazon."

The colonization project

The colonization program was impressive in scope and design, at least on paper. According to the plan, a 100 kilometer strip of land on either side of the Transamazon would pass into the public domain and be distributed for settlement in two forms. The first 10 kilometers were set aside for small farmers who would receive plots of 100 hectares (about 250 acres) for agricultural purposes. The remaining 90 kilometers would be sold in national auctions to investors interested in raising cattle. Additional areas back from the road were reserved for Indians.

A series of administrative and residential centers, located at varying intervals along the road, were part of the organization scheme. The basic unit of the modular plan was the *agrovila*, a residential area of fifty to sixty families that included an administrative center, soccer field, elementary school, health post and a small commercial establishment. At the center of twenty *agrovilas* was the *agrópolis*, the second level of organization that housed a cooperative, a secondary and elementary school, a bank and post office. The largest unit was the *rurópolis*, scheduled at 140 kilometer intervals. The *rurópolis* was to be a service center, the site of an airport, hospital and technical center and would house support industries such as plants to process cotton, rice and sugar.

According to the original plan, incoming colonists would be provided with a medical examination, a monthly wage for six months to tide them over, a modest house, a mutually acceptable 100 hectare lot, guaranteed prices for their agricultural production and education for their children. A battery of government agencies were charged with delivering these services. The responsibility for administering the colonization project fell to the newly created Brazilian Institute for Colonization and Agrarian Reform (INCRA). INCRA provided lots, constructed houses and furnished education and health care until the appropriate ministries were able to take over these tasks. Technical assistance in agricultural matters was left to ACAR (Associação de Crédito e Assistência Rural). The Bank of Brazil was to provide credit at low interest rates, while CIBRAZEM (Companhia Brasileira de Armazenamento) would buy rice at the established price (set by the CFP, Commissão de Financiamento de Produção) and store the produce. CIBRAZEM operated together with a food distribution agency called COBAL (Companhia Brasileira de Alimentos) that was to provide food to colonists at subsidized rates. SESP (Serviço Especial de Saúde Pública) and SUCAM (Superintendência do Controle da Malária)

were responsible for operating mobile health care units and for controlling malaria. To finance these activities, 30 per cent of all fiscal incentives were to be transferred to the National Integration Program for the
period 1971–4.

The goal was to settle 100,000 families between 1971 and 1974, providing sufficient support for the colonists to develop into a "rural
middle class," rather than fall into subsistence agriculture (Sanders
1973a: 7). However, by 1974 INCRA succeeded in settling only a frac-
tion of this target and the support for the colonists fell far short of the
original plan. *Agrópolis* and *rurópolis* centers were never built and
even the smaller *agrovilas* proved unworkable for those farmers whose
lots were distant from the residential centers. By 1976, a large proportion of colonists had moved their houses to their lot sites in order to
avoid long separations from their families and prolonged travel time
back and forth to their land. While early colonists received a six-month
wage and a house, later colonists did not, and educational and medical
facilities in all projects remained pitifully inadequate.

There were serious administrative failures in the support of agricultural production. The colonization project in Marabá had a low output
of basic foodcrops in its first years. This was largely due to inadequate
administration by key support institutions and to poor guidance from
technical advisors, especially in the selection of seed crops. By 1976,
many of these production difficulties were resolved and rice production
soared. But then colonists faced serious problems marketing their produce because the bumper crop created bottlenecks in storage and transportation. The queue to sell rice to CIBRAZEM (and thereby benefit
from the price support policy) sometimes entailed more than a month's
wait. As a result of the delay, many farmers were forced to sell their
produce at much lower prices to private mills (Wood and Schmink
1979).

Colonists had to contend with a host of other problems as well.
Engineers demarcated agricultural plots using a rigid grid-square
method that failed to account for hills, access to water and other critical
variations such as soil quality (Moran 1981; Smith 1981). Credit was
available through the Banco do Brasil at a subsidized interest rate of 7
per cent, yet the cost of obtaining it was high. A study of Altamira
showed that a colonist could spend anywhere from 17 to 20 man-days
formulating a credit plan, having it approved and traveling back and
forth to collect the six payments and to repay the loan. In the end, the
process cost about half of the amount borrowed in the first place
(Moran 1981). Land erosion, malaria and other health problems were

additional constraints (Smith 1981). Finally, it is important to note that INCRA, the key support institution, was itself in a subordinate position within the state bureaucracy. Located in the relatively weak Ministry of Agriculture, the agency was vulnerable to the vagaries of bureaucratic in-fighting which often undercut its ability to fulfill its mandate on the frontier (Bunker 1979). After 1974, budget cuts reduced government support to minimum operating expenditures, and just a few years after its inception, the colonization project was declared a costly failure.

Blaming the victim and the shift in development priorities

In the early 1970s, as the Transamazon pushed westward and the government embarked on the colonization scheme described above, pressures began to build for a change in development priorities. In 1973, a meeting of businessmen from the Center-south foreshadowed a new attitude that would come to dominate the policy agenda. On that occasion the Minister of Planning claimed that the "necessity to avoid a predatory occupation, with a consequent process of deforestation, and to promote the maintenance of ecological equilibrium, leads us to invite large enterprises to assume the task of developing the region."

In 1976, INCRA increased the maximum size of land purchases to 500,000 hectares and encouraged a model of "selective" colonization that was to be carried out by private firms. If the public colonization scheme failed because it was expensive and catered to poor migrants who lacked the required skills, the alternative promised greater success by shifting the cost (and the profit) to private investment projects that would recruit only those colonists with resources to buy into the schemes. By the end of the decade twenty-five projects of this type had been authorized in northern Mato Grosso and southern Pará.

A new regional development program was launched in 1974, called POLAMAZÔNIA. As the acronym implies, the objective was to create growth poles by redirecting public and private investment into areas with economic potential. Later the same year, the president of INCRA, Laurenço Tavares da Silva, signalled his acceptance of the new emphasis, declaring that INCRA would begin a process of occupying the Amazon with the participation of "large enterprises" (Cardoso and Müller 1977: 181 fn). By 1975, this perspective was further elaborated in the Second Development Plan for the Amazon (II Plano de Desenvolvimento da Amazônia, 1975–9, or II PDA). According to this document, the "indiscriminate migration" of poorly educated groups, without capital to invest and using rudimentary technology, only exacerbated problems that already beset the region. From an emphasis on the absorption of excess population in other regions of Brazil, development strategy thus came to favor the expansion of large-scale capitalist ventures.

We can trace the origins of this reversal in development priorities to a number of factors, including the results of the colonization effort itself. At the outset, it is important to recall that incentives to private capital antedated the highly publicized settlement scheme. Moreover, when the colonization program was announced in 1970, there was hardly a consensus regarding the value of the initiative. Because no prior analysis indicated that there was a critical need for the costly Transamazon Highway, conservatives attacked the PIN as a backward step in planning competence. The political left considerd colonization a poor substitute for the real need – full-scale agrarian reform. Politicians in the Northeast greeted the proposal with a noticeable lack of enthusiasm, mainly because it diverted resources to other regions. Within Amazônia, SUDAM's opposition was also intense. The sudden emphasis on colonization challenged SUDAM's leading role in the Amazon development programs and threatened private sector interests benefitted by the fiscal incentive programs administered by the superintendency (Bunker 1984: 1050). Other commentators, wary of the emphasis on mass migration, held that, unless accompanied by enough capital and technological support, Brazil would find itself confronting an Amazon separatist movement of frustrated colonists (Rosenbaum and Tyler 1972: 431).

Against this background, several events were decisive. The completion of the Transamazon suddenly opened vast new areas. This attracted two groups that competed for access to land. Migrants from the NORTHEAST and Central-West, responding to the publicity surrounding the colonization scheme, arrived in the area in numbers that far exceeded INCRA's capacity to absorb in the planned communities. With few other alternatives, the spontaneous migrants staked out whatever land was accessible, laboring under the mistaken assumption that arable land not being cultivated was there for the taking.

Squatters soon came into conflict with a different type of newcomer. Once the Transamazon was completed, it became apparent that enormous profits could be made, particularly in land speculation and livestock. In response to these investment opportunities, industrialists in southern Brazil began to acquire huge tracts of land. Capitalist and peasant interests collided because the property purchased by private entrepreneurs was often already occupied by small farmers (Schmink 1982).

The heavy influx of population, and the front-page publicity given to the violent confrontations between ranchers and squatters, served to undermine the rationale for the INCRA program. By enticing the landless poor to move to Amazônia, the colonization project became linked to the disorderly expansion of the frontier. As the confusion escalated, business interests waged a successful campaign in support of the view that a more "rational" and less "predatory" process of occupation could be achieved by backing the private sector. A key actor in this effort was the São Paulo-based Association of Amazonian Entrepreneurs, whose lobbying efforts within the Congress and the planning bureaucracies played an important role in promoting cattle and later the private colonization of the Amazon (Pompermayer 1979).

In the meantime the colonization project came under increasing criticism for being expensive and for failing to live up to its stated objectives (Moran 1981; Smith 1981). In the tradition of "blaming the victim," the colonists themselves were faulted for their presumed lack of managerial skill and technological sophistication even though many of the problems were hardly of their own making (Wood and Schmink 1979). Indeed there is a cruel irony in the fact that, by the time many of the initial hardships were overcome and agricultural production rose, the fate of the colonization program was firmly sealed.

Land scarcity, violence and the state

Whatever the difficulties associated with the colonization scheme the fact remains that the colonist's claim to his land is reasonably secure. Not all farmers have definite title to the lot they work but, as members of a settlement area, they are afforded a degree of protection from direct appropriation of their land. The much larger contingent of spontaneous migrants to the area have no such protection. Those who attempt to stake out a piece of land beyond the limits of the government-sponsored project are highly vulnerable to speculators, cattle ranchers and others who compete for land on the frontier. With no guarantee that he will be able to hang on to what little land he may have cleared the small farmer migrant is often relegated to a plot too small to meet subsistence requirements.

The expansion and consolidation of the agricultural frontier transforms the character of the relationship between peasant farmers and other social groups. Researchers have attempted to identify the stages by which a region is settled and then incorporated into the national economy. Katzman (1976) refers to change from a "subsistence" to a "market-oriented" frontier. Similarly, Martins (1975) speaks of the "expansion" and "pioneer" fronts, while Foweraker (1981: chapter 2), adding a third category, identifies the "non-capitalist," the "pre-capitalist" and the "capitalist" stages. In an extension of these frameworks, Sawyer (1984) calls attention to the importance of "speculative fronts" where huge unused tracts of land are held by investors seeking a hedge against inflation.

Each of the proposed typologies stress somewhat different factors, yet all of them share essential elements. In the initial stage, the frontier is isolated from the national system of economic production and distribution. Traditional extractive activities exist, but there is no market for land or for labor. Peasant migrants (*posseiros*) informally appropriate unclaimed property for the production of subsistence crops plus a small marketable surplus. Labor exchange, clientage, debt relations and forced labor are common forms of labor control. The subsequent stage (or stages, depending on the scheme adopted), features the in-migration of small farmer migrants, the beginnings of commercial agriculture and the first indications of a market in land and labor. This is followed by the consolidation of a capitalist market for wage labor, the emergence of private property, the concentration of landholdings in the hands of large companies and a decline in the importance of the small farmer. Roads permit access to the national economy and the population grows rapidly. Although the petty commodity sector persists (and may even expand), capitalist social relations of production dominate the regional economy.

Intense social conflict accompanies this reorganization of production and accumulation. The penetration of capitalist production implies the private appropriation of land and the creation of a wage labor force. Small farmers in the non-capitalist sector resist the imposition of these conditions and battle to retain control of the land they have cleared. Disputed claims are resolved through violence or face-to-face negotiation. In other instances the state directly intervenes through bureaucratic or legal institutions.

The escalation of land conflicts in Amazônia forced the Brazilian government to act. Following the successful elimination of a leftist guerilla group in the early 1970s, the army battalion in southern Pará found itself intermittently involved in *ad hoc* interventions in cases of labor and land conflict. In 1977, INCRA formed a special coordinating body for the Araguaia–Tocantins river basins in eastern Amazônia. When this institution proved ineffective, it was replaced in 1980 by GETAT (Executive Group of Araguaia–Tocantins Land), a much more powerful agency that answered directly to the president and to the National Security Council (Schmink 1982).

Armed with the power to cut through red tape, GETAT's primary objective was to defuse tension by resolving the most persistent and threatening cases of land conflict. The agency relied on streamlined bureaucratic authority to accomplish this via a sort of "crisis colonization" program that provided titled land to migrants involved in those areas where land disputes threatened to erupt into a major conflagration. The government has explicitly adopted these methods as a way to weaken its opponents. However, this "administrative" approach represents more of a "mopping up" operation than true solution for the plight of *posseiros* in the region (Schmink 1982: 353).

Events now underway in the Brazilian Amazon have important implications for the frontier's capacity to absorb population. Fiscal incentives fostered land speculation and the expansion of land-extensive, labor-saving economic activities. The needs of the small farmer, once the focus of the public colonization effort, have been de-emphasized. Only in the Northwest Pole Project in the state of Rondônia has semi-directed settlement of migrants continued on a significant scale. Beyond the boundaries of the official settlement area, conditions do not favor the emergence of a stable small farmer sector. Powerful ranchers and other investors with well-placed connections, and aided by federal tax incentives, turn up with "legal" rights to property. The *posseiro* is systematically, often ruthlessly pushed aside to make way for pasture land. The dispossessed join the growing ranks of an itinerant rural proletariat or move farther into the bush only to have the same experience when the frontier catches up to them. Many take up residence in expanding marginal neighbourhoods of frontier towns where they enter the informal sector of the urban labor market. Ironically, the result is a process of land concentration and urbanization that duplicates if not surpasses the very situation in the rest of Brazil that the occupation of Amazônia was intended to resolve.

The volume of migration to the Amazon frontier

The emerging patterns of labor absorption and land use on the frontier raise serious doubts about the capacity of newly settled areas to absorb population. In light of the economic and political importance of these issues, it is important to measure the volume of migration to the Amazon frontier and to assess the relative significance of the estimates. We accomplish this by placing the colonization project and measures of the spontaneous occupation of northern Brazil into the broader context of the overall rural to urban population movement presented in chapter 9.

The colonization projects

The declared intention of the National Integration Plan was to settle 100,000 families in three colonization projects along the Transamazon. However, by 1977 INCRA had succeeded in distributing lots to only 7,839 families in Marabá, Altamira and Itaituba. If we include all federal colonization projects in the North region, the total reached 24,242 families by the end of the 1970s (Sawyer 1984).

In chapter 9 our estimates of rural to urban migration indicated that the total number of net migrants was approximately 13,790,000 between 1960 and 1970, rising to 17,328,000 in the following decade. Here we divide these figures by the average household size in rural Brazil (5.2 people) to yield a rough estimate of the number of households involved in the net migration flow: 2,651,923 in 1960–70 and 3,332,230 in 1970–80. Using these figures it appears that, even if the PIN had succeeded in settling its original goal of 100,000 families, the program would have absorbed only 3.8 per cent of the rural to urban flow in the 1960s or 3.0 per cent in the 1970s. The actual number of families incorporated in the colonization scheme by 1977 gives a more realistic assessment of the project. The 7,839 families settled represent only 0.2 per cent of the total net rural exodus between 1970 and 1980. The total number officially settled in the North region was 0.7 per cent of net rural to urban movement in Brazil during the 1970s.

Total net migration to Amazônia

The colonization projects are only one aspect of Amazônia's potential for labor absorption. In addition to those families who participated in the government-sponsored programs, many more migrated to the North region in search of land. Since the number of families in the colonization projects was relatively small, the volume of people involved in the unplanned settlement process during the 1970s accounted for the bulk of the migration flow to Amazônia.

We estimate the number of migrants who established lots outside of

Table 10.1. *Net migration in Amazônia and Central West by state and territory, 1970–80*

State/territory	Population 1970 (1)	Projected population 1980 (2)	Actual population 1980 (3)	Net migrants (3)–(2) (4)	Net migration rate (5)
A *Amazônia*					
Acre, Amapá,					
Roraima,					
Rondônia	481,607	693,312	1,049,202	+355,890	+203.5
Amazonas	955,253	1,399,715	1,432,066	+32,351	+3.4
Pará	2,167,018	3,033,674	3,411,868	+378,194	+17.5
Subtotal	3,603,878	5,126,701	5,893,136	+766,435	+21.3
B *Central West*					
Mato Grosso	1,597,090	2,093,566	2,511,994	+418,428	+26.2
Goiás	2,938,677	4,000,620	3,865,482	−135,138	−4.6
Subtotal	4,535,767	6,094,186	6,377,476	+283,290	+6.2
C *Amazônia and Central West*					
Total	8,139,645	11,220,887	12,270,612	+1,049,725	+12.9

the official colonization projects or who moved to urban areas in the region by applying the residual method described in chapter 9. In this case the population figures for 1970 are projected forward ten years using the fertility and mortality rates that correspond to the total population of each state or territory of Amazônia. The projected value represents the number of people expected at the end of the decade if no migration occurred. To obtain an estimate of the volume of net migration, we subtract the projected from the actual number of persons enumerated in the 1980 census.

Table 10.1 presents the result of this analysis. The subtotals in panels A and B indicate that in the 1970s net migration added 766,435 people to the population of Amazônia and 283,290 to the Central West region. These figures suggest a total net gain of around 1,049,725 people (panel C).

Disaggregated estimates reveal striking intraregional differences. The state of Goiás (panel B) is especially significant. Between 1970 and 1980 the state experienced a net *loss* of 135,138 people. Whereas Goiás was one of the areas of intense in-migration in the early phase of the northward expansion of the agricultural frontier, the net out-migration of population in the most recent period represents an important reversal. These findings support those who argue that the moving frontier in Brazil leads to an initial expansion of population that is later followed by demographic retraction (Martine 1981; Sawyer 1984).

In Amazônia, the states of Acre, Amapá, Roraima and Rondônia show a net gain of 355,890 people. The net migration rate of +203.5 per thousand is almost entirely due to the intense movement into Rondônia during the 1970s. Unfortunately the advanced tabulations of the 1980 census collapse these four states into a single category, making it impossible to generate separate estimates for each area.

Compared to popular impressions of the massive influx of migrants to the Amazon, the numbers shown in Table 10.1 are surprisingly small. When we place these figures alongside the estimates of total net rural to urban migration for Brazil as a whole, the volume of population movement into the Amazônia region is smaller still. Between 1970 and 1980 the net movement into Amazônia (766,435) was about half the volume of the overall rural exodus *in one year* (1.7 million) and only around 5 per cent of total net rural to urban migration over the decade (17.3 million, Table 9.4). Even if we expand the reference point to include both Amazônia and the Central West, we reach the same conclusion. The total number of in-migrants for the two regions combined (1,049,725) is substantially lower than the yearly number of people who left the rural area in the 1970s and represents only 6 per cent of the total rural exodus in Brazil between 1970 and 1980.

Contrary to what one might expect, the expansion of the frontier into the Central West and Amazônia does not imply an increasingly rural population. With the exception of Rondônia, the rates of population growth between 1970 and 1980 are consistently higher in urban as compared to rural areas. As the data in Table 10.2 show, the rise in the proportion of people living in urban places was particularly evident in Mato Grosso, Mato Grosso do Sul and Goiás where the proportion of people living in urban areas increased by around 20 percentage points. A similar change took place in Acre and Amazonas and, to a lesser degree, in Roraima, Pará and Amapá.

*   *   *

Not since the heyday of the rubber boom at the turn of the twentieth century has Amazônia seen the intensive activity that took place in the 1970s. The colossal road building projects suddenly opened the heart of the lowland tropical basin to the expansion of the national society.

Table 10.2. *Annual rate of increase for rural and urban areas and change in per cent urban in Amazônia and Central West, 1970–80*

| | Annual % increase 1970–80 | | % Urban | | Change in % urban 70/80 (4)–(3) |
	Rural (1)	Urban (2)	1970 (3)	1980 (4)	(5)
A *Amazônia*					
Rondônia	17.6	14.6	53.6	47.3	−6.3
Acre	0.8	8.3	27.6	43.8	16.2
Amazonas	0.4	7.8	42.5	60.0	17.5
Roraima	2.6	10.8	42.8	48.9	6.1
Pará	4.3	5.0	47.2	48.9	1.7
Amapá	3.3	5.2	54.6	59.2	4.6
B *Central West*					
Mato Grosso	2.8	10.9	38.8	57.5	18.7
Mato Grosso do Sul	−1.9	7.3	45.3	57.1	21.8
Goiás	−1.5	6.9	42.1	62.2	20.1

Access to new territories unleashed a land rush of unprecedented scale. Poor farmers were attracted to the colonization areas by the prospect of securing a small plot of land. Enticed by fiscal incentives and in pursuit of lucrative financial returns, large investors also moved into the region. The competition for land, which sometimes led to violent confrontations between capitalist and peasant, propelled the frontier forward, often with disastrous consequences for native Indian groups (Davis 1977). These events profoundly altered the socioeconomic, demographic and ecological profiles of Amazônia.

Official statements in the early 1970s repeatedly claimed that Amazon colonization would solve the problems of population pressure and rural poverty. Policy makers assumed that the massive cityward flow of migrants could be channeled away from metropolitan areas into the newly opened territories thus preventing high urban unemployment from climbing still further. The superficial plausibility of this scenario made it a popular argument in the planning documents of virtually every South American country that has tried to colonize lowland tropical areas (Schmink and Wood 1984).

The persistence of this common theme may also be related to the role such a perception of the frontier plays in the formulation and execution of national development policy. To envision the frontier as the repository of excess population leaves the status quo unchallenged since such a view effectively shifts the object of intervention away from the underlying causes of "surplus" population, such as the concentration of land ownership and the expansion of mechanized commercial agriculture (discussed in chapter 9).

Estimates of net migration to the Brazilian Amazon between 1970 and 1980 tell a different story. The number of persons absorbed by the colonization project and by the frontier in general is minimal in relation to the size of the country's population and the volume of the total rural to urban migration stream. Far from providing a haven for the small farmer, the outcome of current political and economic trends is a highly skewed distribution of land ownership, the growth of land-extensive and labor-saving economic activities and a predominantly urban spatial distribution of population. For the rural poor the once bright promise of Amazônia has faded as the frontier region increasingly mirrors the inequities that mark the rest of Brazilian society.

11

Development and persistent underemployment

An unchallenged doctrine in the development literature during the 1950s and 1960s held that successful economic progress could be realized only through the twin forces of capital accumulation and industrial growth. The conclusion was supported by empirical generalizations of the Western European and North American experiences, described in terms of the continuous transfer of people from low productivity rural agricultural activities to urban-based productive industrial employment. The model pictured a long procession advancing slowly over a difficult terrain, each traveler following the footsteps of preceding ones. "Led by the old, now fully industrialized countries with Japan following close on their heels, that caravan is stretched out in the diminishing order of their per capita national income figures, the poorest straggling several centuries behind" (Leontief 1983: 407).

In W. Arthur Lewis's (1954) two-sector model, development occurs via the transfer of labor from the traditional rural subsistence sector to the urban industrial one. Both the labor transfer and urban employment growth are brought about by output expansion in urban industries. Lewis assumed that, in the initial phase of development, the level of wages in the modern sector would be constant at a fixed rate that exceeds average rural income thereby inducing workers to migrate from their home areas to the city. The speed of modern sector employment creation is determined by the rate of capital accumulation and the reinvestment of these profits in expanded industrial production. An increase in total capital stock causes the total product curve of the modern sector to rise, which in turn induces a shift in the demand curve for labor. Lewis assumed that this process of growth and employment expansion continues until all surplus rural labor is absorbed in the urban industrial sector. From that point on, the labor supply curve becomes positively sloped, both urban wages and employment rise, and the balance of the economic activity shifts from rural agriculture to urban industry.

Lewis's two-sector development model roughly conformed to the historical experience of economic growth in the West, yet the framework did not account for the realities of migration and underdevelopment in Brazil or, for that matter, in most contemporary Third World countries. The assumption that the rate of labor transfer and employment creation in the urban sector is proportional to the rate of urban capital accumulation is especially troublesome. This critical assumption is violated when profits are reinvested in more sophisticated labor-saving capital equipment, as is the case in Brazil. Rapid industrial output failed to generate correspondingly rapid rates of employment growth due to the rising productivity of labor, associated with higher capital/labor ratios. The result was growth in total aggregate output, yet, at the same time, total wages and employment remained unchanged, or failed to keep pace.

But why is there a tendency to use labor-saving technology in developing countries where labor is abundant? After all, the price-incentive model assumes that producers (firms and farms) utilize that combination of capital and labor which minimizes the cost of producing at a desired level of output. If the price of capital is expensive relative to that of labor, a more labor-intensive method of production is anticipated. Since most Third World countries are endowed with abundant supplies of labor, but possess little capital, one would expect firms to adopt labor rather than capital-intensive production methods.

Neoclassical economists blame the low labor absorption rate on price distortions caused by a variety of structural, institutional and political factors that make the actual market price of labor higher and that of capital lower than each of their true (or "shadow") values would dictate. Import substitution industrialization development policies in the postwar period provided subsidies to domestic and foreign firms to invest in favored industries. At the same time, wages in industry were relatively high as a result of protective labor legislation. Hence, the relative price of capital and labor was such as to stimulate the adoption of inappropriate capital-intensive production techniques in manufacturing and agriculture.

Writers in the dependency school find the answer in the technological dependence of peripheral economies. Contrary to conventional economic theory, this approach posits that the excess supply of labor in developing countries does not necessarily translate into an appropriate factor mix when the production process is developed abroad, where labor is scarce and expensive. The kind of development fostered by transnational corporations, therefore, tends to favor labor-saving technology, at least in heavy manufacturing where high quality exports require the latest technology (Cardoso 1972; Dos Santos 1970). The importation of technology contributes to what Furtado (1969: 15) called the "structural deformation" of the peripheral economy. Preference is given to the production of luxury products which, in Amin's (1976: 9) view, results in a "distortion in the allocation of resources in favor of those products and to the detriment of mass consumption goods." For the firms involved, capital intensive production and the low wages paid in the periphery combine to increase the rate of capital accumulation beyond what can be achieved in the center, where labor is scarcer and far better organized to defend its interests.

According to the "products life cycle model" (Wells 1972), over time more and more products will be produced in the periphery. New products, in this view, are first produced and sold in the center, later produced in the center and exported to the periphery and, finally, are produced in the periphery. The last stage occurs only after the technology involved has become routinized such that uncertainties are low and savings from cheap labor are substantial. The process creates jobs in the periphery, but at low wages. Moreover, developing countries must keep wages and living standards at a low level if they are to retain their comparative advantage derived from cheap labor costs. Further technological innovation may undermine the attractiveness of low-wage environments, however. The development of highly advanced technologies diminishes the role of both skilled and unskilled labor as the most important factor of production and as the major component of total costs, thereby eroding a low-wage country's competitive edge. In the case of fully automated installations, the advantage of low wages becomes nil. Current trends indicate that we may yet see another stage in the "products life cycle" model, as the example of the textile industry seems to suggest: "Production of textiles, particularly of the simpler kind such as grey cloth, shifted in the past from the developed to the low-wage, less developed countries; but there are signs that, with the introduction of highly automated equipment, this process has been arrested and is even being reversed" (Leontief 1983: 408).

Another line of reasoning contends that, in the "socially articulated" economies of the center, there is a necessary relation between production and consumption. Because workers are also consumers, the overall rate of profit in economies of the center depends on the long-run need for wages to rise. In "socially disarticulated" economies of the periphery there is no necessary relationship between the demand for capital and the demand for wage goods. Instead, the demand for wage goods, which is generated by returns to labor, is largely met by producers in the traditional sector. Hence, the capacity of the economy to expand does not depend on creating a broad-based home market through wage increases (de Janvry 1981). Moreover, firms in the periphery that buy their equipment and other capital goods from outside transfer back to the center the "multiplier effect" of new investments (Evans 1979). The perpetuation of low wages does not, therefore, imply a structural constraint on expanded industrial production to the same extent that it does in the center economies. According to de Janvry (1981), "social disarticulation" is thus the objective condition that perpetuates low wage levels, and that permits the adoption of repressive labor policies.

Studies by economists of the United Nations Economic Commission for Latin America (ECLA) and by PREALC focus on the structural constraints to the expansion of labor demand in the modern sector, a phenomenon caused by the increasing cost of generating new industrial jobs. Despite the fact that in Latin America the gross investment coefficient was comparable to that in the United States at an earlier period in its history (1870 to 1900), the relative cost of job creation was not. That Latin America entered the process of industrialization quite late implies the advantage of having access to technologies which yield greater productivity without incurring the costs of research and development and technological obsolescence. But, by making more intensive use of capital than labor, the creation of jobs requires more capital than it did in the past (Tokman 1982; Garcia 1982). The rapid expansion in modern sector output does not, therefore, lead to a proportional rise in the amount of labor directly absorbed by modern enterprises (although a dynamic modern sector may induce job creation elsewhere in the economy).

Portes and Benton (1984) accept the conclusion that the high cost of job creation may constrain the rate of employment expansion in the formal sector, yet they note that other factors are also at work. When labor is abundant, the relatively high wage paid in formal employment provides an incentive for employers to make use of the informal sector. This incentive is bolstered by modern labor legislation which makes contractually hired workers more expensive and less subject to arbitrary dismissal. Labor unions impose further restrictions on the ability of employers to vary the size of the workforce in response to market fluctuations. The increased cost and decreased managerial flexibility of contractually hired workers thus makes its rational for employers to draw on the highly elastic supply of informal labor. Employers hire directly on a casual basis and subcontract production or marketing to informal concerns.

The main thrust of these arguments is not that employment in the modern sector has failed to grow. In Brazil, the number of formal non-agricultural jobs rose at an annual rate of 4.4 per cent between 1950 and 1980 (Garcia 1982: Table 1). The point, rather, is that the increase in job creation in Latin America's urban industrial sector has proceeded slowly despite high investment coefficients; secondly, the growth in the supply of labor (due to the high rate of natural increase and heavy rural-to-urban migration) has far outstripped the availability of formal sector positions.

In its simplest formulation, unemployment results from a relatively sluggish growth in labor demand, both in the formal and informal urban sector and in agriculture, combined with a rapid increase in the number of job seekers caused by high rates of population growth and, in urban areas, exacerbated by the influx of rural migrants. The quantity of labor absorbed by the economy, and the wages paid to workers, are determined by the dynamic interplay of a wide range of economic and political forces, including technological innovation, development policy and relative factor prices. The determinants of labor supply involve a different set of factors which we turn to below.

Population growth and labor supply

The number of job seekers in a country depends on the size and the age composition of its population. Two demographic considerations are particularly germane in this regard. First, a high-fertility population, with a rapid rate of growth, is characterized by a relatively large number of people in the younger age groups. Compared to slow-growing populations with low fertility, the age pyramid has a broad base, indicating the high proportion of people under the age of fifteen, and a high dependency ratio (the sum of the population 0–14, plus those 65 years and older, divided by the number of people aged 15 to 64). Second, the impact of a fertility decline on labor force size and age structure does not occur immediately. Population growth has a built in momentum which continues to keep going after the birth rate falls. Young people far outnumber their parents in populations that experienced high fertility in the past. When the new generation reaches adulthood the absolute number of parents will be much larger than at present. Hence, even if these new parents have only two children, the total number of offspring is much larger than previous generations. The result is that the population will continue to increase substantially before the rate of growth begins to level off. Todaro (1977) has shown that a 50 per cent fall in fertility among less developed countries by 1980 would have reduced the male labor force by only 13 per cent by the end of the century. While this reduction is hardly trivial, the essential point is that over the next fifteen years those who will enter the labor force have already been born.

A common method demographers use to estimate the future size of a population is to carry out several projections, each based on different assumptions about fertility and mortality trends. Here we present two different scenarios (Table 11.1). The first projection (panel A) assumes that the fertility rate observed in 1980 stays the same through to the end of the century. These results are useful for comparative purposes but they are not realistic: the fall in the birth rate that began in the 1970s is likely to continue on into the 1980s rather than remain constant. The second projection (panel B) assumes that the rapid fertility decline recorded in the 1970s will continue, although at a diminishing rate from 1980 to the end of the century. This projection, proposed by Brazil's census bureau (FIBGE 1984), begins with a total fertility rate of 4.21 in 1975/80, dropping to 2.91 in 1995/2000.

If fertility remains constant between 1980 and 2000, total population size will reach 194,057,000 by the end of the century. The age structure will stay about the same, with approximately 58 per cent of the population between the ages of 15 and 64. The dependency ratio associated with this age structure is a high 70.2. Although unrealistic, the projection based on constant fertility serves as a useful reference point to compare the more likely estimates shown in panel B.

A continued birth rate decline implies a smaller absolute number of people by the end of the century and a substantially different age structure. The projection in panel B indicates a total population of around 179 million by the year 2000, with 62.84 per cent of the people in the prime working ages (15–64). Compared to panel A, reduced fertility implies a considerable reduction in the dependency ratio, from 70.2 (panel A) to 59.2 (panel B). Analysts generally maintain that a decline in the dependency ratio is economically beneficial because of its positive effect on the aggregate savings rate.

Still, the increase in the absolute size of the population in the working ages poses a serious problem. The number of males aged 15 to 64 will grow from around 35,280,000 in 1980 to 56,068,000 in 2000, a 37 per cent increase in the number of people sure to be seeking employ-

Table 11.1. *Population projections, 1980–2000*

Fertility assumptions	1980	2000	Average annual rate of increase
A *Constant*[a]			
Total Population*	121,286	194,057	2.35
Population 15–64*	70,637	120,730	2.68
% 0–14	37.7	36.5	
% 15–64	58.2	58.7	
% 65+	4.1	4.7	
Dependency Ratio	71.8	70.2	
B *Moderate decline*[b]			
Total Population	121,286	179,487	1.98
Population 15–64	70,637	112,790	2.37
% 0–14	37.7	31.8	
% 15–64	58.2	62.8	
% 65+	4.1	5.4	
Dependency Ratio	71.8	59.2	

* In thousands

[a] Total fertility 4.21 in 1980; life expectancy 61.8 in 1975/80, 63.4 in 1980/85, 64.9 in 1985/90, 66.3 in 1990/95, 67.5 in 1995/2000.

[b] Total fertility 4.21 in 1975/80, 3.81 in 1980/85, 3.46 in 1985/90, 3.16 in 1990/95, 2.91 in 1995/2000; life expectancy, as in projection A (FIBGE 1984).

ment. If we add to that figure the number of women in the same age gorup, the total population of people falling in the main working years reaches 113 million by the end of the century.

Labor absorption

Furtado (1982: 138) estimates that Brazil's Gross Domestic Product has to grow at an average annual rate of 2 per cent in order to absorb a 1 per cent yearly rate of increase in the size of the working age population. Projection B indicates that the population between the ages of 15 and 64 will grow at a yearly rate of 2.37 per cent. GDP must therefore increase at least 4.74 per cent annually for the economy to absorb new entrants into the labor force. These figures portend a sharp rise in unemployment and underemployment if Brazil's economy does not substantially improve over its performance in the early 1980s. The failure to do so will make even worse an employment situation that has already reached dramatic proportions.

The employment picture is far more alarming if, in contrast to Furtado's rough calculation, we examine the Brazilian economy's potential for creating better-paid jobs. It is well-known that official statistics on employment do not accurately reflect the true conditions of the labor force since they include the large number of underemployed, who carry out any job, however poorly paid it might be. The issue transcends the simple question of whether or not people have work and centers, instead, on the opportunity for productive, well-paid employment.

The conventional model of Third World economies draws a distinction between the "formal" and the "informal" sector. The former is characterized by advanced forms of production and organization, where employers hire workers on regular contracts, and observe social security and state labor legislation. The remainder of the economy constitutes the informal sector, defined as a residual category. The development strategies of the 1950s and 1960s envisioned the rapid growth of the formal, or modern, sector sufficient to absorb labor employed in less productive activities, a prediction that proved overly optimistic. Surveys of development performance show that the inability to generate significant employment has been one of the most glaring failures of the development process over the past two decades (Todaro, 1977: 209).

Given the current structure of the Brazilian economy, what are the maximum rates at which the formal sector can absorb the low-skilled population? If the maximum rates are below the values for the predictable forthcoming labor supply, then the Brazilian growth model will alleviate poverty slowly, if at all. To address this question, Lluch (1979) constructed a simple model of growth in the Brazilian formal sector to bracket the likely orders of magnitude for the rate of change in labor absorption into that sector. The simulation, like all such exercises, was premised on a number of simplifications and assumptions. Still, the findings give an approximate idea of the challenge that lies ahead when it comes to the matter of job creation. According to Lluch's model, the unskilled population is estimated to grow at an annual average rate of 2.2 per cent (considerably lower than our estimates of the intrinsic rates of natural increase among the poor reported in chapter 8). He finds that, in an economy growing at a healthy 7 per cent annual increase in GNP, the maximum rate of increase in the demand for formal sector services varies from 2.6 to 4.6 per cent per year. The rate of change in the demand for services is not the same as the demand for workers, however. To translate one into the other we need to subtract from the rate of increase in labor service demand the rate of technical progress associated with the improvements in technology and changes in hours worked. While this rate is not known, values between 1 and 3 per cent cannot be ruled out. These estimates suggest that rates of increase in formal sector employment could be much lower, ranging from −0.4 to 1.6 per cent.

The main conclusion of Lluch's (1979) exercise is that the rate of growth of demand for workers (as distinct from the demand for labor services) by the Brazilian formal sector is, most likely, smaller than the rate of growth of the poor population. This conclusion holds despite the highly favorable conditions assumed for the modern sector growth and employment performance: very large initial size (46 per cent), high output growth (7 per cent) and high saving rates. According to Lluch, the relatively low rate of job creation in the formal sector means that the number of workers making less than the 1970 minimum wage may increase, from 16 to 22 million by the year 2000, despite high growth in output.

12

The demography of inequality in Brazil: summary and conclusion

The ideas in this volume are put forth at a time when the discipline of development studies is in crisis. In a recent article, Hirschman (1981: 1) suggested that (mainstream) development economics is a field in decline. Although "articles and books are still being produced...the old liveliness is no longer there...and the field is not adequately reproducing itself." This state of affairs, according to Weisskopf (1983), is linked to theoretical dilemmas internal to the discipline of economics, as well as to a more general shift in political discourse. Development economics, Weisskopf contends, drew its primary theoretical inspiration from Keynesian principles. This orientation meant, among other things, that economists readily endorsed the premise that a neutral and activist state could, through orchestrated development policies, overcome the structural barriers that could not be resolved by a free market alone.

Events in the last three decades have dashed Keynesian hopes. Stagflation afflicted the developed economies in 1970s, followed by recession in the 1980s. Some Third World nations showed impressive growth. Others did not. Nearly all failed to resolve the problems of inequality, unemployment and political tension. Such setbacks bolstered the position of conservative economists, especially their contention that an unhindered market could and would do the job. Moreover, for reasons having more to do with contemporary politics and ideology than strictly intellectual competition, the right has gained considerable ground. The result has been to weaken both the theoretical underpinnings of the liberal world view, and to question the political acceptability of technocratic reformism – the two elements that once fueled mainstream development economics.

A similar crisis exists on the left, but for different reasons. After more than a decade of vigorous growth, Marxist-influenced sociology of development has reached an impasse. Theoretical positions that were once influential have now been rejected. The apparently promising discussions about basic concepts and methodologies have been inconclusive. The lack of closure has left theoretical and empirical gaps in the field.

Booth (1985) finds the cause of this dilemma in the metatheoretical commitments that have long dominated radical views of development. Researchers on the left have been concerned to demonstrate that the structures and processes found in the less developed world are not only explicable but *necessary* under capitalism. This general formula has two variants. The first is the idea that the attributes of national economies can be "read off" from the laws of motion of capital and the expansion of the capitalist mode of production on a world scale. The second is the teleological functionalism often inspired by Marxist theory. The former ignores systematic variation in development experience between countries, and fosters an economic reductionism laden with evolutionist overtones. The latter reifies social institutions, placing them further beyond human control than is warranted. "These two modes of necessitist metatheoretical commitments," Booth (1985: 777) concludes, "constitute the basic underlying cause of the current impasse of the new development sociology and the main obstacle to be removed if we are to do better in the future."

In the field of population studies, the central concern among analysts of Third World development has been to document the relationships between demographic behavior (fertility, mortality, migration and population growth) and the process of social change. Conventional wisdom acknowledges that population variables and economic development are related to one another. But, beyond this general proposition, there is little agreement about the most appropriate research strategy.

All too often explanations of changes in demographic behavior amount to an eclectic listing of empirical generalizations. Ignoring Stigler's (1969) contention that "there are not ten good reasons for anything," such inventories (e.g., United Nations 1973) simply rattle off a set of fragmented assertions. Accounts of the decline in the birth rate during the demographic transition, for example, typically refer to a number of phenomena ranging from the impact of urban industrial production on the cost of children, to the reproductive consequences of changes in women's attitude (e.g., Notestein 1953). Each assertion may very well be supported by "hard" data. Yet, when you put the findings together, they do not add up to a coherent understanding of the process of structural change, nor of the role played by demographic variables in the development process (e.g., National Academy of Sciences 1986).

Because a general model of social structure is absent in analyses of this kind, it is impossible to sort out the essential from the peripheral, or to separate what is causally prior from what is derivative. The consequence is an implicit tendency to regard every generalization as more or less equal in importance. Lower fertility may indeed be related to both a change in the economic value of children and to the erosion of traditional values, attitudes and gender relations, as the example above suggests. But the two observations are not on the same analytical plane. To treat them as such is to confuse (in our terminology) elements of eco-demographic infrastructure with elements of superstructure. Such an approach not only confuses levels of analysis, but also ignores the causal relationships between the two phenomena.

Most attempts to model eco-demographic relationships are deficient because of their narrow conceptual scope. This limitation characterizes three prominent research traditions in the field of population studies. Formal macroeconomic models (e.g., Coale and Hoover 1958) treat population and economy as aggregates, one acting on the other independently of class structure, institutional setting or historical context. Microeconomic perspectives, on the other hand, cast the study of population at the level of individual cost-benefit decision-making. The socioeconomic and political contingencies that affect the decision process are taken more or less as given. Finally, studies of the proximate determinants of fertility and mortality pay exclusive attention to variables that immediately affect births and deaths, leaving unexamined the origins of the structural processes that cause a change in the proximate determinants.

Important as these perspectives have been in the field of population studies, neither individual-level demographic research nor analyses framed at the aggregate level give much attention to the concepts and relationships that concern students of Third World development. Even a casual review of the temporary development literature shows the importance of such concepts as social class and conflict, the function of the state and its relation to dominant interest groups, the expansion of capitalist social relations of production and the global constraints on national development. With some notable exceptions (especially in the Latin American literature), these issues, if they enter demographic research at all, do so in an *ad hoc* manner.

The conceptual framework developed and applied in this volume begins with the premise that the process of social change and economic growth in developing countries has been characterized by sharp inequalities over time and space, and across social groups. These inequalities are related to demographic behavior because the material conditions that people confront in their daily lives exert a strong impact on the level and timing of births, deaths and the decision to migrate. Differential fertility, mortality and migration rates, in turn, may attenuate or exacerbate inequalities in other aspects of socioeconomic and political organization. It follows that the study of population and development can be advanced by placing the concept of inequality at the center of the conceptualization of social structure and of our empirical analysis of demographic behavior.

In its most general form, the framework presented in chapter 2 draws a conceptual distinction between three different tiers, or analytical levels. The first and most basic element is the eco-demographic infrastructure. Central features of infrastructure include modes of production and modes of reproduction. Production and reproduction interact with one another to determine the structure of the economy (sectoral division; labor demand) and of the population (size, sex ratio, age and spatial distribution, growth rate). The processes and institutions at the level of eco-demographic infrastructure impose limits of possible variation on, and probabilistically determine, the character of a society's stratification system – the model's second analytical tier. The stratification system is defined by the dimensions of inequality created by differential access to resources (land, income, education, public services and social prestige) and political power (e.g., political parties, unions and pressure groups). The third tier – politico-ideological superstructure – encompasses the agencies and institutions of the state apparatus, as well as culture and ideology. Finally, the relationships between all three levels are conditioned by the constraints, opportunities and contingencies associated with a country's position within the global economy.

Like all frameworks, this one does not constitute a formal theory. It is more correctly understood as a "conceptual map" of the terms and relationships that organize the research agenda. If it serves its purpose, the framework provides guidelines for shaping the welter of available data into explanations that are logically situated within a general conception of the social system. Elements of the scheme are separated for expository purposes. In the real world none of the components are as discrete as the diagram might imply. Finally, the model is abstract in the sense that the various elements and relationships merely posit a way of thinking about socio-demographic structure. To apply the framework requires that we "fill in" the institutional details and contingent historical factors relevant to the study of a particular country – in this case, Brazil.

Brazil's early economic history shows that it was population structure that determined the major features of the country's economic organization. During the colonial period, when the demand for sugar assumed increasing importance on the world market, it was the scarcity of population (more precisely, the shortage of labor) that led to the slave mode of production. Slavery, in turn, gave rise to a particular stratification system, and to a politico-ideological superstructure that legally sanctioned and morally justified racial inequality and the brutal exploitation of African peoples. In the eighteenth century, when coffee became the primary export commodity, the inadequate supply of labor prompted the state to subsidize the massive immigration of Europeans into southern Brazil. The result was the *colonato*, a family-based system of agricultural production. By the middle of the twentieth century, however, Brazil entered a period of labor surplus. The evolution of economic structure responded more to the intrinsic logic of the capitalist mode of production than to the constraints imposed by population.

These observations underscore an important theoretical point: the conceptual framework elaborated in chapter 2 makes no a priori commitment as to the direction of the causal relationship between modes of production and reproduction within the eco-demographic infrastructure. Unlike the orthodox Marxist view (which sees population as entirely derivative of the economic), and in contrast to the neo-Malthusian approach (which reverses the causal reasoning), the framework endorses the idea that the relationship between economic and demographic organization is historically variable.

The interaction of modes of production and reproduction also accounts for the changing patterns of migration and population distribution. The export of sugar in the seventeenth century concentrated people and political power along the northeastern seaboard. The subsequent gold rush in Minas Gerais in the 1700s, and the rise of coffee production in São Paulo in the next century, drew the locus of economic activity and of population concentration into central and southern Brazil. In the twentieth century, the fortunes accumulated from the sale of coffee on the international market provided the capital for roads and railways, and stimulated the creation of banks and other financial institutions. By the 1930s, São Paulo emerged as the most economically advanced region of the country while the once-prosperous Northeast lagged behind. Spatial inequalities in living standards were reflected in regional differences in fertility and mortality, and were the cause of inter-regional and rural-to-urban population movement.

The expansion of the industrial sector in the central and southern areas of the country meant the rise of a new class structure. The traditional rural economy based on patron–client relationships gave way in importance to a waged labor force, and to the economic and political ascendance of an urban bourgeoisie. Associated with the rise of new political factions was the hegemony of development ideologies compatible with the economic interests of the growing capitalist class.

After World War II, Brazil's economy grew in size and complexity. Two growth cycles figured prominently in the postwar years: the "inward-looking" Import substitution Industrialization (ISI) from the early 1950s through the mid-1960s; and the "outward looking" export promotion cycle from the 1960s to the present. In the first period, domestically manufactured products began to replace imported consumer durables and intermediate goods. The second period saw the diversification of industrial growth and a closer integration into the world economy. A long-run perspective shows that industrial production, although subjected to cyclical downturns, grew around 7 per cent per year between 1956 and 1984. Non-agricultural employment increased, and the population became increasingly urban. By 1980, over half of the population lived in urban places.

Improvements in the overall quality of life are reflected in the increase in the average number of years of life expected at birth. In 1930/40, life expectancy for the country as a whole was around 41 years. By 1970/80, expectation of life rose to around 62 years. The decline in the death rate was associated with a rise in income, increases in educational attainment and reduced environmental risk due to the increase in the proportion of households with water and sewage facilities and with electrical power. Health policies directed to low-income populations played an important role, especially in recent years. Since 1970, government-financed maternal and child health programs, together with the distribution of food supplements to pregnant women and newborn children, contributed much to reducing infant mortality.

The growth and diversification of Brazil's economy did not eliminate the sharp regional inequalities that have characterized Brazil since the colonial period. Differences between the poverty-stricken NORTHEAST and the more affluent SOUTHEAST are reflected in social indicators such as income, educational achievement and the percentage of households with running water, sewage services and electricity. The impact of these differences in quality of life is expressed by regional disparities in the average number of years of life expected at birth. In 1960/70, life expectancy in the Central Northeast (44.2) was 17.7 years below the number of years of life expected in the South (61.9). In the following decade, life expectancy rose to 49 years in the Central Northeast and to 67.8 years in the South. These findings indicate an increase in regional differences from 17.7 years in 1960/70 to 18.8 years in 1970/80.

Regional inequalities in length of life are considerably wider when the estimates are disaggregated by level of household income. In 1970, the lowest life expectancy rate in the country (42.8 years) was found among the poorest households in the Central Northeast. The highest was found among affluent households in the South. With an average length of life of 66.9 years, the rich in the more developed region of southern Brazil outlived the poor in the least developed area by nearly a quarter of a century (24.1 years).

Differences in length of life by region and household income have important implications for the overall level of life expectancy. This is because the aggregate rate is a weighted average of the rates that correspond to various population subgroups. Hence, the high concentration of income in Brazil, and the large concentration of people in the less developed northeastern region, depress the average length of life for the country as a whole.

The impact of recent economic growth in Brazil on the relative inequality between different socioeconomic groups is a major concern among development and population analysts. We address the inequality issue by focusing on changes over time in the pattern of differential mortality. Estimates of life expectancy for 1960/70 and 1970/80, disaggregated by level of household income, show that mortality gains were more or less evenly distributed across income strata. For the total population, life expectancy rose approximately four years for all income groups in both urban and rural areas of the country. Because of the relatively even increase among all population subgroups, the life expectancy gap between the rich and poor remained about as large in 1960/70 (12.1 years) as it was a decade later (12.4 years in 1970/80).

Comparative analyses of census data provide indispensable information on mortality trends over time. Yet, the census is carried out only every ten years. As a consequence, the results do not capture fluctuations in vital rates that take place during the decade. Yearly estimates of infant mortality derived from São Paulo's vital register clearly show that the long-term trend toward lower mortality is sometimes characterized by short-term reversals. Indeed, fluctuations in the infant death rate reflect the social consequences of economic policy. Soon after the military took power in 1964, development planners endorsed a wage-squeeze strategy to contain inflation and to attract foreign investment. Using the corporatist institutions of labor control forged by Vargas in the 1930s, as well as outright repression, policy makers permitted wage increases to lag behind the rate of inflation. The result between 1965 and about 1975 was a deterioration in the purchasing power of the state-legislated minimum wage and an increase in infant deaths. In the late 1970s, when the real value of the minimum wage rose, the infant mortality rate resumed its downward trend.

The strength of the inverse income–mortality relationship appears to be attenuated in recent years. Direct subsidies to the low-income population in the form of water and sewage services, as well as nutrition and health-related programs, have played an important role in weakening the income effect on infant and child mortality, at least in the more developed regions of central and southern Brazil. If the wage-squeeze development strategy stimulated higher infant mortality by lowering income, public health initiatives and transfer payments to the poor had the opposite result. Economic and social policies of the state thus have important and often contradictory effects on demographic behavior.

The study of the relationship between miminum wage levels and infant mortality rates over time illustrates two important aspects of the conceptual framework set forth in chapter 2. One issue concerns the methodological utility of the three-tiered scheme. The population literature, not to mention common sense, tells us that income and child mortality are inversely related. Yet, the framework invites a more structural and historically-based analysis of the etiology of mortality change. One line of inquiry moves the analytical focus from the distribution of income (stratification system) into the realm of production and social class (infrastructure). The other moves the locus of study to the political institutions and policies (superstructure) that affect both income levels (e.g., minimum wage legislation; corporatist institutions of labor control) and child mortality rates (e.g., nutrition programs and public health initiatives). A change in the level of mortality (as in the case of fertility and migration) can thus be interpreted as the net outcome of the interaction of events analytically situated at the level of infrastructure, stratification and superstructure.

The study of income change and infant mortality in metropolitan São Paulo illustrates another aspect of our conceptual approach to the analysis of population and development. In contrast to structuralist perspectives that characterize the urban poor as passive victims of underdevelopment, the analysis here identified the various means by which people actively attempted to alter their conditions of life. Labor strikes, the creation of neighborhood organizations and occasional outbursts of collective violence were among the ways the population responded to the deterioration in living standards. Inasmuch as these actions fueled the mounting political pressures in the late 1970s to reverse the downward trend in income, such social movements were relevant to the study of infant mortality.

Political mobilization had other demographic outcomes as well. The struggle for a lower cost of living in the 1970s, for example, was led by women in low-income urban neighborhoods. An unintended consequence of these initiatives was to bring to the forefront of daily life the issues of gender inequality and the right of women to control reproduction. By challenging traditional attitudes and dominant ideologies, such actions played an important role in the fertility decline between 1970 and 1980. The action of social groups to defend their interests were also relevant to the analysis of migration and population distribution in Amazônia. The political battles fought within the federal government to influence regional development priorities, as well as the confrontations between peasants and ranchers on the frontier, were crucial elements in understanding the early demise of the public colonization program and the process of land settlement in the tropical lowlands.

Examples of the fertility, mortality and migration consequences of social action point to the general causal principle we invoke to conceptualize the determinations between human agency and socioeconomic and political structure. According to the model in chapter 2, the ecodemographic infrastructure sets limits of variation on the stratification system and superstructure. Nonetheless, social classes, interest groups and the state itself undertake willful actions that transform social organization. Understanding societal change in terms of the interplay of human action and the institutional features of social structure is important for two reasons. Firstly, such a view rejects the dogmatic econominism often associated with base–superstructure schemes. Second, the perspective pays attention to the active and reflexive character of human conduct, thereby distancing itself from the persistent tendency in the social sciences to see human behavior as the result of forces that actors neither control nor comprehend (see Giddens 1984).

Under the recently instated democratic political system, new issues will emerge as focal points of political mobilization. Racial inequality is a likely topic. Mortality differentials by race reveal compelling aspects of Brazilian social stratification not captured by traditional measures of socioeconomic status. Estimates of the average length of life at birth by racial subgroups of the population show that nonwhites were at a considerable disadvantage. In 1950, whites outlived nonwhites by an average of 7.5 years. Between 1950 and 1980, life expectancy rose about nineteen years among both groups, but the difference between them remained high (6.7 years). The persistence of the mortality gap over time suggests that the structural transformation in Brazilian society did little to reduce the relative differences in quality of life between whites and nonwhites. Further analyses showed that race remained a statistically significant variable even after controlling for education, region, household income and the presence of running water in the home. The results indicate that nonwhites in Brazil are subject to disadvantages and to forms of discrimination beyond those associated with lower socioeconomic standing.

Compared to mortality, the drop in the birth rate in Brazil was more recent in origin but no less dramatic. From 1940 to 1970, the total fertility rate remained relatively stable at around six children. Between 1970 and 1980, total fertility fell to 4.5, a decline of nearly 30 per cent in the short span of a decade or so. The sudden decline in the birth rate was primarily due to a rise in the proportion of women using contraception. Increased reproductive control was associated with a number of socioeconomic and ideological changes. The most significant trends included the rise in educational attainment, the increase in the proportion of the population living in urban areas and the greater number of women who entered the labor force. Shifts in values and attitudes, such as the erosion of traditional gender relations, also played a role. The restructuring of Brazilian society altered the incentives and disincentives of large families. The rise in the direct and indirect costs of children reduced the demand for children. The decline in the market and subjective costs of the means of reproductive control permitted couples to adjust their fertility accordingly.

The preference for fewer children was manifest across all social groups in both rural and urban areas. Yet some of the structural factors that led to this common outcome were more or less specific to different sectors of the population. Lower-income urban households were especially hard hit by the erosion in real wages from the mid-1960s to the mid-1970s. Combined with a rise in the price of food, housing and public services, reduced wages meant an increase in the relative cost of children. Income stress also caused women to enter the labor force in greater numbers, primarily in industrial and related jobs. Employment of this type, which is outside the home and characterized by rigid scheduling, is especially incompatible with the demands of childrearing in an urban environment.

Among middle-income families, the acceleration of the fertility decline in the 1970s coincided with a period in which households raised their consumption expectations in favor of material possessions and higher quality children through increased investments in education. High inflation rates and the indexing of credit obligations may have resulted in a gap between a couple's material aspirations and their resources, a condition that depressed the demand for children.

In rural settings, reduced fertility was caused by structural changes in the organization of agricultural production, and in the manner in which labor was recruited and remunerated in the countryside. The old *colono* system, typical of the plantation economy of southern Brazil at the turn of the century, had strong pro-natalist demographic consequences, contributing to high rates of fertility in the countryside. More recently, the *colono* system as well as traditional tenancy and sharecropping are giving way to the wage relationships in which workers are hired individually, often on a seasonal basis. The separation of families from access to land restructured the household decision environment and changed the dominant mode of reproduction in rural settings. The demographic outcomes of the proletarianization of rural labor were a decline in the birth rate and massive rural-to-urban migration.

Estimates of the magnitude of the rural exodus indicate that approximately 13.8 million people abandoned the countryside in the 1960s. The number of urbanward migrants rose to 17.3 million the following decade. The rural out-migration flow was so large in the 1970s that it drained off all of the demographic growth due to the natural increase of the population, and more. The result was an absolute decline in the size of the rural population, from 41,054,000 in 1970 to 38,620,000 in 1980.

Neoclassical economists assume that migration flows are the cumulative result of individual decisions based on a rational evaluation of the benefits to be gained and the costs entailed in moving from one place to another. Inasmuch as the movement of population from rural to urban areas is voluntary, the cost-benefit model applies to the case of Brazil. Yet, the conclusion that people migrate because they find it in their interest to do so hardly explains the structural factors that motivate such a decision. In contrast to the reductionist and ahistorical character of the neoclassical perspective, a structural approach to the study of urbanward migration identifies five aspects of Brazil's agrarian structure that reduce the rural area's ability to retain population.

The first, and undoubtedly most important factor, is the high concentration of land ownership, a phenomenon whose origins can be traced as far back as the colonial period and the mechanisms used by the Portuguese Crown to populate Brazil. In 1975, 52.1 per cent of all rural establishments were less than ten hectares in size and occupied only 2.7 per cent of total land under cultivation. At the other extremes, only 0.8 per cent of farms exceeded 1,000 hectares but controlled nearly half of the land in rural areas. When the means of production are monopolized by a minority of *latifundistas* and the majority of rural inhabitants are relegated to plots of land smaller than the minimum necessary for subsistence, the result is a high rate of rural out-migration. Other factors that contribute to the rural exodus include: the commercialization of agricultural production, the mechanization of the labor process and the impact of credit policies and land price inflation.

In the 1970s, urbanward migration and the interregional flow of people from the Northeast into cities in the Center-south became a major policy concern in Brazil. To counter the increasing size and density of urban areas in industrialized regions, the government launched a plan to redirect the flow of migrants away from the urban south into the sparsely populated Amazon. The Transamazon Highway and an elaborate public colonization project were cornerstones of an ambitious development plan launched in the early 1970s. The colossal road building projects, along with a variety of tax and fiscal incentives, enticed both small farmers and large investors to the region. The competition for land led to violent confrontations between ranchers and farmers, and often had disastrous consequences for native Indian groups.

In view of the expanse of relatively uninhabited territory in the tropical lowlands of northern Brazil, the move to occupy Amazônia presented a seemingly plausible solution to the problem of urbanward migration and population concentration. The plan to populate Amazônia was also politically expedient to the extent that the scheme shifted the object of intervention away from the underlying causes of "surplus" population, such as the concentration of land ownership in the long settled regions of the country. Yet, contrary to the repeated claims that Amazon colonization would solve the problems of population pressure and rural poverty, estimates of net migration to the region between 1970 and 1980 tell a different story. The number of persons absorbed by the colonization project, and by the frontier in general, was minimal in relation to the size of Brazil's population and relative to the volume of the total rural to urban migration stream. Moreover, the highest rates of population growth between 1970 and

1980 within the Amazon region were recorded in urban rather than in rural areas. Far from providing a haven for the smaller farmer, the outcome of recent efforts to populate Amazônia has been a high concentration of land ownership, the deforestation of vast areas, the expansion of highly capital-intensive investments and the growing presence of urban poverty (see Schmink and Wood 1984). Frontier areas in northern Brazil increasingly exhibit many of the same inequities that mark the rest of the country.

Future patterns of Brazilian growth and development will largely depend on the economy's capacity to absorb the growing supply of labor. Population projections to the year 2000 indicate that, even accounting for a continued fertility decline, the number of people in the working ages will increase at a rate of around 2.4 per cent a year. Economists assume that Gross Domestic Product must grow at an average annual rate of 2 per cent in order to absorb a 1 per cent yearly rate of increase in labor supply. If that rule of thumb applies to Brazil, then the country's GDP must grow at an annual rate of 4.7 per cent merely to maintain current employment levels.

Assessment of the Brazilian economy's potential for creating better-paid jobs (as opposed to simple employment) reveal a more alarming picture. Models that simulate the rate of growth of the formal sector find that, even when the overall economy grows at a rate of 7 per cent a year, the rate of increase in formal-sector employment is only around 1.6 per cent (or less). Since the rate of increase in labor supply is much larger (2.4 per cent a year), the findings suggest that, if present trends continue, the formal sector will never fully absorb new additions to the labor force. Analyses of population growth by level of household income indicate that the poor are at a particular disadvantage. Estimates for 1980 show that the poorer sectors of the Brazilian population experience rates of natural increase on the order of about 3 per cent per year. The relatively low rate of job creation in the formal sector and the high rate of increase in labor supply (especially among the poor) mean that, without a fundamental change in the structure of Brazil's economy, the proportion of poorly paid workers will increase even with high rates of economic growth.

The contemporary character of socioeconomic and spatial inequality in Brazil is partly the legacy of its colonial past, and of the peripheral role the country played in the world economy. Before World War II, Brazil depended heavily on the export of raw materials, especially agricultural commodities such as sugar, cotton and coffee. The postwar period saw the expansion of the country's industrial base, the diversification of production through import-substitution and the expansion of a wide range of nontraditional exports. These developments intensified rather than attenuated Brazil's interdependent position in the global system.

No single issue more clearly reflects the consequences of this interdependence on the prospects of Brazilian development than does the country's foreign debt. Extensive borrowing from private banks took place in the mid-1970s when excess liquidity in the banking system made money available at low rates of interest. The size of the debt unexpectedly increased as a result of the sudden rise in interest rates in the late 1970s and early 1980s. During the same period, Brazil's capacity to pay off the debt declined because of the global recession and the associated deterioration in the terms of trade for Brazilian exports. The combined effect of the rise in interest rates and the deterioration in the terms of trade added US$47.5 billion to the size of Brazil's debt. The result in the early 1980s was an economic crisis of unprecedented proportions.

The return to a democratic system in 1985 marked a new era in Brazil's political and economic history. In many ways the new regime inherited an economy on a more solid foundation for future growth than it has ever been in the past. Over the last decade, Brazil reduced its dependence on foreign oil and became self-sufficient in steel, aluminum, plastic and rubber products, as well as many other goods once imported from abroad. Since 1970, manufactured goods rose from 30 per cent of total exports to 50 per cent, reflecting the diversification of production and the inroads Brazilian products have made on the world market. On the other hand, the economy remains troubled by high inflation rates and by the drain on resources caused by the mounting foreign debt. Moreover, despite the recent fertility decline, the population will continue to grow well into the future, magnifying the need for employment creation. In the likely event that current patterns of rural–urban and interregional migration continue in the years ahead, increased population size will also aggravate the already high concentration of people living and looking for work in the country's metropolitan centers.

The success of the Sarney regime, as well as that of its successors, will depend on the ability to juggle a set of complex and often contradictory demands. Meeting popular expectations of an improved standard of living will, at the very least, require a substantial increase in the number of well-paid jobs, as well as redistributive measures to reduce the socioeconomic and regional inequalities documented in this book. But the return to democracy will not, in itself, solve Brazil's current economic crisis. Nor will it necessarily reform the high concentration of income and land ownership, or lead automatically to a more egalitarian development model. Still, the promise of democracy lies in its responsiveness to a plurality of interests, and in its potential to forge a new social and economic future that is more generous to the millions of Brazilians who paid dearly for past development priorities.

APPENDIX

A note on method

Fertility

The registration of vital events in Brazil is far from complete. Although the quality of the vital registration system has greatly improved in recent years, a reliable record of the number of births in the country is still lacking. The absence of data precludes the use of conventional demographic methods that rely on vital registration statistics. Instead, we derive fertility estimates using the indirect method developed by William Brass (1968).

The Brass method requires two kinds of information, classified by the age of women: (1) the number of live births during the twelve months before the census date (current fertility), and (2) the total number of live births (retrospective fertility, or parity). Working with theoretical fertility distributions, Brass developed a series of multipliers to convert cumulated fertility into a measure of mean parity. The correction factors reflect the curvature of an underlying set of model age-specific fertility patterns. The appropriate model (and hence the multipliers) is selected by either of two summary measures derived from the data: the mean age of the fertility schedule, or the steepness of the take-off of the fertility curve (measured by the ratio of current fertility or of mean parity among women aged 15–19 to that of women 20–24 years old).

Under ideal conditions the cumulated fertility distribution of a given cohort of women should exactly match the mean parity of the same group. In practice the two series of fertility data (current and retrospective), after the necessary conversion to make them comparable, will not match one another because of two sources of error: (1) When women are asked about the number of births in the preceding twelve months they may not respond with the correct time span in mind (called "reference period error"). The average length of time covered may include more or less than the intended twelve-month period, often by a margin of several months. (2) Older women may not remember some births they had, especially of children who died soon after they were born. The "memory error" is expected to increase at older ages, reflecting the progressive forgetting of offspring with advances in the mother's age.

The Brass technique uses both current and retrospective data to generate robust estimates of the total fertility rate. The series of current fertility rates of women 15–49 years old provides the age pattern of childbearing. But the age-specific rates derived from the reported number of children in the past year do not accurately reflect the level of fertility because of the effects of reference period error. An adjustment is therefore necessary. The ratio between cumulated fertility (F) and parity (P) of younger women (who are less subject to memory error) provides a factor (P/F) that can be used to correct the entire series of reported current fertility rates.

The matching of current fertility and parity will not produce optimum results even after correcting for reference period error if there have been changes in the level of fertility. This will not cause significant error, however, because the parity used as an adjustment factor is taken from younger women. By virtue of having had their children during a recent period, their cohort fertility distribution would not be too different from the current fertility distribution.

The sum of the adjusted age-specific rates provides an estimate of total fertility. The total fertility rate can be interpreted as the number of children that an average woman would have if her childbearing experience were the same as that of the cross-section of women at the time of the observation.

Fertility estimates for 1930/40 and 1940/50

The 1970 census included questions about the total number of live births and the number of live births in the twelve months before the census, thus permitting the direct application of the Brass method. Earlier censuses did not ask about the number of children in the year before the enumeration. Despite this limitation, Brass estimates were still possible. An analysis of the parity distributions for the ten regions in 1940 and 1950 indicated that there were no significant changes in the age pattern of fertility compared to the 1970 results for eight of the ten regions of the country (Carvalho 1973: chapter 2). It was therefore assumed that the fertility pattern in each region in 1930/40 (with the exception of São Paulo and South) was the same as that observed in

1960/70. The level of fertility in the earlier periods was then obtained by adjusting the 1960/70 level by a factor computed by dividing in each of the eight regions the mean parity of the 20–9 age group in 1940 and 1950 by the same parity for 1970. The São Paulo and South fertility distributions were adjusted using the South and Minas distributions, respectively (see Carvalho 1973). Estimates for the country as a whole were obtained by aggregating the regional estimates.

Fertility rates by income

The application of the Brass method to population subgroups disaggregated by levels of household income raises special issues for analysis and interpretation. As noted above, the age pattern of fertility is adjusted by the P/F ratio, where P is the mean number of children born to women 20–29 years old and F is the sum of the age-specific fertility rates for women of the same age. The level of fertility in each income class is thus determined by the fertility behavior of younger women. This minimizes the confounding effects of a positive correlation between fertility and household income when older children (necessarily born to older women) enter the labor force. When fertility rates are presented by household income, the rates represent the level of fertility implied by the childbearing experience of women 20–29 years of age who were found in households of a given level of monthly monetary income on the census date.

Mortality

The Brass method of estimating mortality entails a simple transformation that generates measures of the probability of death by age x from census data on the number of children ever born and the number of children surviving by age of mother. The proportion of children surviving among children ever born to women aged 20–24, 25–29 and 30–34, when multiplied by the proper correction factors, yield estimates of the probability of death by exact ages 2, 3 and 5. These values correspond to the xqo life table function (in this case, 2qo, 3qo and 5qo).

Although other xqo values can be estimated under ideal conditions, the analyses in this volume use only the 2qo, 3qo and 5qo values. The probability of death by age one (1qo) is excluded because it is especially sensitive to peculiarities in the date. Estimates of survivorship beyond the fifth birthday (above 5qo) are also unreliable. The latter are based on the memory of events by older woman (older than 35 years), which are subject to memory error. Moreover, the values are not representative of current mortality levels. On the other hand, the probability of death by ages two, three and five are acceptable indicators of the levels of recent child mortality. Taken together, the three indicators approximate the average mortality for the decade prior to the census enumeration.

To facilitate intergroup comparison, we converted the three xqo values into a summary measure of the average expectation of life at birth implied by the level of child mortality. In the case of Brazil, this conversion is hampered by the lack of adequate life tables for the country and its ten regions. In the absence of such information, the 1960 life table for Mexico was used. This is an appropriate choice because other analyses indicate that the mortality pattern for Mexico is similar to Brazil's (Carvalho 1973). Having selected this pattern, we estimated the level of mortality by converting the xqo values to life expectancy rates by logit transformation using the Mexican life table as a model pattern.

This method assumes that the 1960 Mexican pattern of mortality approximated that of the total Brazilian population (as demonstrated by Carvalho 1973) and that of its various subgroups. The latter assumption is warranted in light of the remarkable stability of mortality patterns found among groups of geographically linked populations. But, even if the Mexican pattern departs from the true Brazilian one, this would not invalidate our findings because the primary substantive focus is on relative differences between groups rather than on estimating the absolute levels of mortality.

Mortality estimates by household income

When mortality estimates are disaggregated by income, several caveats are necessary. Estimates of the probability of death by, say, age two (2qo) for children born to women in households of income i refer to the mortality over a restrospective period of five to six years before the census date. The survival probabilities can be distorted if mobility took place from one level of income to another. A woman may be recorded in a household with i+1 income in 1970 yet, if she was upwardly mobile within the last five or six years, the mortality of her children corresponds to the income level i (given the retrospective nature of the measure). To minimize this bias, we rely primarily on four broad categories of household income. The more disaggregated estimates of life expectancy are more susceptible to the mobility bias, and should be interpreted with this caveat in mind.

Life expectancy rates by household income should be interpreted as follows: the estimate represents the average life expectancy at birth for the decade (1960/70 or 1970/80). It corresponds to the mortality experience of children born to women who were 20–34 years of age and who were enumerated in households of a given level of monetary earnings at the time of the census.

Time periods and retrospective measures
Estimates of fertility and mortality generated by the Brass method refer to a period of several years before the date of the census enumeration. Estimates of this type are identified in the tables and text using an oblique stroke. A life expectancy of 60 for 1960/70, for example, refers to the average number of years of life expected at birth during the decade of the 1960s. When we refer to a change in the value of a rate or index between two dates, we use "–" (as in 1960–70).

Notes

2 Framework for the study of population, development and inequality

1 We are grateful to a number of colleagues who offered helpful suggestions about the substance and the presentation of the material in this chapter. Thanks to: Harley Browning, Stephen Bunker, Bill Caudill, Mary Castro, Carmen Diana Deere, Diego Hay, Helen Safa, Marianne Schmink, Joachim Singelmann, Rodolfo Tuirán and Peggy Webster. Pamela Richards offered especially helpful substantive and editorial comments.

2 The view associated with Wallerstein characterizes capitalism, not by a specific relation between classes, but rather by the production for profit within a world system of production and accumulation. Hence, Wallerstein sides with the so-called "circulationists" who hold that capitalism emerged in the sixteenth century when it came to depend on the expropriation of surplus from a world division of labor. The view contrasts with that of the "productionists" who claim that capitalism is defined, not by the search for profit alone, but also by the proletarianization of labor and the emergence of the wage relation (the view we endorse). The debate is more than semantic (see Laclau 1971; Portes and Walton 1979: chapter 1). Each definition leads to a fundamentally different historical vision; and, in the contemporary context, each view raises different questions for data collection and analysis.

3 For notable exceptions, see the proceedings of the Congresso Latinoamericano de Población y Desarrollo, Vols. I and II, November, 1983 (UNAM 1983).

4 Evidence of intra-household conflict over goals, incentives and control of resources suggest that the household should not be treated as a homogeneous unit in the study of sustenance strategies (see Fapohunda, forthcoming; Folbre, forthcoming).

5 Mode of production, for Marx, was not a directly observable thing. Instead, Marx treated mode of production as a conceptual object, the product of theoretical reasoning. In this view, a mode of production is a highly abstract concept. It defines a basic structure of social relations – of which there are only a limited number, each characterized by its own laws of motion – and upon which is erected a corresponding superstructure. Marx's conceptual strategy was thus to isolate the simplest and most fundamental represen-

266

tation of different forms of production, exploitation and politico–ideological organization.

The purpose of doing so was methodological. Abstraction was the first step in the research process. Social and economic organization was far too complex to be grasped as an integrated whole straight away. Hence, Marx began with a highly abstract set of concepts and relationships (mode of production, laws of motion) which he then applied to the analysis and interpretation of a concrete situation. The movement from the abstract to the concrete can be thought of in terms of three levels of analysis. This first level, mode of production, is the most abstract. The second, social formation, has come to refer to the specific ways in which different forms of capitalist and non-capitalist relations are combined within a given society. And finally, conjunctural analysis, involves the investigation of societies in terms of the concrete institutional and historical details.

Wright's (1985: 12) analogy clarifies the distinction made between these levels of abstraction and illustrates the methodological principle at hand: "In the scientific study of the chemistry of a lake, the highest level of abstraction involves specifying the particular way the basic elements that go into make water, hydrogen and oxygen, combine to make water, H_2O. The study of different forms of water – ice, liquid water, evaporation, etc. – would be at this most abstract level. The middle level of abstraction corresponding to social formation analysis involves investigating the ways in which this compound, H_2O, interacts with other compounds in lakes. Finally, the conjunctural level involves investigating the myriad contingent factors – nitrogen washed down from farms, chemical waste dumping from factories, etc. – which concretely distinguish a given lake chemically from all other lakes in time and space." The three levels of abstraction noted above serve to clarify the terminology developed in this chapter. The framework portrayed in Figure 2.2 is intended as a heuristic device for guiding empirical research. Thus, when we speak of "modes of reproduction" we are referring to observable differences in, say, the proximate determinants of fertility and child mortality. These observable phenomena apply to a given time, place and social group. Hence, a mode of reproduction is cast at the level of conjuncture. This means that, if we are to retain a consistent level of analysis, we must treat mode of production (the other central element of the eco-demographic infrastructure) at a similar level of concreteness (conjuncture).

That the scheme shown in Figure 2.2 treats mode of production in an empirical fashion, at the level of an historical case, need not imply that we ignore Marx's invaluable insights insofar as abstract modes of production are concerned, nor that we abandon the methodological strategy of moving from these abstract formulations to concrete analyses. It is only to say that, *in our diagram*, modes of production are defined in terms of the social relations that characterize the labor process within empirically observable units of production.

6 Materialist conceptions of the derivative nature of culture are a controversial issue. Worsley (1984), for example, notes that the political economy approach to development often gives short shrift to the importance of culture, a conclusion that few would disagree with. Yet he goes on to reject all frameworks that separate base from superstructure on the (in our view

absurd) grounds that such models imply that production (the base) occurs in the absence of human cognition. He apparently comes to this conclusion because such models treat culture separately, as part of superstructure. What he fails to see is that, if culture is treated separately, the separation is only within a conceptual model that tries to establish causal priorities among different aspects of social organization. It is not a separation that is presumed to exist in the real world. Worsley's wholesale rejection of a materialist perspective is thus premised on an extremely reified interpretation of conceptual models generally.

3 Growth and distribution in historical perspective

1 Immigrants, especially those from Italy, are commonly thought to have played an important role in the industrialization of São Paulo (Dean 1969). They provided labor for the coffee plantations, and later stimulated growth by investing in industry and commerce. Underlying this perception is the notion that the typical immigrant was invariably poor to begin with and that he came to work in agriculture. Once he accumulated sufficient capital, the immigrant became upwardly mobile, moving from farmer to urban entrepreneur.

Reassessments of this important period of Brazil's history paint a more complex picture of these events. In the case of São Paulo, the establishment of the first industries may have begun as early as 1873, as a result of the efforts of Brazilian entrepreneurs drawn from landed families (Martins 1977). Industry nonetheless remained the least attractive undertaking for native capital, a factor that facilitated the increased participation of immigrants in industry and banking in the 1890s. Questioning the mobility hypothesis, Martins (1981) maintains that much of the European population arrived already as capitalists or as members of the urban proletariat.

2 The figures in Table 3.5 cannot be accepted unequivocally. Numerous methodological issues plague longitudinal analyses of the size distribution of income. Wide margins of error, and the use of varying adjustment techniques and conceptual assumptions, have led to alternative intrepretations of the same data. To summarize the many aspects of this complex debate would be both tedious and unnecessary as these issues have been reviewed elsewhere (Bacha and Taylor 1980; Fishlow 1973; Fields 1977). Suffice it to say that the compilations of available findings (Pfeffermann and Webb 1979) conclude that a deterioration in the distribution of personal income occurred between 1960 and 1970. During the 1970s, the distribution profile appears to have remained fairly stable.

4 Income inequality and length of life

1 Because the diffusion of medical and health technologies has depressed the death rate in many countries that remain at relatively low levels of development, it is widely held that mortality rates have become increasingly dissociated from economic conditions (Davis 1956; Stolnitz 1965). The transfer to developing countries of these "exogenous" factors has been estimated to account for approximately 80 per cent of the growth in life expectancy for

the world as a whole between the 1930s and the 1960s (Preston 1975). Using a different sample and somewhat different procedures, the same author obtained a lower estimate (50 per cent) for developing countries during 1940–70, a finding similar to that for Latin America in 1950–70 (Palloni 1979). Yet, these conclusions do not discount the relevance of income as a variable in the study of changes in the death rate. As Preston (1975: 240) argues, despite the fact that the relationship between mortality and national income has shifted upward over the last several decades, at a certain point in time mortality may have become more responsive to income in low-income countries.

2 With regard to the unit of analysis, studies of income distribution offer compelling theoretical and empirical arguments in favor of focusing on the household as opposed to individuals (Kuznets 1955, 1976, 1978). Analyses of the size distribution of income that use smaller entities, such as persons, overestimate the degree of inequality because of the presence of people who may not be engaged in income-earning activities, such as married women, the young and the aged. Such individuals are more properly treated as members of a household, the locus of decisions regarding the generation and disposition of income by economically active and dependent members of the unit (Kuznets 1976: 7).

5 Wage policy, infant mortality and collective social action in São Paulo

1 We restrict the scope of the investigation to São Paulo because of the lack of data for other places, and because the figures for São Paulo are of much better quality compared to other cities that report infant mortality rates.

2 Unlike the survey in 1972, the household income measure used in 1976 includes non-monetary income. The lack of comparability between the surveys is especially significant at the lower end of the income range since the proportion of total household income from resources received in kind is greater among low-income groups.

There is an added problem of definition. Because of the deterioration in the purchasing power of the minimum wage, the meaning of the minimum salary as an index of poverty or wealth changed over the period. It is therefore unclear whether the percentage of households at or below the minimum wage actually declined or not. It should be noted, however, that the effect of both sources of bias (the inclusion of non-monetary income in 1976; a lower real wage in 1976) is to reduce the proportion of households in the lowest income stratum. This suggests, in turn, that the observed reduction in the percentage of households below the minimum salary, which was already small, may be little more than a statistical artifact.

6 Racial inequality and child mortality

1 Since the census item is based on self-identification, the classification must be taken in the social and cultural sense, making no claims as to its validity as a physical or genetic typology.

2 We have collapsed the "black" and "brown" into a single "nonwhite" cat-

egory for both practical and substantive reasons. In practical terms, the number of blacks is very small, a factor that limits our ability to cross-classify the data in meaningful ways. Moreover, the substantive findings of research by Silva (1985) and Hasenbalg (1985) show little differences between the two, thus allowing us to treat them as a single group.

3 Several methodological issues come to mind when we observe the increase in the white–nonwhite mortality gap among children of upper income and more highly educated women, a pattern that appears for the country as a whole and also for estimates of life expectancy within the NORTHEAST (not shown). If there is any truth to the common expression in Brazil that "money whitens," then the findings are counter-intuitive as we would expect discrimination to be less significant among upper income groups leading to a narrower mortality differential. On the other hand, it is possible that the "money whitens" concept means that poor or middle-income persons, who once considered themselves black or brown, subjectively reclassify themselves as their social standing rises. This implies that the most successful individuals "migrate" from the nonwhite to the white category. If "success" is not adequately measured by income and education, then "less successful" persons may remain in the nonwhite group. If this takes place on a large scale, then we would expect to find what the data show: a widening of the white–nonwhite mortality gap among upper income children.

How much importance should we give to these considerations? On the basis of currently available data, it is impossible to answer this question with certainty. However, we can speak indirectly to the issue using a crude but revealing forward-survival method. From census data we know the number of nonwhites between the ages of, say, 10 and 25 (in five-year intervals) in 1950. If we subject these values to nonwhite adult mortality rates (derived from model life tables) over the thirty-year interval (1950/60, 1960/70 and 1970/80), we obtain a projected estimate of the number of nonwhites aged 40 to 55 in 1980. This number can then be compared to the actual number of nonwhite persons aged 40 to 55 counted in the last census. If our estimates of adult mortality are correct, then the projected number of people should equal the number enumerated, provided that individuals have not reclassified themselves in the interim. In other words, the difference between the actual and the projected number of nonwhites in 1980 for a given cohort is an indirect measure of the extent to which individuals change their racial classification. If the "money whitens" thesis operates in this fashion, we expect the projected value to be higher than the actual one (because nonwhites in 1950 "migrated" into the white category in 1980), and that the difference will be large (because income and other indicators of social standing rose considerably since 1950).

The results of this analysis show that the projected number of nonwhites in 1980 is inded higher than the actual number counted in the census. Yet, the difference is only 7.1 per cent. Keeping several methodological caveats in mind (especially the accuracy of nonwhite adult mortality rates), this exercise suggests that racial reclassification may take place, as the "whitening" hypothesis predicts, but that the phenomenon is not widespread.

4 Because the distribution of MI is bounded by zero, other techniques, such as TOBIT analysis, may be more appropriate. However, as Trussell and

Preston (1982) demonstrate, using ordinary least squares yields the same substantive results.

7 The "baby bust"

1 During the 1970s the Brazilian Census Bureau carried out a series of national household surveys (called PNADs) which included questionnaire items that permit estimates of fertility using the Brass method. While the surveys do not provide national coverage and are subject to larger sample bias (Carvalho, Paiva and Sawyer 1981: 7–11), the findings derived from these sources confirm the rapid drop in the level of fertility. Because the 1972 and 1976 PNADs provide interim data between the decennial censuses, the data offer an indication of the timing of the fertility change. Although numerous methodological problems exist (e.g., the design of the 1976 survey may have produced an overstatement of the decline), the results of the surveys, together with the estimates of the 1980 census, suggest that the fertility decline began in the late 1960s, proceeded at a relatively rapid pace through about 1976, after which the decline continued but probably at a slower pace.

8 Income distribution and population growth

1 Projections to the year 2000 were carried out using a program prepared by the Population Council (Shorter 1978). Projections of the 1970 population were based on the stable age distributions that correspond to the fertility and mortality levels specific to each of the major categories of household income. This assumption is plausible in light of the fairly constant fertility rates that characterized Brazil in the decades prior to the 1970 census. Comparing the stable distributions of the population aged 15 to 49 with the actual distributions for the same age range reveals only minimal differences between the two (less than 1 per cent at each five-year interval) except in the highest income category where the stable model tended to underestimate the proportion of the population in the younger ages.

The total population of Brazil in 1970 was 93 million. The base number used here is lower because it excludes people who were not members of households and does not include families with zero income. The analysis therefore stresses the change in relative proportions of the population by household income rather than the absolute size of population.

Finally, it is important to note that we do not consider the probable occurrence of other effects that are likely to obtain in the real world, such as: the increase or decrease in wages that may occur because of the shortage or excess of labor that results from different rates of population growth; the impact of lower or higher rates of social investments or transfer payments, the benefits of which might be differentially distributed among subgroups of the population; or changes in average income that result from savings and investments. The growth of total income by 2000 and the changes in the distribution of that income are clearly important issues. But, to incorporate these factors here would carry us far beyond our objective. The analysis, which assumes constant per capita income within the income categories, is restricted to an analysis of the demographic side of the income distribution question.

2 Brass's methods of estimating fertility and mortality assume constant vital rates (see the Appendix). This assumption is less problematic in the case of fertility which, until the late 1960s, remained fairly stable. Mortality rates, on the other hand, declined in recent decades (chapter 4). Since the Brass method is based on a retrospective time period, there is the likelihood that mortality levels may be overestimated among those socioeconomic groups that experienced sharp reductions in the period just prior to the 1970 census. However, the objective here is to estimate rates of natural increase by strata of monthly household earnings. Since the rate of growth is the difference between births and deaths, an overestimate of mortality leads to a conservative bias in our estimates of the subgroup rates of demographic increase.

3 The total fertility rate for the highest income stratum is 2.0, below replacement. Yet, the projection indicates a slightly positive rate of growth (+0.3). This is due to the age distribution of the population in this income bracket. The intrinsic rate of increase associated with a total fertility rate of 2.0 and a life expectancy of 63.9 years is slightly negative (−.55 per cent per year, as shown in Table 8.4).

4 Studies of mobility in Brazil suggest high levels of structural mobility stemming from changes in the economy and the labor market. However, these conclusions are based on comparisons of fathers' and sons' occupational status (Pastore and Haller 1977) and offer no indication of the magnitude of intragenerational movement. In the absence of such information, the projections here are based on hypothetical mobility rates.

9 Agrarian structure and the rural exodus

1 This procedure generates an estimate of net migration that consists of the real movement of persons, plus the transfer of individuals by boundary change and reclassification. As the city limits move outward over time, people are added to the urban (and subtracted from the rural) population by boundary movement, rather than the actual migration of people. Similarly, when urban areas are defined on the basis of an administrative criterion, as is the case in Brazil, the urban population may grow (and the rural one may decline) by administrative decision. All three types of population change (actual migration, boundary shifts and reclassification) are treated here as part of net migration. Fortunately, however, the number of *municípios* created during the period was minimal due to legislative changes that made the creation of new administrative areas more difficult than in the past.

2 This measure of net out-migration includes the number of people who left for urban places (direct effect), plus the children born to migrants in the intercensal period (indirect effect). It is possible to estimate the relative importance of the two effects on the size of the rural population using a separate projection for the net migrant population. For 1960–70, the results indicate that 75 per cent of the reduction in rural population is due to the direct loss of migrants. The remaining 25 per cent can be attributed to the transfer to the cities of the children of migrant parents.

3 We obtained the input data for the regional projections by calculating a

weighted average of state-level rural fertility and mortality rates, using as weights the size of population in the states comprising each region. Regional birth and death rates for the projection period 1970–5 were derived by inter-polating the values for 1960–70 and 1975–80.

Bibliography

Adelman, Irma & Cynthia Taft Morris. 1973. *Economic Growth and Social Equity in Developing Countries.* Stanford University Press.

Ahluwalia, Montek S. 1976. "Inequality, poverty and development." *Journal of Development Economics* 3 (December): 307–42.

Almeida, A. L. Ozório de. 1980. "Produtividade em serviços: alguns problemas para a nova política salarial." *Conjuntura Econômica* 34(4): 70–6.

Almeida, Angela Mendes & Michael Lowy. 1976. "Union structure and labor organization in the recent history of Brazil." *Latin American Perspectives* 3 (Winter): 98–119.

Almeida, M. H. de. 1981. "Tendências recentes da negociação coletiva no Brasil." *Dados* 24(2): 161–89.

Álvaro, Moisés José 1979. "Current issues in the labor movement in Brazil." *Latin American Perspectives* 6 (Fall): 1–21.

Ambercombie, K. C. 1972. "Agricultural mechanization and employment in Latin America." *International Labor Review* 105–6: 11–45.

Amin, Samir. 1974. "Modern migrations in Western Africa." *Modern Migrations in Western Africa*, ed. S. Amin, pp. 65–124. London: Oxford University Press.

   1976. *Unequal Development: An Essay on the Social Formation of Peripheral Capitalism.* New York: Monthly Review Press.

Antonovsky, A. 1967. "Social class, life expectancy and over-all mortality." *The Milbank Memorial Fund Quarterly* 45 (April): 31–73.

Azevedo, Thales de. 1953. *As elites de cor: um estudo de ascensão social.* São Paulo

Bacha, Edmar & Lance Taylor. 1980. "Brazilian income distribution in the 1960s: Facts, model results and the controversy." In *Models of Growth and Distribution in Brazil.* (eds.) L. Taylor et al., pp. 296–341. New York: Oxford University Press.

Bacha, Edmar L. 1980. "Selected issues in post-1964 Brazilian economic growth." In *Models of Growth and Distribution for Brazil.* (eds.) Lance Taylor et al., pp. 12–48. New York: Oxford University Press.

Baer, Werner. 1965. *Industrialization and Economic Development in Brazil.* Homewood, Ill.: Richard D. Irwin, Inc.

   1979. *The Brazilian Economy: Its Growth and Development.* Columbus, Ohio: Grid Publishing, Inc.

Baer, Werner & Carlos Von Doellinger. 1978. "Determinants of Brazil's foreign economic policy." In *Latin America and the World Economy: A Changing International Order* (ed.) J. Grunwald, pp. 147–61. Beverly Hills: Sage.

Baer, Werner & Adolfo Figueroa. 1981. "State enterprise and the distribution of income: Brazil and Peru." In *Authoritarian Capitalism, Brazil's Contemporary Economic and Political Development*, (eds.) T. C. Bruneau & P. Faucher, pp. 59–83. Boulder, Colorado: Westview.

Balán, Jorge. 1973. "Migrações e desenvolvimento capitalista no Brasil: ensaio de interpretação histórico-comparativo." *Estudos CEBRAP* 5: 7–79.

Banco do Brasil. 1983. *Annual Report, 1983*. Rio de Janeiro: Banco do Brasil.

Bartra, R. 1975. "Sobre la articulación de modos de producción en America Latina: algunos problemas teóricos." *Historia y Sociedad* 5 (Spring): 5–19.

Becker, Gary. 1980. "An economic analysis of fertility." In *Universities-Bureau of Economic Research, Demographic and Economic Change in Developed Countries*. Princeton University Press.

BEMFAM/DHS (Sociedade Civil Bem-Estar Familiar no Brasil and Demographic and Health Surveys). 1986. *Brazil: Demographic and Health Survey, 1986*. New Jersey: Institute for Resource Development, Westinghouse.

Benton, Ted. 1984. *The Rise and Fall of Structural Marxism: Althusser and his Influence*. New York: St. Martin's Press.

Berg, A. 1973. *The Nutrition Factor: Its Role in National Development*. Washington, DC: The Brookings Institute.

Bergsman, Joel. 1970. *Brazil: Industrialization and Trade Policies*. London: Oxford University Press.

Berquó, Elza S. & M. A. Gonçalves. 1974. "A invasão de óbitos no município de São Paulo." *Cadernos CEBRAP* No. 19.

Berry, Albert & Ronald Soligo. 1980. "The distribution of income in Columbia: an overview." In *Economic Policy and Income Distribution in Columbia*, pp. 14–17. Boulder, Colorado: Westview Press.

Birdsall, Nancy. 1980. *Population and Poverty in the Developing World*. Washington, DC: World Bank, Working Paper No. 404.

Bongaarts, John. 1978. "A framework for analyzing the proximate determinants of fertility." *Population and Development Review* 4(1): 105–32.

Bongaarts, John & Jane Menken. 1983. "The supply of children: a critical essay." In *Determinants of Fertility in Developing Countries*. (eds.) Rodolfo Bulatao & Ronald D. Lee, vol. 1. pp. 27–60. New York: Academic Press.

Bongaarts, John & Robert G. Potter. 1980. "The fertility inhibiting effects of the intermediate fertility variables." *Working Papers, No. 57*. New York: The Population Council, Center for Policy Studies.

1983. *Fertility, Biology and Behavior: An Analysis of the Proximate Determinants*. New York: Academic Press.

Booth, David. 1975. "André Gunder Frank: an introduction and appreciation." In *Beyond the Sociology of Development*, (eds.) T. Barnett & David Booth, pp. 50–85. London: Routledge and Kegan Paul.

1985. "Marxism and development sociology: interpreting the impasse." *World Development* 13(7): 761–87.

Boserup, Ester. 1965. *The Conditions of Agricultural Growth: The Conditions of Agrarian Change under Population Pressure.* Chicago: Aldine.

1981. *Population and Technology.* Oxford: Basil Blackwell Publishers.

Brass, W., A. J. Coale, P. Demeny, D. F. Heisel, F. Lorimer, A. Romaniuk & E. Van de Walle. 1968. *The Demography of Tropical Africa.* Princeton University Press.

Brookfield, Harold. 1975. *Interdependent Development.* University of Pittsburgh Press.

Browning, H. L. & J. Singelmann. 1978. "The emergence of a service society and its sociological implications." *Journal of Politics and Society* 8 (Nos. 3–4).

Bulatao, Rodolfo & Ronald D. Lee. 1983. "A framework for the study of fertility determinants." In *Determinants of Fertility in Developing Countries.* (eds.) R. Bulatao & R. D. Lee, vol. 1, pp. 1–26. New York: Academic Press.

Bunker, Stephen G. 1979. "Power structures and exchange between government agencies in the expansion of the agricultural sector." *Studies in Comparative International Development* 14(1): 56–76.

1984. "Modes of extraction, unequal exchange, and the progressive underdevelopment of an extreme periphery: the Brazilian Amazon, 1600–1980." *American Journal of Sociology* 89(5): 1017–64.

Burns, Bradford E. 1970. *A History of Brazil.* New York: Columbia University Press.

Caldwell, John C. 1976. "Toward a restatement of demographic transition theory." *Population and Development Review* 2 (3 and 4): 321–66.

1980. "Education as a factor in mortality decline: an examination of Nigerian data." In *Proceedings of the Meeting on Socioeconomic Determinants and Consequences of Mortality, Mexico City, June 19–25.* Geneva: WHO.

Camargo, Cândido Procópio Ferreira de. 1982. "A igreja do povo." *Novos Estudos, CEBRAP* 1(2): 49–53.

Camargo, Cândido Procópio Ferreira de (et al.) 1978. *São Paulo: Growth and Poverty.* London: Boverdean Press.

Cardoso, Fernando Henrique. 1962. *Capitalismo e escravidão no Brasil meridional.* São Paulo: Difusão Européia do Livro.

1972. "Dependency and development." *New Left Review* 74 (July–August): 83–95.

1973. "Associated dependent development: theoretical and practical implications." In *Authoritarian Brazil,* ed. Alfred Stepan, pp. 142–78. New Haven: Yale University Press.

1977. "The consumption of dependency theory in the United States." *Latin American Research Review* 12(3): 7–24.

1982. "A questão da democracia." In *Brasil: do "Milagre" à "Abertura."* ed. Paulo J. Krischke, pp. 103–19. São Paulo: Cortez Editora.

Cardoso, Fernando Henrique & Enzo Faletto. 1979. *Dependency and Development in Latin America.* Berkeley: University of California Press.

Cardoso, Fernando Henrique & Geraldo Müller. 1977. *Amazônia: Expansão do capitalismo.* São Paulo: Brasiliense.

Cardoso, Ruth. 1982. "Duas fases de uma experiência." *Novos Estudos CEBRAP* 1(2): 53–8.

1983. "Planejamento familiar: novos tempos." *Novos Estudos CEBRAP* 2(3): 2–7.

Carneiro, Robert L. 1967. "On the relationship between size of population and complexity of social organization." *Southwest Journal of Anthropology* 23(3): 234–43.

Carnoy, Martin. 1984. *The State and Political Theory*. Princeton University Press.

Carvalho, José Alberto Magno de. 1973. "Analysis of regional trends in fertility, mortality and migration in Brazil, 1940–1970." Unpublished PhD Dissertation. London School of Economics.

Carvalho, José Alberto Magno de & Paulo de Tarso Almeida Paiva. 1976. "Estrutura de renda e padrões de fecundidade no Brasil." In *Fecundidade: Padrões brasileiros*, ed. Manoel Costa, pp. 21–38. Rio de Janeiro: Altiva Gráfica e Editora Ltda.

Carvalho, J. A. M., Paulo de Tarso Almeida Paiva & Donald R. Sawyer. 1981. *A recente queda da fecundidade no Brasil: evidências e interpretação.* Belo Horizonte, Brazil: CEDEPLAR Monograph No. 12.

Carvalho, Livio de. 1984. "Brazilian wage policies." *Brazilian Economic Studies* 8: 109–41.

Carvalho, J. A. & Charles Wood. 1978. "Mortality, income distribution and rural–urban residence in Brazil." *Population and Development Review* 4 (September): 405–20.

Cassen, R. H. 1976. "Population and development: a survey." *World Development* 4(10,11): 785–830.

Castells, Manuel. 1983. *The City and the Grassroots*. Berkeley: University of California Press.

Castro, Mary Garcia. 1987. *Family, Gender and Work: The Case of Female Heads of Household in Brazil, 1950–1980*. Unpublished Dissertation, Department of Sociology, University of Florida, Gainesville, FL.

CEPAL (Commisión Económica para América Latina). 1983. "Latin American development problems and the world economic crisis." *Cepal Review* 19 (April): 51–83.

Chayanov, A. V. 1966. In *The Theory of Peasant Economy*. (eds. and translators) Daniel Thorner, B. Kerbley & R. E. F. Smith. Homewood, Ill.: American Economic Association.

Chen, Lincoln C. 1983. "Child survival: levels, trends and determinants." In *Determinants of Fertility in Developing Countries*, (eds.) R. Bulatao & R. Lee, pp. 199–232. New York: Academic Press.

Chenery, H. 1974. *Introduction. Redistribution with Growth*, (eds.) H. Chenery et al., pp. xii–xx. London: Oxford University Press.

Chenery, H., M. S. Ahluwalia, C. L. G. Bell, J. Duloy & R. Jolly. 1974. *Redistribution with Growth*. London: Oxford University Press.

Chilcote, Ronald. 1974. "Dependency: a critical synthesis of the literature." *Latin American Perspectives* 1 (Spring): 4–29.

Chilcote, Ronald & Dale L. Johnson. 1983. *Theories of Development: Mode of Production or Dependency?* Beverly Hills, California: Sage.

Clark, Colin. 1940. *The Conditions of Economic Progress*. London: Macmillan.

Clausen, A. W. 1984. "Priority issues for 1984." Remarks delivered before the European Management Forum, Davis, Switzerland, January 26.

Coale, A. J. 1973. "The demographic transition." In *Proceedings of the International Union for the Scientific Study of Population (IUSSP)*, Liège, Belgium: IUSSP.

Coale, Ansley & E. M. Hoover. 1958. *Population Growth and Economic Development in Low Income Countries*. Princeton University Press.

Cochrane, S. 1979. "Education and fertility: what do we really know?" World Bank, Population and Human Resources Division, Development Economics Department. Preliminary Draft.

Conjuntura Econômica. 1980. "Política social e emprego." *Conjuntura Econômica* 34(2): 40–54.

Corrêa do Lago, Luiz Aranha. 1980. "Relações trabalhistas e salário real no Brasil, 1952–78." *Conjuntura Econômica* 34(4): 62–9.

Cravioto, J. & E. R. de Licardie. 1973. "The effect of malnutrition on the individual." In *Nutrition, National Development and Planning* (eds.). A. Berg et al., pp. 3–21. Cambridge: MIT Press.

Davis, Kinglsey. 1956. "The amazing decline of mortality in underdeveloped areas." *The American Economic Review* 46: 305–18.

——— 1973. "Cities and mortality." pp. 259–82 in International Population Conference. Liège, Belgium: International Union for the Scientific Study of Population (IUSSP).

Davis, Kingsley & Judith Blake. 1956. "Social structure and fertility: an analytic framework." *Economic Development and Cultural Change* IV (April) 211–35.

Davis, Shelton H. 1977. *Victims of the Miracle: Development and the Indians of Brazil*. New York: Cambridge University Press.

Dean, Warren. 1969. *The Industrialization of São Paulo, 1880–1945*. Austin: University of Texas Press.

——— 1971. "Latifundia and land policy in nineteenth-century Brazil." *The Hispanic American Historical Review* 51 (November): 606–25.

Deere, Carmen Diana. 1978. *The Development of Capitalism in Agriculture and the Division of Labor by Sex: A Study of the Northern Peruvian Sierra*. Unpublished PhD Dissertation, Agricultural Economics, University of California, Berkeley.

Deere, Carmen Diana & Alain de Janvry. 1979. "A conceptual framework for the empirical analysis of peasants." *American Journal of Agricultural Economics* 61, no. 4 (November): 601–11.

Degler, Carl N. 1971. *Neither Black nor White*. New York. Macmillan.

D'Incão e Mello, M. C. 1976. *O Bóia-Fria: Acumulação e Miséria*. Petrópolis, Brazil: Vozes.

De Janvry, Alain. 1981. *The Agrarian Question and Reformism in Latin America*. Baltimore: The Johns Hopkins Press.

Delacroix, Jacques. 1977. "The export of raw materials and economic growth: A cross-national study." *American Sociological Review* 42 (October): 795–808.

Denslow, David & W. Tyler. 1984. "Perspectives on poverty and income inequality in Brazil." *World Development* 12(10): 1019–28.

Dickenson, John P. 1978. *Brazil*. Boulder, Colorado: Westview.

DIEESE (Departamento Intersindical de Estatística e Estudos Sócio-econômicos). 1974. "Família assalariada: padrão e custo de vida." *Estudos Sócio-econômicos* 1(2). São Paulo: DIEESE.

— 1975. "Dez anos de política salarial." *Estudos Sócio–Econômicos* 1:3. São Paulo: DIEESE.

Dos Santos, Teotônio. 1970. "The structure of dependence." *American Economic Review* 60 (May): 231–6.

Duque, J. & E. Pastrama. 1975. "Las estrategias de supervivencia económica de las unidades familiares del sector popular urbano: una investigación exploratoria." Santiago, Chile: FLACSO

Easterlin, Richard A. 1975. "An economic framework for fertility analysis." *Studies in Family Planning* 6:54–63.

— 1976. "The conflict between aspirations and resources." *Population and Development Review* 2 (September/December): 417–25.

— 1980. *Population and Economic Change in Developing Countries.* University of Chicago Press.

— 1983. "Modernization and fertility: A critical essay." In *Determinants of Fertility in Developing Countries.* (eds.) Rodolfo Bulatao & Ronald D. Lee, vol. 2. pp. 562–86. New York: Academic Press.

Enke, Steven. 1960. "The gains to India from population control." *Review of Economics and Statistics* 42(2): 175–81.

Emmanuel, Arghiri. 1972. *Unequal Exchange: A Study of the Imperialism of Trade.* London: New Left Books.

Erickson, Kenneth Paul & Keven J. Middlebrook. 1982. "The state and organized labor in Brazil and Mexico." In *Brazil and Mexico: Patterns in Late Development.* (eds.) Sylvia Ann Hewlett & Richard S. Weinert, pp. 213–63. Philadelphia: ISHI.

Escudero, Jose Carlos. 1980. "On lies and health statistics: some Latin American examples." *International Journal of Health Services* 10 (3): 421–34.

Esman, Milton. 1978. "Landlessness and near-landlessness in developing countries." Ithaca, NY: Rural Development Committee, Cornell University.

Evans, Peter. 1979. *Dependent Development. The Alliance of Multinational State, and Local Capital in Brazil.* Princeton University Press.

— 1985. "Transnational linkages and the economic role of the state: an analysis of developing and industrialized nations in the post-World War II period." In *Bringing the State Back In.* (eds.) P. Evans, D. Rueschmeyer & T. Skocpol, pp. 192–226. Cambridge University Press.

Evans, Peter, D. Rueschmeyer & T. Skocpol (eds.) 1985. *Bringing the State Back In.* Cambridge University Press.

Fapohunda, Eleanor. Forthcoming. "The nonpooling household: a challenge to theory." In *A Home Divided: Women and Income in the Third World.* (eds.) D. H. Dwyer & J. Bruce. Stanford: University of California Press.

Faucher, Philippe. 1981. "The paradise that never was: the breakdown of the Brazilian authoritarian rule." In *Authoritarian Capitalism: Brazil's Contemporary Economic and Political Development.* (eds.) Thomas C. Bruneau & Philippe Faucher, pp. 11–39. Boulder, Colorado: Westview.

Feder, Ernest. 1978. "The peasant." *Latin American Research Review* 13 (3): 193–204.

Felix, David. 1983. "Income distribution and the quality of life in Latin America: patterns, trends and policy implications." *Latin American Research Review* xvii (2): 3–33.

Fernandes, Florestan. 1969. *The Negro in Brazilian Society.* New York: Columbia University Press.

FIBGE (Fundação Instituto Brasileiro de Geografia e Estatística). 1972. *Pesquisa Nacional por Amostra de Domicílios, 1972.* Rio de Janeiro: Fundação IBGE.

1975a. *Anuário Estatístico do Brasil.* Rio de Janeiro: FIBGE.

1975b. *Censo Agropecuário,* Brazil, Rio de Janeiro: Fundação IBGE.

1976. *Pesquisa Nacional por Amostra de Domicílios, 1976.* Rio de Janeiro: FIBGE.

1979. *Indicadores sociais.* Rio de Janeiro: Fundação IBGE.

1982. *Perfil estatístico de crianças e mães no Brasil: características sóciodemográficas, 1974–75.* Rio: FIBGE.

1984. *Brasil: Estimaciones y Proyecciones de Población, 1950–2025.* Rio de Janeiro: FIBGE.

Fields, Gary S. 1977. "Who benefits from economic development? A reexamination of Brazilian growth in the 1960's." *American Economic Review* 67 (4): 570–82.

Figueroa, Adolfo & Richard Weisskoff. 1980. "Viewing social pyramids: income distribution in Latin America." *Consumption and Income Distribution in Latin America,* ed. Robert Ferber, pp. 257–94. Washington, DC: Organization of American States.

Fischer, A. G. B. 1935. *The Clash of Progress and Security.* London: Macmillan.

Fishlow, Albert. 1972. "Brazilian size distribution of income." *Papers and Proceedings of the American Economic Association* 62 (May): 391–402.

1973. "Some reflections on post-1964 Brazilian economy policy." In *Authoritarian Brazil,* ed. A. Stepan, pp. 69–118. New Haven: Yale University Press.

Folbre, Nancy. Forthcoming. "A black four of hearts: toward a new paradigm of household economics." In *A Home Divided: Women and Income in the Third World.* (eds.) D. H. Dwyer & J. Bruce. Stanford: University of California Press.

Fontaine, Pierre-Michel (ed.) 1985. *Race, Class and Power in Brazil.* Los Angeles: University of California, Center for Afro-American Studies.

Fordyce, James E. 1977. "Early mortality measures as indicators of socioeconomic well-being for whites and non-whites: a re-appraisal." *Sociology and Social Research* 6 (January): 125–37.

Foster-Carter, Aidan. 1978. "The modes of production controversy." *New Left Review* 107: 47–77.

Foweraker, Joe. 1981. *The Struggle for Land: A Political Economy of the Pioneer Frontier in Brazil, 1930 to the Present.* London: Cambridge University Press.

Frank, André Gunder. 1967. *Capitalism and Underdevelopment in Latin America.* New York: Monthly Review Press.

1969. *Latin America: Underdevelopment or Revolution.* New York: Monthly Review Press.

Frazier, F. 1944. "A comparison of Negro–White relations in Brazil and in the United States." *New York Academy of Sciences* 6:251–69.

Freedman, D. S. 1963. "The relation of economic status to fertility." *American Economic Review* 53: 414–27.

Freyre, Gilberto. 1946. *The Masters and the Slaves.* New York: Alfred A. Knopf.

Frish, R. E. 1975. "Demographic implications of the biological determinants of female fecundity." *Social Biology* 22: 17–22.

Furtado, Celso. 1963. *The Economic Growth of Brazil: A Survey from Colonial to Modern Times.* Berkeley: University of California Press.

    1969. *Um Projeto para o Brasil.* Rio de Janeiro: Editora Saga, SA.

    1982. *A nova dependência: dívida externa e monetarismo.* Rio de Janeiro: Paz e Terra.

Garcia-Bouza, Jorge. 1980. *A Basic Needs Analytical Bibliography. OECD Development Centre.* New York: Random House.

Garcia, Norberto E. 1982. "Growing labour absorption with persistent unemployment." *CEPAL Review* (December): 45–64.

Gerth, H. H. & C. Wright Mills. 1946. *Max Weber: Essays in Sociology.* London: Oxford University Press.

Ghai, Dharam P. 1975. "Population growth, labour absorption and income distribution." *The Population Debate: Dimensions and Perspectives.* ed. United Nations, pp. 502–9. New York: United Nations.

Giddens, Anthony. 1984. *The Constitution of Society.* Los Angeles: University of California Press.

Gonzales, E. N. & M. I. Bastos. 1975. "O trabalho volante na agricultura brasileira." *Reforma Agrária* 5 (May–June): 2–44.

Goodman, David & Michael Redclift. 1977. "The 'boias-frias': rural proletarianization and urban marginality in Brazil." *International Journal of Urban and Regional Research* 1(2): 348–64.

    1982. *From Peasant to Proletarian: Capitalist Development and Agrarian Transitions.* New York: St. Martin's Press.

Gouldner, Alvin. 1980. *The Two Marxisms.* New York: Seabury.

Graham, Douglas & Sérgio Buarque de Holanda. 1972. "Interregional and urban growth and economic development in Brazil." Paper presented at the I Simpósio de Desenvolvimento Econômico e Social, Belo Horizonte, 13–14 April.

Graham, Richard. 1970. "Action and ideas in the abolitionist movement in Brazil." In *Race and Class in Latin America,* ed. Magnus Mörner, pp. 51–69. New York: Columbia University Press.

Graziano da Silva, J. R. (coordinator). 1978. *Estrutura agrária e produção de subsistência na agricultura brasileira.* São Paulo: Hucitec.

Gross, D. R. & B. A. Underwood. 1971. "Technological change and caloric costs: Sisal agriculture in Northeastern Brazil." *American Anthropologist* 73 (June): 725–40.

Guimarães, A. Passos. 1963. *Quatro séculos de latifúndio.* Rio de Janeiro: Fulgor.

Gurley, John G. 1983. *Challenges to Communism.* San Francisco: W. H. Freeman and Company.

Gwatkin, D. 1980. "Indications of change in developing country mortality trends: the end of an era?" *Population and Development Review* 6 (4): 615–44.

Harris, J. R. & M. Todaro. 1970. "Migration, unemployment and development: a two sector analysis." *American Economic Review* 60 (March): 139–49.

Harris, Marvin. 1964. *Patterns of Race in the Americas*. New York: Walker & Co.

1979. *Cultural Materialism: The Struggle for a Science of Culture*. New York: Random House.

Harris, Marvin & Eric Ross. 1987. *Death, Sex and Fertility: Population Regulation in Preindustrial and Developing Societies*. Columbia University Press, New York.

Hasenbalg, Carlos A. 1985. "Race and socioeconomic inequalities in Brazil." In *Race, Class and Power in Brazil*, ed. Pierre–Michael Fontaine, pp. 25–41. Los Angeles: University of California.

Henry, L. 1961. "Some data on natural fertility." *Eugenics Quarterly* 8 (2): 81–91.

Heynig, Klaus. 1982. "The principal schools of thought on the peasant economy." *CEPAL Review* No. 16 (April): 113–39.

Hicks, Norman & Paul Streeten. 1979. "Indicators of development: the search for a basic needs yardstick." *World Development* 7.

Hirschman, Albert O. 1981. *Essays in Trespassing: Economics to Politics and Beyond*. London: Cambridge University Press.

Hoffman, Rodolfo. nd. "Evolução da desigualdade da distribuição da posse da terra no Brasil no período 1960–80." Mimeo.

1972. "Tendências da distribuição da renda no Brasil e suas relações com o desenvolvimento econômico." Paper presented at XXIV meeting of the SBPC, São Paulo. Reprinted in *A controvérsia sobre distribuição de renda e desenvolvimento*. (eds.) R. Tolipan & A. C. Tinelli, pp. 105–23. Rio de Janeiro: Zahar (1975).

Hoffman, R. & J. F. Graziano da Silva. 1975. "A estrutura agrária brasileira." In *Tecnologia e desenvolvimento agrícola*, ed. C. B. Contador, pp. 233–65. Rio: IPEA/INPES, Monograph No. 17.

Ianni, Octávio. 1972. *Raças e classes sociais no Brasil*. Rio de Janeiro: Civilização Brasileira.

Jagger, Alison M. 1983. *Feminist Politics and Human Nature*. Totowa, NJ: Rowman and Allanheld.

Katsman, Martin. 1976. "Paradoxes of Amazonian development in a 'resource-starved' world." *Journal of Developing Areas* 10 (July): 445–60.

Keller, A. F., F. Samano, L. Nuñez & O. Mojarro. 1981. *Lactancia materna: tendencias recientes en la experiencia mexicana*. Mexican City: Dirección General de Salúd Materno–Infantil y Planificación Familiar de la Secretaria de Salubridad y Asistencia.

King, T., et al. 1974. *Population Policies and Economic Development, A World Bank Staff Report*. Baltimore: Johns Hopkins University Press.

Knight, Peter R. 1981. "Brazilian socioeconomic development: issues for the eighties." *World Development* 9 (11/12): 1083–96.

Knight, P. T., D. Mahar & R. Moran. 1979. "Annex III: health, nutrition and education." In *Brazil: Human Resources Special Report*. Washington, DC: World Bank.

Kocher, James E. 1973. *Rural Development, Income Distribution and Fertility Decline*. New York: Population Council.

Kohl, Barbara A. 1981. "State and capital: agricultural policy in post-coup Brazil." PhD Dissertation, Ohio State University.

Kucinski, Bernardo. 1982. *Brazil: State and Struggle*. London: Latin American Bureau.

Kuczynski, Pedro-Pablo. 1983. "Latin American debt: Act Two." *Foreign Affairs* 62 (1): 17–38.

Kuznets, Simon. 1955. "Economic growth and income inequality." *American Economic Review* 45 (1): 1–28.

 1976. "Demographic aspects of the size distribution of income: an exploratory essay." *Economic Development and Cultural Change* 25 (October): 1–94.

 1978. "Size and age structure of family households: exploratory comparisons." *Population and Development Review* 4 (June): 187–224.

Laclau, Ernesto. 1971. "Feudalism and capitalism in Latin America." *New Left Review* 67 (May–June) 19–38.

Laclau, Ernesto & Chantal Mouffe. 1985. *Hegemony and Socialist Strategy: Towards Radical Democratic Politics*. London: Verso.

Langoni, Carlos Geraldo. 1973. *Distribuição da renda e desenvolvimento econômico do Brasil*. Rio de Janeiro: Editora Expressão e Cultura.

Latin American, Regional Report (LARR). 1983. "Fighting for jobs, not wages." *LARR*:B, 18 March: 6–7.

Latin American Weekly Report (LAWR). 1985. "How to make a social pact?" *LAWR*, 25 January: 10–11.

Laurenti, R. 1975. "Fontes de erros na mensuração da mortalidade infantil." *Revista de Saúde Pública* (9): 529–37.

Leff, N. H. 1969. "Dependency rates and savings rates." *American Economic Review* 59 (5): 886–96.

Leibenstein, H. 1954. *A Theory of Economic and Demographic Development*. Princeton University Press.

Leontief, Wassily. 1983. "Technological advance, economic growth, and the distribution of income." *Population and Development Review* 9 (3): 403–10.

Lerner, S. 1980. "Población y familia o grupo doméstico." Paper presented at Reunión Nacional de Investigación Demográfico in Mexico, Consejo Nacional de Ciencia y Tecnología (CONACYT), Mexico City.

Lernoux, Penny. 1984. "Debt obligations breed political and economic instability." *Latinamerican Press* 16, March 29.

Leser, W. 1974. "Crescimento da população e nível de saúde na cidade de São Paulo." *Problemas Brasileiros* 16 (October): 17–36.

Lesthaege, R. 1981. "Lactation and lactation-related variables, contraception and fertility: an overview of data problems and world trends." Paper prepared for the Seminar on Breastfeeding and Fertility Regulation, World Health Organization, Geneva.

Levine, Robert M. 1982. "Brazil: The dimensions of democratization." *Current History* 81: 60–3.

Lewis, W. A. 1954. "Economic development with unlimited supplies of labour." *The Manchester School of Economic and Social Studies* 22: 105–38.

Lluch, Constantino. 1979. "Employment, earnings and income distribution." *Annex II of Human Resources Special Report: Brazil*. Washington, DC: World Bank.

Long, Norman. 1977. *An Introduction to the Sociology of Rural Development*. London: Tavistock Publications Ltd.

   1984. *Family and Work in Rural Societies. Perspectives on Non-Wage Labor*. London: Tavistock.

Lopes, Juarez Brandão. 1973. "Desenvolvimento e migrações: uma abordagem histórico–estrutural." *Estudos CEBRAP* 6: 125–42.

   1977. "Empresas e pequenos produtores no desenvolvimento do capitalismo agrário em São Paulo." *Estudos CEBRAP* 22 (October/December): 41–110.

   1978. "Capitalist development and agrarian structure in Brazil." *International Journal of Urban and Regional Research* 2 (March): 1–11.

Macedo, Roberto. 1981. "Minimum wages and income distribution in Brazil." *Luso–Brazilian Review* 18 (1): 59–75.

Mahar, Dennis J. 1979. *Frontier Development Policy in Brazil*. New York: Praeger.

Mandel, Ernest. 1975. *Late Capitalism*. London: New Left Books.

Margolis, Maxine L. 1979. "Seduced and abandoned: agricultural frontiers in Brazil and the United States." In *Brazil: Anthropological Perspectives, Essays in Honor of Charles Wagley*. (eds.) Maxine L. Margolis & William E. Carter, pp. 160–79. Columbia University Press.

   1973. *The Moving Frontier*. Gainesville: University of Florida Press.

Martine, George. 1986. "As migrações de origem rural numa perspectiva histórica: algumas notas." Paper presented at the meeting of the Associação Brasileira de Estudos Populacionais (ABEP), Águas de São Pedro, Brazil, October 12–16.

Martine, George & J. C. P. Peliano. 1977. *Os migrantes nos mercados de trabalho metropolitanos*. Brasília: Projeto de Planejamento de Recursos Humanos, Relatório Técnico Número 32.

Martinez-Alier, V. 1975. "As mulheres do caminhão de turma." *Debate e Crítica* 5: 59–85.

Martins, José de Souza. 1975. *Capitalismo e tradicionalismo: estudos sobre as contradições da sociedade agrária no Brasil*. São Paulo: Pioneira.

   1977. "O café e a gênese da industrialização em São Paulo." *Contexto* 3: 1–17.

   1981. "Empresários e trabalhadores de origem italiano no desenvolvimento industrial brasileiro entre 1880 e 1914: o caso de São Paulo." *Dados* 24 (2): 237–64.

McKeown, T. 1976. *The Modern Rise of Population*. London: Academic Press.

McKeown, T. & R. Record. 1962. "Reasons for the decline of mortality in England and Wales during the nineteenth century." *Population Studies* 16: 94–122.

McKeown, T., R. G. Record & R. D. Turner. 1975. "An interpretation of the decline of mortality in England and Wales in the twentieth century." *Population Studies* 29 (November): 391–422.

McKintosh, M. 1981. "The sexual division of labour and the subordination of women." In *Marriage and the Market*. (eds) K. Young, C Wolkowitz & R. McCullagh. London: CSE Books.

McNicoll, Geoffrey. 1978. "Population and development: outlines for a structuralist approach." *The Journal of Development Studies* 14 (July): 79–99.

Merrick, Thomas W. 1976. "Population, development, and planning in Brazil." *Population and Development Review* 2 (June): 181–99.

1978. "Fertility and land availability in rural Brazil." *Demography* 15 (August): 321–36.

1985a. *Recent Fertility Declines in Brazil, Colombia, and Mexico*. World Bank Staff Working Papers, No. 692, Population and Development Series, No. 17. Washington, DC: The World Bank.

1985b. "The effect of piped water on early childhood mortality in urban Brazil, 1970 to 1976." *Demography* 22 (1): 1–23.

Merrick, Thomas W. & Douglas H. Graham. 1979. *Poplation and Economic Development in Brazil: 1800 to the Present*. Baltimore: Johns Hopkins University Press.

Merrick, Thomas W. & Elza Berquó. 1983. *The Determinants of Brazil's Recent Rapid Decline in Fertility*. Washington, DC: National Academy Press.

MINTER (Ministério do Interior). 1976. *Mudanças na composição do emprego e na distribuição da renda: efeitos sobre as migrações internas*. Brasília: MINTER.

Mintz, Sidney W. 1985. *Sweetness and Power: The Place of Sugar in Modern History*. New York: Viking.

Miró, Carmen A. & Joseph E. Potter. 1980. *Population Policy: Research Priorities in the Developing World*. London: Frances Printer Ltd.

Moisés, José Álvaro. 1979. "Current issues in the labor movement in Brazil." *Latin American Perspectives* 6 (4): 51–70.

Moisés, José Álvaro & Verena Martinez-Alier. 1978. "A revolta dos suburbanos ou patrão o trem atrasou." In *Contradições urbanas e movimentos sociais*, ed. Centro de Estudos de Cultura Contemporânea, pp. 13–63. Rio de Janeiro: Paz e Terra.

Molineaux, David J. 1984. "Roots of debt: new role of banks, old dependency." *Latinamerican Press* 16: March 29.

Monteiro, Carlos Augusto. 1982. "Contribuição para o estudo do significado da evolução do coeficiente de mortalidade infantil no município de São Paulo, SP (Brasil) nas tres últimas décadas (1950–1979)." *Revista de Saúde Pública* 16: 7–18.

Moran, Emilio F. 1981. *Developing the Amazon*. Bloomington: University of Indiana Press.

Moreira, Morvan de Melo, Lea Melo da Silva & Robert McLaughlin. 1978. *Brazil*. New York: The Population Council, Country Profiles.

Moser, Caroline & Kate Young. 1981. "Women of the working poor." *Institute of Development Studies Bulletin* 12 (3): 54–62.

Munck, Ronaldo. 1980. "State, capital and crisis in Brazil: 1919–1979." *Insurgent Sociologist* ix (Spring): 39–58.

Nag, Moni. 1983. "The impact of sociocultural factors on breastfeeding and sexual behavior." In *Determinants of Fertility in Developing Countries*. (eds.) R. Bulatao & R. Lee, vol. 1, pp. 163–98. Nw York: Academic Press.

National Academy of Sciences. 1986. *Population Growth and Economic Development: Policy Questions*. Washington, DC: National Academy Press.

Notestein, Frank W. 1953. "Economic problems of population change." In *Proceedings of the Eighth International Conference of Agricultural Economists*. London: Oxford University Press.

O'Donnell, Guillermo. 1973. *Modernization and Bureaucratic Authoritarianism: Studies in South American Politics*. Berkeley: University of California at Berkeley.

Offe, Claus. 1985. *Disorganized Capitalism*. Cambridge, Massachusetts: The MIT Press.

Oliveira, Lúcia Elena Garcia, Rosa Maria Porcaro & Tereza Cristina N. Araújo Costa. 1981. *O Lugar do negro na força de trabalho*. Rio de Janeiro: FIBGE.

Olivera, M. C. 1982. "Notas acerca da família nos estudos demográficos." Paper presented at the VII meeting of Grupo de trabajo sobre proceso de reproducción de la población, Mexico City.

Paiva, Paulo. 1982. "As necessidades de geração de emprego no Brasil durante os anos oitenta." Mimeo.

Palloni, Alberto. 1979. "Mortality decline in Latin America." Paper presented at the annual meeting of the Population Association of America, April 26.

1981. "Mortality in Latin America: emerging patterns." *Population and Development Review* 7 (4): 623–49.

Pang, Eul-Soo. 1983. "Brazil's new democracy." *Current History* 82: 54–7.

Parsons, Talcott & E. Shils (eds.) 1951. *Toward a General Theory of Action*. New York: Harper and Row.

Pastore, J. & A. Haller. 1977. "The socioeconomic status of the Brazilian labor force." *Luso-Brazilian Review* 14: 1–28.

Pfeffermann, G. 1985. "The social cost of recession in Brazil." Mimeo.

Pfeffermann, Guy P. & Richard Webb. 1979. *The Distributions of Income in Brazil*. Washington, DC: World Bank Staff Working Paper No. 356, The World Bank.

Pierrucci, Antonio Flávio de Oliveira. 1982. "Comunidades eclesiais: origens e desenvolvimento." *Novos Estudos CEBRAP* 1(2): 48–9.

Pierson, Donald. 1967. *Negroes in Brazil*. Southern Illinois University Press.

Piven, Francis Fox & Richard A. Cloward. 1971. *Regulating the Poor: The Functions of Public Welfare*. New York: Vintage.

Pompermayer, Malori José. 1984. "Strategies of private capital in the Brazilian Amazon." pp. 419–38 in M. Schmink and C. H. Wood (eds) *Frontier Expansion in Amazonia*. Gainesville, University of Florida Press.

Poppino, R. E. 1968. *Brazil: The Land and People*. New York: Oxford Press.

Portes, Alejandro. 1978a. "Migration and underdevelopment." *Politics and Society* 8 (1): 1–48.

1978b. "The informal sector and the world economy: notes on the structure of subsidised labour." *IDS Bulletin* 10 (4): 589–611.

1985. "Latin American class structures: their composition and change during the last decades." *Latin American Research Review* xx (3): 7–39.

Portes, Alejandro & John Walton. 1981. *Labor, Class and the International System*. New York: Academic Press.

Portes, Alejandro & Lauren Benton. 1984. "Industrial development and labor absorption: a reinterpretation." *Population and Development Review* 10 (4): 589–611.

Portes, Alejandro & John Walton. 1981. *Labor, Class and the International System.* New York: Academic Press.

Poulantzas, Nicos. 1973. *Political Power and Social Classes.* London: New Left Books.

Prado Júnior, Caio. 1971. *História econômica do Brasil.* 14th edn. São Paulo: Ed. Brasiliense.

Prebisch, Raul. 1950. *The Economic Development of Latin America and its Principal Problems.* New York: United Nations.

1984. "The global crisis of capitalism and its theoretical background." *CEPAL Review* 22: 159–78.

Preston, Samuel. 1975. "The changing relation between mortality and level of economic development." *Population Studies* 29 (July): 231–48.

1976. *Mortality Patterns in National Populations with Special References to Recorded Causes of Death.* New York: Academic Press.

Puffer, R. R. & C. V. Serrano. 1973. *Patterns of Mortality in Childhood.* Washington, DC: PAHO/WHO, Scientific Publication Number 262.

Repetto, R. G. 1974. "The relationship of the size distribution of income to fertility, and the implications for development policy." *Annex A of Population Policies and Economic Development.* Washington: International Bank for Reconstruction and Development.

1977. "Income and fertility change: a comment." *Population and Development Review* 3 (December): 486–9.

1978. "The interaction of fertility and the size distribution of income." *The Journal of Development Studies* 14 (July): 22–39.

Rich, W. 1973. "Smaller families through social and economic progress." Washington, DC: Overseas Development Council, Monograph Series.

Riding, Alan. 1986. "Brazil gets back on the fast track." *New York Times*, October 12, 1986.

Rodgers, G. B. 1978. "Demographic determinants of the distribution of income." *World Development* 6: 305–18.

Rosenbaum, H. J. & W. G. Tyler (eds.) 1972. *Contemporary Brazil: Issues in Economic and Political Development.* New York: Praeger.

Rostow, W. W. 1960. *The Stages of Economic Growth: A Non-Communist Manifesto.* New York: Cambridge University Press.

1978. *The World Economy: History and Prospects.* Austin: University of Texas Press.

Rothenberg, J. 1977. "On the microeconomics of migration." In *International Migration: A Comparative Perspective.* (eds.) A. Brown & E. Neuberger, pp. 183–205. New York: Academic Press.

Roxborough, Ian. 1979. *Theories of Underdevelopment.* London: Macmillan Press Ltd.

Russell, L. B. & C. S. Burke. 1975. *Determinants of Infant and Child Mortality: An Econometric Analysis of Survey Data for San Juan, Argentina.* Washington, DC: National Planning Association.

Sanders, T. G. 1973a. "Colonization of the Transamazonia Highway." *Ameri-*

can Universities Field Staff, East-Coast South American Series, vol. XVII (3).

1973b. "The Brazilian model." *American Universities Field Staff, East-Coast South American Series*, vol. XVII, No. 8: 1–12.

Sawyer, Diana Oya & I. S. Soares. 1982. "Mortalidade na infância em diferentes contextos no Brasil." Paper presented at the Brazilian Population Association meetings, Vitória, Brazil, October 11–15.

Sawyer, Donald R. 1984. "Frontier expansion and retraction in Brazil." In *Frontier Expansion in Amazonia.* (eds.) Marianne Schmink & Charles H. Wood, pp. 180–203. Gainesville, FL: University of Florida Press.

Schmink, M. 1979. "Community in ascendance: urban industrial growth and household income strategies in Belo Horizonte, Brazil." Unpublished PhD Dissertation, University of Texas at Austin.

1982. "Land conflicts in Amazonia." *American Ethnologist* 9: 2 (May): 341–57.

1984. "Household economic strategies: review and research agenda." *Latin American Research Review* 19 (3): 87–101.

Schmink, Marianne & Charles H. Wood (eds.) 1984. *Frontier Expansion in Amazonia*. University of Florida Press.

Schmitter, P. C. 1973. "The 'Portugalization' of Brazil." In *Authoritarian Brazil*, ed. A. Stepan, pp. 179–232. New Haven: Yale University Press.

Schultz, T. Paul. 1981. *Economics of Population*. Reading, Mass.: Addison–Wesley Publishing Co.

Schutjer, W. A. & C. S. Stokes (eds.) 1984. *Rural Development and Human Fertility*. New York: Macmillan.

Scott, J. 1978. "Some notes on post-peasant society." *Journal of Peasant Studies* 7 (Summer): 139–54.

Scrimshaw, S. C. M. 1978. "Infant mortality and behavior in the regulation of family size." *Population and Development Review* 4 (September): 338–403.

Seccombe, Wally. 1983. "Marxism and demography." *New Left Review* 137 (January–February): 22–47.

Serra, José. 1982. "A economia constrangida." *Novos Estudos CEBRAP* 1 (4): 2–8.

Shaw, Paul. 1975. *Migration Theory and Fact: A Review and Bibliography of Current Literature*. Philadelphia: Regional Science Research Institute.

Shorter, F. 1978. *Computational Methods for Population Projections with Particular Reference to Development Planning*. New York: The Population Council.

Silva, Nelson Do Valle. 1978. "Black–white income differentials: Brazil 1960." PhD Dissertation, University of Michigan.

1985. "Updating the cost of not being white in Brazil." In *Race, Class and Power in Brazil*. ed. Pierre-Michel Fontaine, pp. 42–55. Los Angeles: University of California Press.

Simões, Celso C. & L. A. P. de Oliveira. 1986. "Considerações sobre o recente declínio da mortalidade infantil no Brasil." *Proceedings of the Fifth meeting of the Brazilian Population Association (ABEP)*, Águas de São Pedro, SP, 12–16. October.

Simon, Julian. 1976. "Population growth may be good for LDCs in the long run: a richer simulation model." *Economic Development and Cultural Change* 24 (2): 309–33.

Simonsen, Roberto C. 1969. *História Econômica do Brasil, 1500–1820.* 6th edn. São Paulo: Companhia Editora Nacional.

Singelmann, Joachim. 1978. *From Agriculture to Services: The Transformation of Industrial Employment.* Beverly Hills, California: Sage

Singer, Paul. 1972. "O 'Milagre Brasileiro' causas e consequências." São Paulo: CEBRAP, Caderno 6.

1973. "Migrações internas: considerações teóricas sobre o seu estudo." In CEDEPLAR (ed.), *Migrações internas e desenvolvimento regional,* vol. 1. Belo Horizonte, Brasil: CEDEPLAR

1982. "Neighborhood movements in São Paulo." In *Towards a Political Economy of Urbanization in Third World Countries,* ed. H. Safa, pp. 283–304 Delhi: Oxford University Press.

Sjaastad, L. A. 1962. "The costs and returns of human migration." *The Journal of Political Economy* 70 (October): 80–93.

Skidmore, Thomas E. 1973. "Politics and economic policy making in authoritarian Brazil 1937–71." In *Authoritarian Brazil,* ed. A. Stepan, pp. 3–41 New Haven: Yale University Press.

1974. *Black into White.* New York: Oxford University Press.

1978. "The years between the harvest: the economics of the Castelo Branco presidency, 1964–1967." *Luso-Brazilian Review* 15 (2) 157–77.

1985. "Race and class in Brazil: Historical perspectives." In *Race, Class and Power in Brazil,* ed. Pierre-Michel Fontaine, pp. 11–24. Los Angeles: University of California Press.

Smith, Nigel. 1981. "Colonization lessons from a tropical forest." *Science* 214 (4522): 755–61.

Smith, T. L. 1972. *Brazil: People and Institutions.* 4th edn. Baton Rouge: Louisiana State University Press.

Soares, Gláucio Ary Dillon. 1976. *A questão agrária na América Latina.* Rio de Janeiro: Zahar.

1979. "As políticas de cassações." *Dados* 21: 69–85.

1978. "After the mircale." *Luso-Brazilian Review* 15 (2): 278–301.

1980. "The Brazilian political system: old parties and new cleavages." Mimeo.

1985. "Brazil: from fable to legend." Paper presented at the Conference on Recent Electoral Changes in the Americas, University of California, San Diego, February 22–6.

Sorj, Bernardo. 1980. *Estado e classes sociais na agricultura brasileira.* Rio de Janeiro: Zahar.

Souza, Amaury de & Bolívar Lamounier. 1981. "Governo e sindicatos no Brasil: a perspectiva dos anos 80." *Dados* 24 (2): 139–59.

Souza, Paulo R & Paulo E. Baltar. 1975. "Salário mínimo e taxas de salários no Brasil." *Pesquisa e Planejamento Econômico* 9 (3): 629–60.

Spengler, J. & G. Myers, 1977. "Migration and socioeconomic development: today and yesterday." In *Internal Migration: A Comparative Perspective.* (eds.) A. Brown & E. Neuberger, pp. 11–35. New York: Academic Press.

Standing, Guy. 1983. "Women's work activity and fertility." In *Determinants of Fertility in Developing Countries*. (eds.) R. Bulatao & R. Lee, pp. 517–46. New York: Academic Press.

State of São Paulo. 1979. "Infant mortality: positive results of new health policy." São Paulo: State Secretariat for Economic Planning.

Stavrianos, L. S. 1981. *Global Rift: The Third World Comes of Age*. New York: William Morrow and Co.

Stepan, Alfred. 1985. "State power and the strength of civil society in the southern cone of Latin America." In *Bringing the State Back In*. (eds.) P. Evans, D. Rueschmeyer & T. Skocpol, pp. 317–43. Cambridge University Press.

Stigler, George. 1969. "Does economics have a useful past?" *History of Political Economy* 1 (Fall): 217–30.

Stolcke, Verena. 1984. "The exploitation of family morality: labor systems and family structure on São Paulo coffee plantations, 1950–1979. In *Kinship, Ideology and Practice in Latin American*, ed. Raymond T. Smith, pp. 24–91. Chapel Hill: University of North Carolina Press.

Stokes, C. Shannon & Wayne A. Schutjer. 1984. "Access to land and fertility in developing countries." In *Rural Development and Human Fertility*. (eds.) Wayne A. Schutjer & C. Shannon Stokes, pp. 195–215 . New York: Macmillan Publishing Co.

Stolnitz, G. 1965. "Recent mortality trends in Latin America, Asia and Africa: review and reinterpretation." *Population Studies* 19(2): 117–38.

Sunkel, Osvaldo. 1979. "The development of development thinking." In *Transnational Capitalism and National Development: New Perspectives on Dependence*, José H. Villamil, pp. 19–30. Atlantic Highlands, New Jersey: Humanities Press.

Todaro, Michael R. 1969. "A model of labor migration and urban unemployment in less developed countries." *American Economic Review* 3 (March): 138–48.

   1977.. "Development policy and population growth: a framework for planning." *Population and Development Review* 3 (March and June): 23–43.

   1981. *Economic Development in the Third World*. 2nd edn. New York: Longman.

Tokman, Victor. 1982. "Unequal development and the absorption of labour." *CEPAL Review* (August): 121–33.

Toplin, Robert Brent. 1981. *Freedom and Prejudice: The Legacy of Slavery in the United States and Brazil*. Westport, Connecticut: Greenwood Press.

Torrado, S. 1980. "Sobre los conceptos de estrategias de vida' y proceso de reproducción de la fuerza de trabajo'." PISPAL Seminar, Buenos Aires.

Trussell, T. & S. H. Preston, 1982. "Estimating the covariates of childhood mortality from retrospective reports of mothers." *Health Policy and Education* 13 (1).

Turchi, B. 1975. *The Demand for Children in the United States*. Cambridge, Mass.: Ballinger Press.

Tyler, William G. 1984. "Stabilization, external adjustment and recession in Brazil: perspective on the mid-1980's." Paper presented at the Conference on the Crisis in Brazil, University of Florida, Gainesville, November 15–16.

UNAM (Universidad Autónoma de Mexico). 1983. *Memorias del Congreso Latino Americano de Población y Desarrollo*, 8–10 November, Mexico City, Mexico.

United Nations. 1973. *The Determinants and Consequences of Population Trends*. New York: United Nations, Department of Economic and Social Affairs.

1980. *World Population Trends and Policies: 1979 Monitoring Report*. vol. 1. New York: Department of International Economic and Social Affairs: United Nations.

Valenzuela, Samuel J. & Arturo Valenzuela. 1979. "Modernization and dependence: alternative perspectives in the study of Latin American Underdevelopment." In *Transnational Capitalism and National Development*, ed. José Villamil, pp. 31–65. Atlantic Highlands, New Jersey: Humanities Press.

Vetter, Donald Michael & Celso Cardoso da Silva Simões. 1980. "Acesso à infra-structure de saneamento básico e mortalidade." *Boletim Demográfico* 10 (4): 4–29.

Wagley, Charles. 1952. *Race and Class in Rural Brazil*. New York: Columbia University Press.

1971. *An Introduction to Brazil*, revised edn. New York: Columbia University Press.

Wallerstein, I. 1974. *The Origins of the Modern World System I: Capitalist Agriculture and the Origins of the European World-Economy in the Sixteenth Century*. New York: Academic Press.

Walton, John. 1986. *Sociology and Critical Inquiry: The Work, Tradition and Purpose*. Chicago: Dorsey Press.

Ward, Kathryn Barbara. 1982. "The influence of the world economic system on the status of women and their fertility behavior." Unpublished PhD Dissertation, Sociology, University of Iowa.

Webster, Andrew. 1984. *Introduction to the Sociology of Development*. London: Macmillan Publishers Ltd.

Weisskoff, R. & A. Figueroa. 1976. "Traversing the social pyramid: a comparative review of income distribution in Latin America." *Latin America Research Review*, 1: 71–112.

Weller, Robert H., John Macisco Jr. & George Martine. 1971. "The relative importance of the components of urban growth in Latin America." *Demography* 8 (May): 225–32.

Wells, Louis T. 1972. *Product Life Cycle and International Trade*. Boston: Harvard Graduate School of Business Administration, Harvard University.

Willems, Emilio. 1972. "The rise of a rural middle class in a frontier society." In *Brazil in the Sixties*, ed. Riodan Roett, pp. 325–44. Nashville: Vanderbilt University Press.

Williams, Eric. 1944. *Capitalism and Slavery*. Chapel Hill: University of North Carolina Press.

Wolf, Eric R. 1982. *Europe and the People Without History*. Berkeley: University of California Press.

Wolpe, Harold (ed.) 1980. *The Articulation of Modes of Production*. London: Routledge and Kegan Paul.

Wood, Charles H. 1981. "Structural change and household strategies: a conceptual framework for the study of rural migration." *Human Organization* 40 (4) 338–43.

1982. "Equilibrium and historical–structural perspectives on migration." *International Migration Review* 16 (2): 298–319.

Wood, Charles H. & José Alberto M. de Carvalho. 1982. "Population growth and the distribution of household income: the case of Brazil." *The Sociological Quarterly* 23 (Winter): 49–65.

Wood, Charls H. & Stephen D. McCracken. 1984. "Underdevelopment, urban growth and collective social action in São Paulo, Brazil." *Studies in Third World Societies* 29 (Sept.): 101–40.

Wood, Charles H. & Marianne Schmink. 1979. "Blaming the victim: small farmer production in an Amazonian colonization project." *Studies in Third World Societies* 7: 77–93.

Woortman, Klaus. 1984. "Família trabalhadora: um jeito de sobreviver." *Ciência Hoje* 3 (13): 26–31.

World Bank. 1979. *Human Resources Special Report: Brazil.* Washington, DC: World Bank.

1983. *The World Bank Annual Report, 1983.* Washington, DC: The World Bank.

Worsley, Peter. 1984. *The Three Worlds: Culture and World Development.* University of Chicago Press.

Wright, Eric Olin. 1979. *Class, Crisis and the State.* London: Verso.

1985. *Classes.* London: Verso.

Yone, Paula & I. A. F. Barreira. 1984 "Saques e desemprego." *Ciência Hoje* 2 (12): 26–33.

Yunes, J. & V. S. Ronchezel. 1974. "Evolução da mortalidade geral, infantil e proporcional no Brasil." *Revista de Saúde Pública* 8 (supplement): 3–48.

Index

CAMBRIDGE LATIN AMERICAN STUDIES